Jason Godesky

Thirty Theses

Edited by Lothric Wildman

2024

ISBN : 978-1-4461-6792-2

CONTENTS :

*

Jason Godesky

Thirty Theses

What are these?

We all have basic assumptions about the world, human nature, and the relationship between the two. We are taught certain perspectives as children, and this recieved wisdom forms the common ground for communication. Ultimately, when we see the whole picture, our major disagreements are squabbles over details. Should gays be allowed to marry? We assume here a common understanding of what "marriage" means. Should we raise or lower taxes? We assume the legitimacy of government, and of *taxes* at all!

What happens when the disagreement occurs at an even more basic level? Like, whether or not our civilization is even a good thing?

The case is complex, but in truth no more complex than our "common ground" of unexamined, recieved wisdom. In many cases, it is much *less* complex. But it *is* different. Since forming these ideas, I have faced an increasing obstacle in communication. Unspoken, differing assumptions force me routinely to return to the same arguments again and again. So I resolved some time ago to crystalize my philosophy into a single, comprehensive work, which could from a base for further communication.

There have been several failed attempts at this, the most recent being "The Anthropik Canon." *The Thirty Theses* recycles much of my previous work, but extends and elaborates on all of it, as well. This is my latest attempt to develop a comprehensive treatment of my core philosophy, reduced to thirty pronouncements which I individually defend.

Jason Godesky

Neo shaman,

Tribe of Anthropik

anthropik.com

28 July 2005

Thesis #1: Diversity is the primary good.

Humans are social animals, and also capable of abstract, independent thought. The combination requires some form of social standards. Bees think with a single hive mind, and solitary animals do not encounter one another often enough to require a rigid system of morality and ethics. Without social norms, however, human society would break down. We have evolved in such societies, and require other humans to live. A single human, on his own, has little chance of survival.

Some rules are nearly universal, such as the injunction against murder. Society cannot long endure if everyone is murdering one another. Other taboos are less common; theft, for example, is generally found only in those societies where resources are limited in some regard. Rules of morality and ethics vary widely from culture to culture, adapted to given circumstances. Our ethics and morality are another means we have of adapting to new and different environments.

Basic rules of behavior are required for our survival, and conscience is an adaptation we have evolved to continue our existence. Such a conscience must at once be deeply felt, and culturally constructed. It must be adapted to those rules, taboos, and guidelines a given society requires in a given place and time, but be too deeply felt to be ignored. The human brain is incredibly malleable, made to be adapted to the cultural context it finds itself in. Enculturation is a powerful process which should never be underestimated. What you learn as a child can never be completely shaken; it becomes an inextricable part of who you are, as intrinsic to your being as your DNA.

As necessary as ethics may be, that does not make them correct. Nor does the depth of our conviction. I, like most Westerners, feel a very strong revulsion at the thought of pedophilia, for example. Yet, in the cultural context of the Etoro, the Marind-ani, and 10–20% of all Melanesian tribes, it is the only acceptable form of sex. While I cringe at the thought, I have no argument that it is "wrong" beyond my gut feeling of disgust — a result of my enculturation. As much as I prefer monogamous, heterosexual relationships, it was monogamous heterosexuals who committed the Holocaust. There is no similar act in Melanesian history.

The arbitrary nature of such ethical rules led many of our early ancestors to posit the final authority for such decrees with divine will. This is good and that is not because the gods said so, end of story. This made things nice, neat and easy. In the early days of polytheism, this worked nicely. Worshippers of Apollo and Ra alike could live in peace with one another. Most polytheists were willing to accept the gods of another as equally real as their own pantheon. Religious wars and intolerance were quite uncommon; after all, what's one more god? Early religion was inextricably bound to politics, and so ancient states would enforce worship of the state gods — often including the emperor or king — alongside one's own gods. Usually, this was not a problem; again, what's one more god? Even monolatry — the worship of a single god, amidst the acknowledgement of many — was not much of a problem. Ra is my god and Apollo is yours, but we're both worshipping the sun. I worship the ocean, and you worship the harvest, but both are equally real.

It was the emergence of monotheism that first posed a serious challenge. If only one god exists, then all other gods are false. If this is also combined with a charitable disposition towards the rest of mankind, crusades, missionaries, and other attempts to save the heathens from their error ensue. In a world where morality is determined by the will of the gods, such a conflict comes to a head.

If morality follows from divine will, are there no ethics for atheists? And what of the heathens? Yet, these individuals still have pangs of conscience as acute — and sometimes more — than their monotheistic cousins. This led to many philosophers trying to find some other basis for ethics, besides divine will. Such philosophies generally come in one of three types.

The first harks back to the old days of the divine will; deontological ethics focuses on duties we are required to either fulfill or refrain from. The seminal figure of this school is Immanuel Kant, who formulated the categorical imperative. Kant argued that an act is ethical if it could be done by everyone without breaking down society. This was later refined by Sir David Ross with his *prima facie* values — things that simply are good without question. Individual acts can then be judged by how well they comply to those values. The past fifty years have seen the re-emergence of "virtues," as found in ancient philosophy. The four Stoic virtues of temperence, fortitude, justice and prudence work in a manner similar to Ross's values — acts may be judged by how well they cling to these virtues.

Both of these systems share the same flaw as the ancient systems of ethics; they cannot exist apart from divine revelation. Even if there is such a god handing down such ethical systems, how can we ever be sure which of us has the "true" revelation? Every culture has different values, virtues, morals and ethics. Each believes that its way is the *right* way. Simply reiterating that position is not sufficient, and all claims to the superiority of one's own scripture require one to first accept the superiority of one's own scripture.

Unlike the foregoing systems, however, consequentialist ethics like John Stuart Mill's theory of Utilitarianism do the best job of creating an ethical system independent of divine powers. Utilitarianism tries to maximize the utility — roughly, the "happiness" — of all parties involved. An action is "right" insofar as it makes everyone more satisfied, more happy, than they were before. This is not simple hedonism, as the welfare of all must be considered — your family, your friends, your society. Sitting at home tripping on acid is not an ethical action in Utilitarianism, for as much as it may raise your own utility, it carries with it a slight negative impact on everyone in the form of your support for a global network of drug dealers and smugglers connected to various forms of crime, oppression and terrorism.

Utilitarianism is often disparaged in philosophical circles, with counter-examples as the following. Take a thousand people, and some magical means of measuring utility numerically. One of them is extremely annoying. Killing him would drop his own utility from its current "100" to zero, while raising everyone else's from "100" to "101." That means that the overall effect of utility would be 999–100=899. Ergo, killing annoying people is a very good thing!

Obviously, Utilitarianism needs some other goal that mere "happiness," but what? Once again, we run up against the wall of needing to decipher the divine will. Everyone has their own ideas, beliefs, dogmas and scriptures. How can we possibly know what the gods desire of us?

Perhaps one good start is to stop pouring over the texts they supposedly inspired, and instead look to the only thing we know for certain came from them (if they exist at all): the world around us. It turns out the universe has been screaming a single, consistent value at us from the beginning of time.

From a single, undifferentiated point of energy, the universe unfolded into hundreds of elements, millions of compounds, swirling galaxies and complexity beyond human comprehension. The universe has not simply become more complex; that is simply a side-effect of its drive towards greater diversity.

So, too, with evolution. We often speak of evolution couched in terms of progress and increasing complexity. There is, however, a baseline of simplicity. From there, diversity moves in all directions. If evolution inspired complexity, then all life would be multi-celled organisms of far greater complexity than us. Instead, most organisms are one-celled, simple bacteria — yet, staggeringly diverse. As organisms become more complex, they become less common. The graph is not a line moving upwards — it is a point expanding in all directions save one, where it is confined to a baseline of simplicity. From our perspective, we can mistake it for "progress" towards some complex goal, but this is an illusion. Evolution is about diversity.

Physics and biology speak in unison on this point; if there are gods, then the one thing they have always, consistently created is diversity. No two galaxies quite alike; no two stars in those galaxies quite alike; no two worlds orbiting those stars quite alike; no two species on those worlds quite alike; no two individuals in those species quite alike; no two cells in those individuals quite alike; no two molecules in those cells quite alike; no two atoms in those molecules quite alike. That is the pre-eminent truth of our world. That is the one bit of divine will that cannot be argued, because it is not mediated by any human author. It is all around us, etched in every living thing, every atom of our universe. The primacy of diversity is undeniable.

With that, we can suppose another form of consequentialist ethics, like Mill's Utilitarianism, but with a different measure of "good." It is not happiness, but diversity that should be our measure. Diversity of life, of thought, of action.

So, killing the annoying person becomes "bad"; as annoying as he is, he adds diversity to the group. Nor does this give license to everything under the cause of increasing diversity. Our own civilization is a unique data point, but its existence requires the expansion of its markets and influence. It gobbles up other cultures to create new customers. Though it is itself another point of diversity, it requires many other points to be sacrificed. Its overall effect, like sitting at home on acid, is profoundly negative.

7

Thesis #2: Evolution is the result of diversity.

The concept of progress is actually rather new. Most prehistoric and ancient peoples saw history as a constantly repeating cycle, incompatible with any notion of advancement or degradation. The first conceptions of linear time are found only in the historical era. Confucius, the Greeks and the Jews all believed that the world was, in fact, becoming *worse*. In this, they did concieve of history as linear, but as the *opposite* of progress. The Greeks held that the first, "Golden Age" had been the best era, with each succeeding age diminished from its predecessor's glory. In Judaism, the "Fall of Man" in Genesis paints humanity in a fallen, exiled state. Later Jewish prophets outlined a messianic and eschatological timeline which extended this into an on-going societal free-fall that would end only by divine intervention with the Messianic Age. This final hope of the Messianic Age sowed the first seeds of the idea of progress.

In many ways, we can thank Christianity for the concept. In reconciling their belief in Jesus as the messiah, and the very obviously unfulfilled predictions of the Eschaton and the Messianic Age, Christians began to develop a more progressive concept of history. Their Christology immediately separates history into "before Christ" and "after Christ." They mark the passage of years as *Anno Domini*-the "Year of Our Lord." Since the New Covenant is, in the Christian mind, immediately superior to the Old — as Paul argues in his Letter to the Galatians — we already have fitted all of history into a broad sweep of progress. The condition of mankind was improved by the life of Christ. History has progressed.

The concept proved adaptable to changing memetic environments. The Enlightenment was a response to the superstitious worldview that preceded it, and like so many philosophical responses, was prone to attempts to counter-balance its opponents by going equally far in the opposite direction. The Enlightenment defined humanity as unique for its faculty of Reason, and celebrated that Reason as the seat of mankind's "redemption" from its state of ignorance and savagery. The Enlightenment promised an optimistic future, where humanity triumphed over every obstacle in its way thanks to the unstoppable power of Reason. As E.O.Wilson described it in *Consilience*:

« *Inevitable progress is an idea that has survived Condorcet and the Enlightenment. It has exerted, at different times and variously for good and evil, a powerful influence to the present day. In the final chapter of the*

8

Sketch [for a Historical Picture of the Progress of the Human Mind], "The Tenth Stage: The Future Progress of the Human Mind," Condorcet becomes giddily optimistic about its prospect. He assures the reader that the glorious process is underway: All will be well. His vision for human progress makes little concession to the stubbornly negative qualities of human nature. When all humanity has attained a higher level of civilization, we are told, nations will be equal, and within each nation citizens will also be equal. Science will flourish and lead the way. Art will be freed to grow in power and beauty. Crime, poverty, racism and sexual discrimination will decline. The human lifespan, through scientifically based medicine, will lengthen indefinitely. »

Though the Enlightenment placed its faith in Science, rather than in deities, this belief in progress remains no less a leap of faith for it. The idea of progress — particularly of humanity's constant self-improvement through the application of Reason — became as fundamental a belief for the secular humanists as the redeeming power of Christ was for the Christians they proceeded. The beliefs fulfilled similar needs, as well, by promising similar outcomes — even if brought about by entirely different processes. Both comforted their believers with the promise that the current misery was only temporary, and that a new, better day was waiting on the horizon for those who soldiered on.

Little wonder, then, that when Darwin challenged the conceit of our species' superiority by suggesting we were mere animals, those that did not reject the evidence entirely instead comforted themselves with the myth of progress. In the popular mind, the word "evolution" became nearly a synonym for "progress," the process by which species "improve" themselves. In fact, evolution has nothing to do with "progress" at all.

Evolution, technically defined, is merely a change in allele frequency in a population over time. In one generation, 15% have a given gene; in the next, it is only 14.8%. Iterated over generations, this may lead to the complete extinction of the allele. The idea of evolution predates Darwin, as such change is immediately observable and undeniable. Darwin made two contributions to this; the first was defining the first mechanism for evolution in the process of natural selection, the second his contention that such evolution satisfactorily explains the origin of species.

Since the Neolithic, herders have practiced artificial selection with their livestock. If a given cow produces more milk than the others, or is more docile and easy to control, then you simply give that cow more time with the bulls, so that she will have more children. The next generation of the herd will have more docile cows that produce more milk. The herder has artificially selected for traits he desires. Over enough generations, this could lead to the entire herd being docile and producing more milk.

Darwin's concept of natural selection merely suggests that this can also happen without the conscious guidance of a herder. A giraffe with a slightly longer neck may be able to reach foliage in trees more easily. He will be better and more easily fed, giving him more time to dally with the ladies and concieve young, who are also more likely to have slightly longer necks. Over enough generations, this could easily explain the modern state of the giraffe, the same as artificial selection sufficiently explains the state of the modern cow herd. The difference being, no single entity was consciously guiding the giraffes to that end.

The seeds of these thoughts were planted during Darwin's time aboard the *Beagle*. During this time, he visited the Galapagos Islands, and noted both the similarities and differences of birds on those islands to birds on the mainland. He noted the similarities suggesting they had once been a single species, and the differences specifically adapted to the Galapagos' unique ecology. Darwin allowed the implications of his natural selection to play out. If two populations of a given species are separated, each will continue changing with each generation, but now separated, their changes will diverge. Over sufficient generations, the two groups will become too divergent to interbreed any longer. Two new species will have formed.

In its truest essence, then, evolution is nearly irrefutable. "Survival of the fittest," is a true shorthand, if we understand "fittest" to refer to the ability to produce young, as well as being severely restricted to a given locale. In this case, it becomes a tautology; if a creature possesses some trait that will make it more likely to have young, then it is more likely to have young. The controversy comes from the implication of this statement. If true (and how could it not be?), then all the diversity of life can be accounted for in a natural fashion. Gods can still be invoked if one insists; evolution could be seen as G-d's paintbrush, or Genesis as a poetic account of evolution, as all but the most hardline, fundamentalist Christians believe, but they are not necessary. The existence of life itself is no longer a proof for the existence of G-d.

Evolution, then, is simply a consequence of diversity. All organisms are subject to "dumb luck," and untold heritages of the world were pre-emptively snuffed out by rocks falling at the most inopportune moments.

Yet, the diversity of populations of organisms played with the probability of that dumb luck. Falling stones did not kill the swift and the slow in equal measure. Trees with flame-retardant seeds inherited the earth after enough forest fires had gone through. Evolution happens, as the inevitable consequence of a diverse world. As Dawkins abstracted it in *The Selfish Gene*, the diversity of possible chemical reactions meant that, eventually, a reaction would occur that reproduced itself. Such a reaction would have a higher probability of occuring again, as it was no longer relying on pure chance to do so. Anything that reproduces itself — even ideas — are subject to natural selection and evolution.

What, then, is the "goal" of evolution, if we can speak of such a thing? The marriage of evolution and progress has left many with the notion that evolution is driving towards some endpoint, that we are progressing ever closer to some perfect state. Usually, this is formulated as evolution's drive towards greater complexity. Such a "drive" towards complexity, however, is ultimately a mirage, an illusion created by the unique myopia of our scale.

There is a certain baseline of simplicity for all things. No atom can be simpler than hydrogen, for example. There is a baseline for DNA where, if it were any simpler, it would not be able to reproduce itself, and thus would no longer be DNA. There is a baseline, somewhere around the complexity of the virus — whether above or below is a matter of some debate — where any more simplicity would yield something no longer alive. From this baseline, there is nowhere to go but up. Diversity spreads out in all possible directions. There is infinite diversity in the space that is equally simple, hugging close to the baseline. Diversity also moves up, towards more complex. If we were to graph such dispersion, it would not look like an arrow shooting up into the stratosphere of complexity; it would be a hemisphere against a solid floor, with its radius constantly growing.

The evidence for this view is clear and intuitive. If evolution drives ever greater complexity, rather than simply diversity, why then is the vast majority of life on earth single celled? Instead, this distribution of life — with almost all of it existing at lower orders of complexity, and the numbers of species diminishing as we climb into greater levels of complexity — is *exactly* the hemisphere of diversity. Nowhere do we see the straight line of "progress," unless we track only our own, specific evolutionary path, and ignore everything else. If we stare at the radius pointing straight up and ignore the rest of the hemisphere, then, and only then, can we convince ourselves that evolution is about "progress."

Consider the case of the Neanderthal. Larger, stronger and faster than normal humans, our success (and their failure) was once attributed to their inferior intellect. In fact, their brains were noticeably larger than our own. While this may simply be a matter of ennervating muscle tissue, it means their physical faculties were at least the equal of our own, if not superior. Culturally, the only evidence of adaptation to changing stimulus we have in the Paleolithic is the Châtelperronian toolset, an ingenious integration of Acheulean and Mousterian technology. It is not found associated with "modern" humans, however, but with Neandertals. With their intellectual abilities in greater doubt, many turned to Bergman's Rule to explain their demise: Neandertals were cold-adapted, and could not survive in the changing climate of the end of the Pleistocene. However, Neandertals have been found throughout the Middle East in areas which, while once colder than they are now, were never so cold as to justify the idea that Neandertals were doomed by their cold adaptation.

There is yet no angle to the Neandertals' extinction besides sheer, dumb luck that does not present a host of problems. It seems, regardless of which attribute we value most, Neandertals were at least our equals, and perhaps even our betters. Their extinction, and our success, may be a case of evolution picking the *worse* candidate; it may simply be randomly choosing between two equally qualified candidates. What it seems very strongly to not represent is a case of "progress." Instead, it is simply change.

This highlights one of the last important traits of evolution: its ambivalence. A friend of Darwin's once tried to develop a system of ethics based on the conviction that, while evolution is inevitable, it is also a monstrous process, and that which helps it along is itself immoral. I argue that evolution can, indeed, be monstrous, but is not always so. Like everything else, good and evil are matters of proximity. Evolution sometimes makes things better; sometimes, it makes them worse. Evolution is driven by diversity, and in general creates even more diversity, but it is also blind and unconscious. It operates on immediate results, leaving long-term errors to be resolved by time. It is a process of continual trial and error, as it allows long-term mistakes to correct themselves with self-destruction. Thus, at any given point, we must be careful to declare anything an evolutionary "success" by its current survival — as it may just as easily be a terrible mistake in the midst of eliminating itself.

Thesis #3: Humans are products of evolution.

As we saw in the second thesis, natural selection is a tautology: anything that possesses some trait that makes it more likely to propogate itself, is more likely to propogate itself. Played out over a sufficiently long timeline, this can easily explain the origin of species. It was an explosive idea; not because it was theoretically lacking, nor even for lack of evidence. It was not even explosive for what it ruled out. Rather, it was explosive for what it *allowed*: namely, a world with no intelligent designer. The opposition came primarily from the most fundamentalist of religious organizations. Evolution does not preclude the existence of G-d, but neither does it require it. It was this that made it "evil," because it removed the existence of life itself as a proof for the existence of G-d.

Yet it was not evolution in general that bothers these religious zealots. Many are even willing to concede "microevolution," or the change of species over time. The laser-like focus of their ire has always been *human* evolution in particular.

This is not without reason, of course. These same religions teach a myth of humanity as a higher, nobler order of creation. Jews, Christians and Muslims all share the Genesis account, where humanity was the crown of creation — something made in G-d's own image. "Then God said, 'Let us make man in our image, in our likeness, and let them rule over the fish of the sea and the birds of the air, over the livestock, over all the earth, and over all the creatures that move along the ground.'" (Genesis 1:26) In Islam (7:11–18) — as well as in Christian folklore and exegesis — Lucifer and his angels are cast from heaven because they refuse to bow to humanity, and accept their primacy as the greatest of G-d's creation, superior even to the angels.

Such beliefs are widespread, if not universal. In Iroquois belief, humans were descended from the superhuman, utopian Sky People, while mere beasts already existed in the world. The Australian Aborigines believed humans were the children of the Morning Star and the Moon. The Sun Mother "made them superior to the animals because they had part of her mind and would never want to change their shape." The Ju'/hoansi also make humanity special; first in our ability to master fire, and then in the fear that fire inspired in other animals, separating us from the rest of creation.

Ultimately, such stories are merely another iteration of ethnocentrism and tribalism, writ large. Rather than simply suggesting that one's own group is superior to all others, this suggests that one's own species is superior to all others. Such sentiments serve the same evolutionary function: they help maintain group cohesion. Enlightened self-interest and intolerable arrogance both serve equally well to keep individuals from straying off and dying alone in the wilderness. Social life is not always easy, and interpersonal problems arise even in the most idyllic of societies. When these things happen, a personal commitment to the group becomes necessary. Ethnocentrism is a universal among all human cultures; it helps keep them together as a culture. That said, its evolutionary usefulness speaks nothing to the sentiment's basis in reality. It is a useful belief to hold, but is it *true*?

Starting with the Renaissance, our mythology of self-importance took a series of hard blows. First, Copernicus published his *Revolutions of the Celestial Bodies* posthumously, shattering the geocentric theory that the earth lay at the center of the universe. Copernicus' heliocentric theory has been heralded as the beginning of the scientific revolution; indeed, it is from the title of his book that the term "revolution" took on its current meaning of an overthrow of established ways, ideas and governments. Galileo proved that not all heavenly bodies orbited the earth when he observed the largest four of Jupiter's moons — known now as the Galilean moons. He was placed on trial for his heresy; on the possible threat of torture and execution, Galileo recanted, though legend says that he whispered under his breath, "*E pur si muove!*" — "But it *does* move!"

Just as we began to accept that the planet made for us was not the center of the universe, Darwin closed the vise even more, facing us with the idea that we were animals like any other, no better and no worse. Neither gods nor kings, angels nor demons, not the children of Sky People or the Divine Sun, but mere beasts as any other. Darwin challenged our dominion by suggesting that we were products of evolution, rather than the crown of creation. Ultimately, this is the root of the argument over evolution: are humans mere animals, or are we something better?

We've grasped at a lot of straws to prove that we're special. The first was the soul. Of course, we can't even prove *we* have souls, much less that other animals don't, so the modern, scientific mind has locked onto a related concept: intelligence. The problem is that this supposedly unique human trait is not uniquely human. We've found significant intelligence among nearly all the great apes, dolphins, parrots, and crows. This intelligence even extends to tool use and communication, other traits we have variously used to define our unique status as "higher than the animals."

14

Perhaps, then, we can find the key to our uniqueness in culture? When we define culture tautologically, then yes, of course, only humans have culture. But if we choose not to define "culture" as "what humans do," but instead "things we learn," then suddenly we see quite a few animal cultures. We know there are orangutan cultures, chimpanzee cultures, and even though he can't prove it, George Dyson just can't shake the notion of interspecies co-evolution of languages on the Northwest Coast.

« *During the years I spent kayaking along the coast of British Columbia and Southeast Alaska, I observed that the local raven populations spoke in distinct dialects, corresponding surprisingly closely to the geographic divisions between the indigenous human language groups. Ravens from Kwakiutl, Tsimshian, Haida, or Tlingit territory sounded different, especially in their characteristic "tok" and "tlik."* »

Which brings us to communication. Surely humans are unique in language? Again, it all depends on how niggardly we define the word. It makes sense to consider only verbal communication, and so eliminate the complexity of bees' dances and the pheramone waltz of ant colonies, but we routinely understate the complexity and nuance of chimpanzee calls, bird song, and other animal communication in order to elevate our own achievements. We denigrate these means of communication by insisting on the difference of our particular languages' use of discrete elements and grammar, or by pointing out that chimpanzees do not use the same range of sounds humans do (though, *no* language uses the full range of possible human sounds, either). These criteria of "language" are selected specifically to dance around the fact that other animals also have very complicated means of communication, sufficiently complicated to bear some comparison to a crude, simple human language.

In each of these regards — intelligence, culture and language — humans have achieved a degree of nuance and sophistication that surpasses everything else in the animal kingdom. We are not the only intelligent creatures in the world, but we are certainly the *most* intelligent. We are not alone in possessing culture, but our cultures are the most far-reaching. All animals communicate, but ours is more nuanced and complex than any other. These are differences of degree, not kind. We are not unique in our *possession* of these traits, only in *how much* we have of them.

Every species is unique in some regard. They must be, in order to be species. If there was no trait that differentiated us from chimpanzees, then we would not be humans — we would be chimpanzees. That does not mean that any one of our unique traits are unique in the entire universe. Nor do these unique traits make us a different order of being, any more than the unique attributes of chimpanzees make them a different order of being.

The evidence for human evolution is incontrovertible. It is easy to see how insectivorous rodents simply moved their eye sockets forward to gain binocoluar vision and depth perception to climb up trees and exploit the insect colonies there. It is easy to see the changes in their physiology as some of them adapted to eat fruit. It is simple to trace the development of the great apes as they adapted to life in small communities, the rise of Australopithecus as a grasslands scavenger, and the development of our own genus as we came to rely on hunting. Darwin despaired of a "missing link," a phrase still exploited by creationists. That link is no longer missing — we have an entire fossil continuum clearly outlining the descent of man.

Humans are quite clearly the products of evolution, like every other organism on this planet. Each of us is heir to a genetic heritage stretching back to the dawn of life a billion years ago. We are not gods or kings enthroned by a despotic, short-sighted deity, separated from our domain by the insulation of superiority. We are not damned to an icy tower under the burden of rulership, cut off from all life. We are part of this world, through and through. In a very real sense, everything that lives are siblings to one another, all descended from that first self-propogating protein. We are bound to one another in mutual dependence in complex networks and feedback systems, a system screaming with life. We are not apart from this. We can partake fully in what it means to live — and all it will cost is our illusion of dominion.

Thesis #4: Human population is a function of food supply.

Thomas Malthus was one of the most influential thinkers of all time. His father knew Hume and Rousseau, and his own paper — *An Essay on the Principle of Population* — forever changed the way we think about populations and food supplies. It has informed food security policies worldwide, and provided the basic underpinnings of our modern concern with overpopulation. In *The Origin of Species*, Darwin called his theory of natural selection an application of the doctrines of Malthus in an area without the complicating factor of human intelligence. Yes, Malthus' work has been a major underpinning and influence on everything since. It's a shame he was so incredibly *wrong*.

Malthus' case is simple: population grows "geometrically" (exponentially), but food supply only grows arithmetically. So Malthus warned of a coming crisis where we would not be able to feed our burgeoning population — the "Malthusian catastrophe." Of course, the failure of such a catastrophe to come to pass took a lot of wind out of Malthus' sails. Malthusianism was declared dead after the 1960s and 1970s saw the greatest increases in human population ever seen, accompanied with *higher* calories per capita, thanks to the abundance of the Green Revolution. Cornucopians rejoiced as they saw the evidence come in that increasing population meant increasing prosperity for all: the realization of Jeremy Bentham's credo, "the greatest good for the greatest number."

If it seems too good to be true, that's because it is. Even Bentham knew that the two factors needed to be balanced against one another, and that increasing one necessarily meant decreasing the other. As Garrett Hardin refuted it in his classic article, "The Tragedy of the Commons":

A finite world can support only a finite population; therefore, population growth must eventually equal zero. (The case of perpetual wide fluctuations above and below zero is a trivial variant that need not be discussed.) When this condition is met, what will be the situation of mankind? Specifically, can Bentham's goal of "the greatest good for the greatest number" be realized?

No — for two reasons, each sufficient by itself. The first is a theoretical one. It is not mathematically possible to maximize for two (or more) variables at the same time. This was clearly stated by von Neumann and Morgenstern, but the principle is implicit in the theory of partial differential equations, dating back at least to D'Alembert (1717–1783).

The second reason springs directly from biological facts. To live, any organism must have a source of energy (for example, food). This energy is utilized for two purposes: mere maintenance and work. For man maintenance of life requires about 1600 kilocalories a day ("maintenance calories"). Anything that he does over and above merely staying alive will be defined as work, and is supported by "work calories" which he takes in. Work calories are used not only for what we call work in common speech; they are also required for all forms of enjoyment, from swimming and automobile racing to playing music and writing poetry. If our goal is to maximize population it is obvious what we must do: We must make the work calories per person approach as close to zero as possible. No gourmet meals, no vacations, no sports, no music, no literature, no art...I think that everyone will grant, without argument or proof, that maximizing population does not maximize goods. Bentham's goal is impossible.

So why were the Cornucopians so right, and Malthus so wrong? Because Malthus got the entire problem almost completely backwards — and it has remained backwards ever since.

Science has never been as unbiased as it would like to be — how could it? Skewing results is easily noticed, and rightfully condemned — as happened with such forgeries as Piltdown Man. Much more insidious is a lack of curiousity. We do not question recieved wisdom, and what we do not question we cannot understand. From Genesis 1:28 to the present day, we've viewed population growth as an inherent property of human nature. It has gone unquestioned. Certainly an Anglican country parson like Malthus would not question it. Malthus' problem was how to feed so many people — a problem that could only be solved by misery, vice (i.e., contraception) or moral restraint (i.e., abstinence). The country parson, naturally, favored the same kind of abstinence programs in favor by the United States' current conservative regime.

This is entirely backwards. What are all these people made of, fairy dust and happy thoughts? No, they are made of proteins — of food! Without a sufficient food supply, such a population cannot be achieved. We understand this as a basic biological fact for every other species on this planet, that population is a function of food supply. Yet we continue to believe that the magic of free will exempts us from such basic biological laws.

The usual counter-argument goes something like this: Humans are different from other animals. We can think. We can rationally observe the situation, and decide for ourselves how many children to have. While this is certainly true of individuals, groups are governed by much more deterministic criteria. For every individual who decides to be responsible and only have 2.1 children, another will take advantage of the space that individual has opened by having seven. The variation in values, thought patterns, beliefs and feelings of social responsibility ensure that the fertility rates of a group will rise to the carrying capacity possible, regardless of the intelligent, responsible choices of others in the community. Charles Galton Darwin, the grandson of *that* Charles Darwin, said, "It may well be that it would take hundreds of generations for the progenitive instinct to develop in this way, but if it should do so, nature would have taken her revenge, and the variety *Homo contracipiens* would become extinct and would be replaced by the variety *Homo progenitivus*."

Education is often proposed as a solution, but Garrett Hardin already offered the best counter-argument to that strategy, again in "The Tragedy of the Commons":

The long-term disadvantage of an appeal to conscience should be enough to condemn it; but it has serious short-term disadvantages as well. If we ask a man who is exploiting a commons to desist "in the name of conscience," what are we saying to him? What does he hear? — not only at the moment but also in the wee small hours of the night when, half asleep, he remembers not merely the words we used but also the nonverbal communication cues we gave him unawares? Sooner or later, consciously or subconsciously, he senses that he has received two communications, and that they are contradictory: 1. (intended communication) "If you don't do as we ask, we will openly condemn you for not acting like a responsible citizen"; 2. (the unintended communication) "If you do behave as we ask, we will secretly condemn you for a simpleton who can be shamed into standing aside while the rest of us exploit the commons."

Every man then is caught in what Bateson has called a "double bind." Bateson and his co-workers have made a plausible case for viewing the double bind as an important causative factor in the genesis of schizophrenia. The double bind may not always be so damaging, but it always endangers the mental health of anyone to whom it is applied. "A bad conscience," said Nietzsche, "is a kind of illness."

We can see this problem of overpopulation and education as a case of the Prisoner's Dilemna. The best case scenario is cooperation; if neither prisoner confesses, both go off free. If we are all responsible, then we can save ourselves from self-destruction. But this is not what usually happens. The fear of abandonment prompts players to pre-emptively abandon the other. The question becomes a simple one of game theory, and the challenge to stop overpopulation by education, a contradiction of human nature.

All of this, however, is theoretical. This hypothesis is easy to test: calculate carrying capacity, and compare it to actual human population numbers. This is precisely what Russell Hopfenberg of Duke University did in his 2003 study, "Human Carrying Capacity is Determined by Food Availability. As you might imagine from such a title, he found that the numbers lined up almost perfectly.

There is a significant complication in this, however, which critics of this stance are eager to point out. The First World is facing a population growth decline — the world's richest nations are growing by the smallest percentages. Italy has been very concerned with its low growth rate, only 0.11% according to a 2003 estimate. Italy has the 201st highest population growth, and the 100th highest agricultural growth. Meanwhile, Singapore has the sixth highest population growth rate, and the 147th highest agricultural growth rate — out of 147.

If population is a function of food supply, why is the most significant growth taking place in those areas producing the least food?

The answer, I think, lies in globalization. How much of what you ate today came from your own bioregion? Unless you do a significant amount of your grocery shopping at Farmers' Markets or eat only USDA-certified organic food, probably not a lot. In 1980, the average piece of American *fresh produce* was estimated to have traveled 1,500 miles before it was consumed. Interestingly, those same countries which produce so much food but don't see it translate into their population, are also the heaviest exporters, and the impoverished countries with significantly rising growth rates are often the recipients. When the First World rushes in with foreign aid, food, and humanitarian aid to a desert area in the midst of a famine, we serve to prop up an unsustainable population. That drives a population boom in an area that already cannot support its *existing* population. The result is a huge population dependent on outside intervention that itself cannot be indefinitely sustained. Eventually, that population will crash once outside help is no longer possible — and the years of aid will only make that crash even more severe. In the same way that the United States' policy of putting out all forest fires in the 1980s led to an even worse situation in its forests, our benevolence and good intentions have paved the way to a Malthusian hell.

Another part of the answer lies in our ecological footprint. In the passage above, Garrett Hardin made the distinction between the calories it takes to maintain a human body, and the "work calories" humans use to do anything else. While it is certainly true that population is a function of food supply, standard of living — how many work calories we recieve, in addition to mere maintenance — is an important factor in that equation. Not only how much food is available, but how much food each individual demands. The dwindling First World has the largest ecological footprint; the growing Third World has the smallest. Italy comes in at #25 with 5.51 hectares per person (1996); Somalia is #114 with 0.97.

This is ultimately why education appears to have an effect on population: because higher education raises the standard of living, increasing the ecological footprint so that fewer people can live off the same amount of food, reducing the population. However, the problem we face is not one of Malthusian catastrophe. If we could not feed our population, we would not *have* such a population in the first place. The problem is the ecological consequences of such resource exploitation. Expanding ecological footprints do nothing to lessen this. Also, this trend can only continue so far, because the First World *needs* the Third. Our prosperity comes from the triumph of the corporate model, but the corporation itself runs on externalized costs. Our economy could never function if we had to pay the full and total cost for the luxuries we enjoy. Consider simply our oil costs — never mind the way it is built in to, say, our food. The Arab population oppressed under Saudi rule pays the balance for our cheap oil. Low prices at WalMart are made possible by cheap Third World labor. It is a grim economic reality that, given ten apples and ten people, for one person to have nine apples, the other nine must split one between them. In the conclusion to their 1996 study on ecological footprint, Wackernagel and Rees stated, "If everybody lived like today's North Americans, it would take at least two additional planet Earths to produce the resources, absorb the wastes, and otherwise maintain life-support." Since we have but one earth, this conclusion can also be spun around in the form that each of us essentially has three slaves whose existence is one of constant misery for our benefit.

Intelligence does not exempt us from basic biological laws — just as it has not exempted dolphins, crows or chimpanzees. Groups reproduce to the best of their ability, and the carrying capacity — their food supply — creates the ceiling of that ability. Populations will rise to their carrying capacity, and no further — even human populations. So Malthus has the problem entirely backwards. The problem is not how to feed so many people; of course we have the means to feed them, because if we didn't, the population would not exist. The problem is the implications of so many people.

Every year, there is a certain amount of energy generated by the sun. This energy radiates in all directions, so there is only a small given percentage of it that falls on the earth. The total amount of solar energy available to our planet per time unit has a hard limit — what is called the photosynthetic capacity of the planet. This energy can be used in any number of ways. Plants turn solar energy into sugar; animals turn plant sugar into kinetic energy. Animals can eat other animals, and obtain the energy stored in their bodies, which they obtained from plants, which they obtained from the sun. But none of these conversions are perfect, and some energy is lost in each one; this is why an animal that eats other predators is almost unheard of. Also, each individual likely used some of the energy, before it was taken by the next link in the chain. As animals, we are always at least one step removed — and as omnivores, we're just as often two steps removed. Also, we're only one of millions, if not billions of species, all sharing the same, set amount of energy from the sun.

With the agricultural revolution, we found a way to convert biomass into human flesh, by reducing biodiversity in favor of our own foods. We increased the percentage of the planet's photosynthetic capacity that we recieved. Solar energy that fell on an acre of forest would be divided amongst all the creatures, plant, animal and otherwise, that lived there. Solar energy that fell on an acre of wheat would go exclusively to humans. Our carrying capacity increased; not just that we had more food, but in more abstract terms, we were helping ourselves to more energy. Our population increased, so we cultivated more land. We had more people, so obviously we needed more food. We cultivated more land, and occasionally improved our technology to increase our yields per acre, but more food simply led to more people. Who required more food ... the Food Race. But lurking high above our heads was an absolute limit: photosynthetic capacity.

In the 1960s, we saw the latest, greatest "win" in the Food Race: the Green Revolution applied the potential of petroleum to farming, allowing for vastly increased yields. We found a bit of a "cheat" to the natural order in fossil fuels. Now, we can burn through decades of solar energy every day to escape the limits of photosynthetic capacity. Essentially, we burn our past and take credit against our future in order to ensure our continued, exponential growth.

The Green Revolution set our carrying capacity to — well, whatever we wanted it to be. The population responded accordingly, with a huge initial jump, slowing as it reaches its asymptote. The scientists say that asymptote lies at 9 billion, and who am I to disagree? It seems like a perfectly reasonable figure. The population growth curve fits exactly what you would expect for a population adjusting to a suddenly raised carrying capacity — a huge jump, peaking relatively early, and extinguishing as it reaches the new "stable."

Of course, it's unlikely that this will remain the case for long. The Food Race goes on. 9 billion people will leave millions — billions, even — starving. Those people need to be fed. We need another "win" in the Food Race!

But 9 billion people is not sustainable. 6.4 billion is not sustainable. There is no sustainble solution for so many people. Only the Green Revolution can feed that many, and the Green Revolution is inherently unsustainable, because it relies on the consumption of a non-renewable resource.

The human race currently consumes some 40% of the earth's photosynthetic capacity. This monopoly on the earth's resources is having a devastating effect. We are seeing the extinction of some 140 species every day, some thousands of times higher than the normal background rate. Today, right now, we are seeing extinction rates unparalleled in the history of the earth. We are undeniably in the midst of the seventh mass extinction event in the history of the earth — the Holocene Extinction. Unlikely previous extinction events, however, this one is driven by a single species.

This is the true danger of overpopulation, not our inability to feed a growing population. As much as we would deny it, we depend on the earth to live. Dwindling biodiversity threatens the very survival of our species. We are literally cutting the ground out from under our feet.

Increasing food production only increases the population; our current attitudes about food security has locked us into what Daniel Quinn called a "Food Race," by comparison to the Arms Race of the Cold War. Garrett

Hardin began his famous article with this dilemna, and I'll close with his assessment:

« In our day (though not in earlier times) technical solutions are always welcome. Because of previous failures in prophecy, it takes courage to assert that a desired technical solution is not possible. Wiesner and York exhibited this courage; publishing in a science journal, they insisted that the solution to the problem was not to be found in the natural sciences. They cautiously qualified their statement with the phrase, "It is our considered professional judgment...." Whether they were right or not is not the concern of the present article. Rather, the concern here is with the important concept of a class of human problems which can be called "no technical solution problems," and more specifically, with the identification and discussion of one of these. »

It is easy to show that the class is not a null class. Recall the game of tick-tack-toe. Consider the problem, "How can I win the game of tick-tack-toe?" It is well known that I cannot, if I assume (in keeping with the conventions of game theory) that my opponent understands the game perfectly. Put another way, there is no "technical solution" to the problem. I can win only by giving a radical meaning to the word "win." I can hit my opponent over the head; or I can falsify the records. Every way in which I "win" involves, in some sense, an abandonment of the game, as we intuitively understand it. (I can also, of course, openly abandon the game — refuse to play it. This is what most adults do.)

The class of "no technical solution problems" has members. My thesis is that the "population problem," as conventionally conceived, is a member of this class. How it is conventionally conceived needs some comment. It is fair to say that most people who anguish over the population problem are trying to find a way to avoid the evils of overpopulation without relinquishing any of the privileges they now enjoy. They think that farming the seas or developing new strains of wheat will solve the problem — technologically. I try to show here that the solution they seek cannot be found. The population problem cannot be solved in a technical way, any more than can the problem of winning the game of tick-tack-toe.

Thesis #5: Humans are neither good nor evil.

Are humans essentially good, or essentially evil? This is one of the most basic, perennial questions in philosophy. Many identify our individual answers to this question as determing our political spectrum — conservatives believe humans are inherently evil, and require strict rules to make them good, while liberals believe humans are inherently good, and must simply be free to act on such goodness. Both positions are unrealistic. Humans are products of evolution, and evolution is unconcerned with such abstractions as "good" or "evil." As Aristotle said, humans are social animals. We are neither "good" nor "evil." We are only inherently *social*.

From the beginning of our civilization, our vision of ourselves has suffered from a sort of schizophrenia, pulled between these two unrealistic poles of good and evil. Plato posited that we each had an angelic spirit in our mind, and a bestial demon in our belly, with all our actions, emotions, and passions torn between them. This provides a foreshadowing of Descartes' dualism, which remains a powerful idiom today, even though modern medicine has conclusively proven the strong interdependence of mind and body. Though I doubt it was a conscious modelling, it would be a mistake to overlook the obvious philosophical heritage this provides to Freud's formulation of the id, ego and superego. This dichotomy was only made more severe by the influence of Zoroastrianism. Once adopted by Judaism prior to the splintering of Christianity, and later Islam, this vision of the universe at war between good and evil was combined with the ancient Greek concept of macrocosm and microcosm to only further this "bizarre superstition." Even Jesus makes reference to this idea in the gospels with, "The spirit is willing, but the flesh is weak." (Matthew 26:41) In this vision, humanity itself is neither good nor evil, but only because each individual human is a spiritual battleground between the two. It is a vision of human nature that is not inherently good, nor inherently evil, but instead, inherently *schizophrenic*. Though widely accepted, it is a rather crude attempt to reconcile "the better angels of our nature" with the ugly facts of our history. Descartes' dualism, once fundamental to the early practice of medical science, has since become an impediment. Neurology, psychiatry and biopsychology have all highlighted how closely knit the mind and the body are. In fact, any separation is now recognized as utterly lacking in any basis in reality.

Another concept, equally ancient, dismisses such ambivalence by simply claiming that humans are inherently evil. Perhaps the earliest formulation of this came from Plato, who argued that men act ethically only for fear of punishment. This sits well with the concept of "original sin" we find in the Abrahamic traditions. In Christianity, the inherent sinfulness of humanity necessitated the sacrifice of Christ, and subsequently, obedience to Holy Mother Church. On the other side, it is argued that altruism is an illusion, because every seemingly altruistic act is motivated by some selfish desire, even if it is only a desire for a feeling of self-fulfillment. Dawkins' central thesis in *The Selfish Gene* is an argument grounding this concept in biology: that altruism arises as a genetic strategy of propogating itself.

This vision of humanity found its ultimate fulfillment in the work of Thomas Hobbes. *"Bellum omnium contra omnes"* — Hobbes' "war of all, against all" — was the first word on the "state of nature." It was a hypothetical then, a possible time when humans may have existed without government. Philosophers were only beginning to consider the possibility of the scientific method, and Hobbes was a strong proponent of the superiority of philosophical thought experiments. Anthropological data was only beginning, and even what little there was, was generally of the form of imperial apologia, describing the horror of barbaric pagan ways, and how desperately they needed the salvation of Christendom and European civilization. Hobbes' "state of nature" owed much to the Christian conept of the inherent sinfulness of humanity, and much to the trauma of his own childhood. His mother went into labor prematurely when she became panic-stricken with news of the Spanish Armada's approach, leading Hobbes to later remark, "Fear and I were born twins." The individual human in the "state of nature" was, in Hobbes' philosophy, a solitary predator whose cruelty was matched only by his cowardice. The result of such "anarchy," in the traditional, pejorative sense of the word, was a life that was "solitary, poor, nasty, brutish, and short."

This idea of human nature is more often associated with the right side of the political spectrum. It argues that humanity is inherently evil, and that a just society is only possible when humans are compelled to act justly by the threat of force. This idea underlies our concepts of law, justice, and punishment at a very basic level. One might consider rhetoric of "deterrance" as a euphemism for this philosophy of terrorizing others into compliance. Hobbes is a powerful underlying current in the philosophy of the neoconservatives.

In counterpoint to this is the view that humans are inherently *good*. We might find faint echoes of this in Abrahamic mythology of humanity as the "crown of creation," but Christianity has traditionally emphasized the fallen nature of humanity, over its exalted nature. The concept that human nature is essentially good is much more modern, finding its roots primarily in the changing strategies of colonial apologia in the 1600s and 1700s.

Where Hobbes' "state of nature" was supported by the tales of cruel heathens and their primitive ways, with the obvious call to colonize those lands and save the savages by giving them Christ's redemption and civilization's benefits, by the time of Jean-Jacques Rousseau, imperial apologists had turned to a different strategy. Evoking the imagery of an Edenic existence, they wove a myth of the "Noble Savage." The term "noble savage" first appeared in English with John Dryden in 1672, though it originated earlier, in 1609, with Lescarbot's *Histoire de la Nouvelle France*. Lescarbot noted that among the Mi'kmaq, everyone was allowed to hunt — an activity enjoyed only by Europe's nobility. This led Lescarbot to remark that "the Savages are truly noble," thus referring to nobility of birth, rather than nobility of character. However, to trace the etymology of a popular phrase is a very different problem from the history of that idea it expresses. In this new form of apologia, indigenous peoples are presented as innocent, unspoiled by civilization. They are innocent, honest, healthy, moral people living in harmony with nature and one another. The savage is like the child, innocent of the "real world" and all its concomitant iniquities. And just as children must be protected by their parents, so too must these innocent savages be protected by more mature, worldly European powers.

In *The Myth of the Noble Savage*, Ter Ellingson argues that the myth of the noble savage was never widely believed — a straw man made to be universally debunked. She points to the racist work of John Crawfurd in 1859 popularizing the concept, attributing it to Rousseau to give it intellectual weight. I haven't read Ellingson's account, so I can't speak much to it except that it seems to contradict the entire body of Romantic thought. Though Crawfurd may have been the first to introduce the racist messages of the "Noble Savage" myth of *"ein Volk, ein Land,"* the two ideas have become inextricably linked in Romantic philosophy. It became a primary basis for Nazi ideology in the 1920s.

Yet, these ideas contradict Rousseau's own argument in many ways. The myth of the "Noble Savage" states that savages are innately good because of their race. Rousseau argues that *all* humans are innately good, regardless of race, and that we are "corrupted" by civilization.

This myth has been thoroughly debunked by writers, philosophers and anthropologists, who highlight the darker side of "savage" life. In *War Before Civilization*, Lawrence Keeley highlights the violence of Neolithic and horticultural "primitives," and shows that, *per capita*, they experience more violent casualties from war than civilizations do. Another favorite criticism is the "overkill theory," but this particular argument is deeply flawed: though humans were no doubt involved in the extinction of the megafauna, our contribution was likely no greater than any other alpha predator would have made. Tribal societies suffer from the same ethnocentrism as all other human societies. Tribal societies are not idyllic utopias, and their members are not angels. In the "state of nature," humans are not always and invariable "good." These arguments are sufficient to prove Rousseau wrong about the essential nature of our species.

If, then, Hobbes is wrong to project his own fear to the entire species, and Rousseau is wrong to project his idealism the same way, where does that leave the truth of who we are? If we are neither good nor evil, what are we? What manner of creature has evolution created in us?

In my study, I have identified several characteristics that I would call the essential hallmarks of "human nature." If I had to sum them up into a single, pithy slogan, I would take Aristotle's: humans are social animals.

1. **Society**. Humans are social animals. In rare and extraordinary circumstances, in areas barely fit for human habitation, there have been collapses of even the simplest forager societies, such as among the Ik. This is an exceptional extreme of social collapse. In general, humans need some sort of society to survive.
2. **Culture**. Culture is not unique to humans, but we have certainly emphasized it to an unprecedented degree. Our brains are hard-wired to recieve culture. The acculturation process can stir us as powerfully as genetic impulses. This is highlighted as simply as the old (useless) debate on "nature versus nurture." To consider an analogue from the world of technology, Herbert Simon helped write the General Problem Solver (GPS) in 1957. Prior to this, programs were written to solve specific problems. This was perhaps the first instance of a more generalized approach: the GPS could be fed information on specific problems, and then solve them. It is the difference between a machine that is hard-wired to do a specific task, and a machine that can be programmed to do any number of tasks. This is the difference culture makes; it allows for another layer, and gives humans an adaptive edge.

It also means that we have much less of an essential "nature" than other animals, since we more closely resemble Rousseau's "*tabula rasa*."

3. **Egalitarianism**. There are ambiguously gendered humans. This in itself shows a degree of sexual dimorphism among the lowest in the entire animal kingdom. Males are not significantly larger than females, and morphological differences are minimal, particularly when compared to many of our closest primate cousins. Male baboons are three times the size of females, and mandrill males sport distinctive coloring that make them almost look like an entirely different species. Sexual dimorphism throughout the animal kingdom is correlated with gender equality. Emperor penguins have as little sexual dimorphism as we, and they split child-rearing responsibilities evenly. This physical evidence strongly suggests that gender equality is part of human nature. Egalitarianism in general is supported by a total lack of evidence for any form of hierarchy in our species, except in cases of exceptional abundance and surplus (that is, after the Neolithic, except for the singular exceptions of the Kwakiutl and the burial sites of Sungir). This is further corroborated by the universality of egalitarianism among modern foragers. Even in hierarchical societies, in all times and places, there is a universal aspiration towards more egalitarian forms of society — even where population pressure and complexity will not allow for egalitarianism. Thus, it seems that we should consider egalitarianism part of human nature.

4. **Technology.**. The genus *Homo* suffers from one of the most ridiculous distinctions in all of biology, thanks to the powerful force of anthropocentrism: we are defined by our tool use. Though other primitivist writers define themselves by a rejection of technology, even the most primitive societies use tools of some kind. Tool use, though, is a very different proposition from an almost messianic belief in the power of technology to save us from all problems. Technology is morally ambivalent, capable of good or evil depending on how it is used. Yet the creation and use of tools *of some kind* is a universal human trait, and one that figures prominently in our evolution. The creation of the first stone tools is strongly correlated to the exponential increases in cranial capacity that defines *Homo habilis* from *Australopithecus afarensis*. It is also strongly correlated to handedness (a rather unique quirk we possess in the animal kingdom), and another crucial aspect of human nature:

5. **Language**. Though humans are not unique in their use of an advanced and nuanced communication system, there is little that can compare to the complexity of human language. Much of the human brain is hard-wired to use some kind of language. There is a "universal grammar" born instinctively in every human child. All human societies have some kind of language. The implications of this are far-reaching, from abstract thought to Wittgenstein's philosophies.

6. **Story-telling**. Australopithecines were almost certainly scavengers, competing in the African savanna — an environment where the emergence of "super-predators" had given rise to one of the most competitive ecosystems in the history of the planet. They could hardly compete with some of the other scavengers, such as hyenas and vultures, and so developed tools to get to a kill site first, grab the meat, and get out before other scavengers arrived. As tool use became more sophisticated, early humans began to hunt for themselves. This innovation required a range of skills, including story telling. Tracking has a great deal to do with weaving a story. The tracks, scat and other signs are, themselves, meaningless, unless one can weave that evidence into a narrative of the animal's state, size and progression. This combines with human's capacity for language and abstract thought to create a creature that tells stories. Scientific explanations of the Big Bang and evolution are as much stories as ancient myths and legends. Any narrative that links elements in a linear, causal line is a story. This article is a story.

What does this say to the essential question of whether humans are "good" or "evil"? Nothing. Humans are neither. We are not good, we are not evil, and we are not torn between the two. There are characteristics of human nature, but none of those characteristics can truly be called "good" or "evil." We are what we are, and nothing more. We live more easily, and more fully, when we work with that rather than against it. That nature, though, is neither "good" nor "evil" — it simply *is*.

Thesis #6: Humans are still Pleistocene animals.

In 1833, Charles Lyell introduced the name "Holocene," or "Recent Whole," for our current geological epoch, stretching back only 10 or 12 thousand years. This makes the Holocene an incredibly young geological epoch, the shortest by far. The International Geological Congress in Bologna adopted the term in 1885, and it has been the accepted terminology ever since. The preceding geological epoch was the "last ice age," the Pleistocene. It lasted for two million years, and while it was marked by significantly advanced glaciation, this was not the unremitting state of affairs. The Pleistocene had regular interglacial periods, during which the weather would turn warmer and the glaciers would temporarily recede — just like today. These interglacials typically lasted an average of 10 — 20 thousand years — just like ours. In short, the "Holocene" is not a new geological epoch, as much as we might think that the grandeur of human civilization's appearance should be reflected in the ages of the earth. It is a perfectly typical interglacial. The Pleistocene — the "last ice age" — never ended. We're still in it — we're simply in a bit of a warm spell.

If anything, our current interglacial is most remarkable for its brevity. If it ended this week and the glaciers returned (and, while *The Day After Tomorrow* certainly pressed the point too far, these things *do* happen *very* suddenly), it would be marked as the shorter side of normal. In fact, it would have ended some 5,000 years ago— an interglacial of just 5 to 7 thousand years — were it not for the ecological devastation of the Agricultural Revolution. The first farmers were responsible for massive deforestation, and raising huge herds of livestock that polluted the atmosphere with incredible amounts of methane — enough to hold the glaciers in check. For 5,000 years, our civilization has lived on borrowed time, extending our "Holocene" by balancing the earth's natural cooling trend against our reckless environmental abuse. The Industrial Revolution was not a change in kind, but in scale — a significant increase in our ability to harm the earth's ecosystems, destroying all semblance of balance that our previous rampages had so precariously struck.

Amazingly, much of the reporting on Ruddiman's findings, like the FuturePundit entry cited above, argue that this is evidence that humans *should* try to engineer the planet's climate. Our agricultural civilization is utterly dependent on the peculiar climate of the Holocene interglacial, this is true. It is a unique product of that climate, and if that climate ends, so will it. In the same fashion, humans are children of the Pleistocene. It is our home, through and through. We have changed far too little in the past 10,000 years to be well-adapted to the epochal changes in our lifestyle that we have seen. We are maladapted to our cultural context. The ecological damage we have done for these past millennia have only extended this state of affairs. Civilization may not be able to survive the end of the Holocene interglacial, but *humanity* certainly can. We are Pleistocene animals.

The Pleistocene was preceded by the Pliocene, an epoch cooler and drier than the preceeding Miocene. Temperatures and rainfall were similar to that of today; in most regions, this meant a colder, drier climate. This was the case in Africa, where jungles shrank and grasslands took their place. Our ancestors were those primates who did not retreat with the jungle, but instead attempted to make their living in the wide, open grasslands. It was in this new challenge that our ancestors, the australopithecines, first defined themselves: by walking upright.

Habitual bipedality is unique in the order primates, though certainly not across the animal kingdom. Australopithecine anatomy shifted to accomodate a vertical, rather than horizontal, alignment. Greater height gave australopithecines the ability to see farther over the grasses, and it gave them a new mode of locomotion in walking.

Walking has unqiue advantages. It is not by any means the fastest mode of transport. Most animals can run faster than humans. However, such locomotion is supported primarily by powerful muscles. This means they tire quickly. Cheetahs can run at over 110 km/hr (70 mph), but it cannot sustain this speed for very long. Most cheetahs will stalk their prey closely, but the final chase will rarely last more than one minute. Walking is very different. Walking does not rely on muscle, but on bone. Walking is a controlled fall, which shifts the body's weight onto the leg bones, thanks to the locked knee. This means that there is less energy involved in each individual step a bipedal human takes, compared to most quadrupedal animals. Humans may not move as quickly, but they can move more often. The result is an animal that won't run as quickly, but at the end of the day can cover much more ground.

This tells us something about the changing diet of australopithecus. Many other apes are opportunistic scavengers, and sometimes even hunters. However, this is rarely their primary sustenance. The innovation of walking suggests that australopithecines were relying more on meat than their ancestors had.

The superpredators of Africa had created a harsh Darwinian niche for scavengers, leading to powerful packs of hyenas and flocks of vultures that could easily overpower australopithecines. Instead, australopithecines adopted a strategy of finding the kill site first, getting to it first, grabbing their meat, and retreating before other, more powerful scavengers showed up. Walking upright allowed them to see farther across the grasslands, but a kill site could be *anywhere*. The more ground a scavenger covers in a day, the more likely that scavenger is to stumble upon a kill site. Scavengers don't necessarily need to be fast — the dead rarely outrun them — they just need to keep moving as long as possible and cover as large a range as possible. The larger their daily range, the higher their chances of finding a kill site. That's precisely what walking allows for, and australopithecine anatomy was built for nothing quite so perfectly as walking.

We retain those traits even today, which is precisely what makes walking such an important activity. Thomas Jefferson remarked, "Walking is the best possible exercise. Habituate yourself to walk very far." For more than 99% of our history, humans have been foragers — which meant, more than anything else, walking. While foragers work markedly less than we do, that work consisted almost exclusively of walking: up to four hours every day. The effects of the automobile in the 1950s not only gave us dating, it also destroyed our communities. Resources were no longer grouped together, as walking from place to place became impossible and automobiles became a requirement for existence. Face-to-face interaction died off, and so did the habit of walking — resulting in our current obesity crisis. This doesn't mean that cars and dating are bad — what it means is that we now live in a context to which we are not adapted.

* * *

Two million years ago, the Pliocene became colder and drier still, as the Pleistocene began. The last of these walking australopithecines, *Australopithecus afarensis*, was nearly identical to the first member of our own genus, *Homo habilis*, save in one, crucial regard: *Homo habilis*'s skull was twice the size of the australopithecus'.

Thanks mostly to anthropocentrism, our genus, *Homo*, suffers from what may well be the single most ridiculous defining criteria in all of science: *we use tools*. Of course, we have found tool use in other animals (as we touched on in thesis #3), and it is entirely likely that various australopithecines used wooden tools at least as complicated as those fashioned by modern-day chimpanzees or crows. Chimpanzees have even been observed with the rare *stone* tool. But the primary reason that this distinction is so laughable as a biological genus is that it is entirely behavioral, and *utterly divorced from biology!*

That is not to say that our tool use isn't important. Quite the opposite. The explosion in cranial capacity that separates the two contemporary hominid genera seems quite significant. It is very clearly tied to tool use, for while australopithecines may well have fashioned any manner of wooden tools, we only find stone tools associated with *Homo habilis.*

The Oldowan tool set is the oldest set of technology we know of. It emerged 2.4 million years ago, as the long cooling of the Pliocene — the era of the australopithecines — gave way to the deeper cold of the Pleistocene — the era of our own genus. The making of these stone tools required changes in *Homo habilis*'s brain structures. We find the first evidence for handedness among these earliest members of our genus. We have also learned that handedness, tool use, and *language* are all linked functions in the human brain. Even if *Homo habilis* could not speak, the neurological foundations for it were laid with tool use.

These tools made *Homo habilis* a more efficient scavenger. With choppers and other stone tools, *Homo habilis* could butcher a dead animal more quickly, allowing them to clear out of the kill site more quickly, giving them an evolutionary edge. Yet for all its importance, the Oldowan tool kit changed little in the million years that it was used by *Homo habilis* and the myriad species thrown together into the waste-basket called "*Homo erectus.*" These tools made our genus a far more efficient scavenger. The greater amounts of meat this afforded provided the protein for the explosion in cranial capacity that marked the seperation of the hominid genera.

One of the various "*Homo erectus*" species developed the Achulean tool set; others learned how to use and control fire. Hominids became better scavengers. Now they might have used their weapons to scare off other scavengers, rather than butchering quickly and running from the site. They may have begun to prey upon that gray area ever carnivore treads. No predator will pass up a perfectly good, recent kill — and many scavengers are more than willing to finish off a wounded animal. Or, with sufficient coordination and/or weaponry, a hale and healthy animal. It was in the "*Homo erectus*" period that hominids transitioned from scavengers, to hunters.

Through the 1960s and 1970s, the "Man the Hunter" theory dominated thinking on this topic, explaining human evolution in terms of hunting practices. It was closely linked to thinking on "killer apes," and a generally Hobbesian view of human nature, painting humans as inherently violent killers. It drew ire from feminists who charged that it neglected the role of females in evolution, while other researchers hoped for evidence to distance human nature from such a grim, violent picture. That theory has declined in recent years, largely due to political correctness.

The feminist critique is rather weak. Since every female has a father, any strong natural selection exerted on one gender will easily cause changes throughout the species, in *both* genders. Any strong natural selection exerted on women will show up in the male population, as well. There is a much stronger criticism in the analyses of forager diets showing that they rely much more on plants than animals. Richard Lee showed that foragers relied more on plant matter than meat, leading some to refer to "gatherer-hunters" rather than "hunter-gatherers." However, critics of Lee highlighted his complete reliance on the Ju/'Hoansi, who have an atypical love affair with the mongongo nut. More cross-cultural studies found that forager diets correlated to latitude: foragers closer to the equator ate more plants, foragers closer to the poles ate more meat. They also found significantly more meat than Lee: near 100% for such polar extremes as the Inuit, but only 14% of forager cultures in total got even half of their diet from plants. Despite this solid refutation, much is still made of Lee's findings. An emerging concensus supports this "gatherer-hunter" model, though nearly all arguments for it are based on political correctness.

For the opponents of the "Man the Hunter" theory, acquiescing that hunting was an important part of human evolution is to normalize and excuse violence. It rests on an idea that is very old in Hinduism and Buddhism, which has only in recent decades formed vegetarian thought in the West: the idea of meat-eating as an inherently violent act. The presumption of this argument is that violence is only violence if enacted upon animals; that one cannot by violent towards plants. There is an assumption in this that while animals are alive, plants really aren't. This is also a very old idea. The name "animal" derives from the Latin *animus* or spirit, because animals are *animated* — moved by a spirit — while plants are not. Even in shamanic and animistic schemes, animal life is often elevated above plant life.

The underpinnings for this belief have little basis in fact. As animals, animals are closer to us, and thus enjoy some special concern from us for their proximity. At its base, this is simply one more concentric circle in the widening ripples of anthropocentrism. As Giulianna Lamanna highlighted in her article, "The Hypocrisy of Vegetarianism," there is even some intriguing indications of the possibility that plants may even *feel* in some strange way. Violence against a carrot is every bit as much violence, as violence against a cow.

Yet the proponents of "Man the Hunter" have predicated it upon an inherently evil and violent human nature; its detractors have predicated it upon an inherently good and gentle human nature. Both are idealized and misguided. We do not think of other predators as evil or violent, do we? Do we conceive of lions, or sharks, or bears, or spiders in such ways? Predators are important parts of the natural world. The return of the wolves to Yellowstone restored the park's ecology which had been thrown out of balance by the predator's departure.

We have already seen that both views of humans as good and humans as evil are overly simplistic (thesis #5). The issue of humanity and hunting is a fine example of such an issue that cuts both ways. Tracking requires careful observation, but even that alone is insufficient. Careful observation yields only an assemblage of data points. The tracker must assemble those points into a narrative, to weave a story around that data that not only says where the animal was and what it did, but predicts where it is going, as well. The needs of the tracker provide the natural selective pressure for human cognition as we know it.

But hunting is never a sure thing. Sometimes you bag yourself a big, juicy kill, and sometimes you come home empty-handed. Skill has a lot to do with it — but so does luck. Among foragers, it's been calculated that on any given hunt, a hunter only has a 25% chance of making a kill. Yet our ancestors not only derived most of their protein from meat, they derived most of their daily energy from meat, as well. How did they do this, if they only ate one day out of four? While the probability that one hunter will fail on a given day might be 0.75, the probability that four hunters that all go out on the same day will all fail to catch something is 0.316. In other words, if four hunters all agree to share whatever they kill between them, then there is generally a 68% chance that all four of them will eat that day — where alone, their chances drop to 25%.

The risks involved in hunting made cooperation an important human strategy. Unlike other primates, our bonds formed into small, open, cooperative, *egalitarian* groups. The adoption of human society to mitigate hunting risks emphasized that any hunter could be the one bringing home dinner that night, and ultimately the conviction that everyone has value to the group. Sharing evolved not as a virtue, but as a necessity. In forager groups today, sharing is not considered "nice," it's simply expected as a social baseline, and as a requirement for survival.

Hunting inhabits a morally ambiguous position, then. The act itself is violent, yet its risks gave us the very notion of society and its attendant virtues of sharing, cooperation, and compassion — the very same virtues vegetarians seek to promote by denying that very thing that created them. The risks of hunting instilled in our ancestors their first sense of wonder and reverence. They saw the animals they killed not as trophies as we might, but as sacrifices necessary for survival. They worshipped the animals they consumed, using the narrative cognition tracking bestowed upon them to yield the first philosophy and religion humans would ever have. As shamans charted the expanses of human consciousness, art, music and science followed. The first hominids made their lives as communal scavengers, but as they learned to hunt, they became human *[On this topic, see the work of Paul Shepard]*.

* * *

But man does not live by meat alone, but by every nut, berry, tuber and leafy green that comes from the hand of woman. While the supposition that foragers were "gatherer-hunters" is little more than political correctness projecting itself back into our evolutionary history, neither can we ignore the importance of gathered foodstuffs. Foragers *did* divide labor roughly along gender lines, with males usually taking up most of the hunting, for obvious, biological reasons. Even though it was hunting that provided not only the protein our bodies required, but also most of the energy we used, it would be a mistake to discount the role of women.

Besides energy and protein, our bodies require smaller amounts of vital micronutrients. We do not need them in large quantities, but we do very much need them. Without sufficient vitamin A, children go blind. Insufficient vitamin D leads to rickets. If you don't get enough vitamin C, you'll come down with a case of scurvy. Wild edible plants provided these in abundances our modern domesticates cannot hope to match. Two cups of dandelion leaves contain more vitamin C than four glasses of orange juice; dandelions have more beta carotine than carrots, and more potassium than potatoes or spinach — alongside healthy doses of iron and copper. You'll find wild edibles replete with quantities of vitamins, minerals, omega 3 fatty acids and all manner of other nutrients that float in our public consciousness precisely because our modern diet so clearly lacks them.

The line between food and medicine was not so clear, either. Common, broadleaf plantain is, along with dandelion, probably one of the most nutritious plant in the world, but plantain is also a powerful pain-killer, as well as having anti-toxic, anti-microbial, and anti-inflammatory properties. When ingested, it is a demulcent, a diuretic, and an expectorant. By the same token, dandelions can be used as a general tonic that helps strengthen the liver, gall bladder, pancreas, spleen, stomach, and intestines. They improve bile flow and reduce inflammation in cases of hepatitis and cirrhosis.

Women did not simply gather side dishes crucial to nutrition and survival; they provided medicines that not only cured sickness, but improved health, as well. Where male hunters cultivated spacial perception and risk-sharing strategies, could it have been the needs of female gatherers that gave us much of our abilities for memory and memorization?

* * *

As Paleolithic foragers, humans were beginnning to develop a new strategy to survive the Pleistocene. Many animals learn a great deal, and use this to supplement their instincts. Orangutans have identifiable cultures, and similar observations have been made of chimpanzees. Humans took this to an extreme, with very few inborn instincts. Instead, our brain became hard-wired not for any specific behavior set, but for recieving culture. In the acculturation process, we learn the rules and taboos of the culture we are born into, and incorporate them on a very deep level. Things that disgust us, for example — particularly food and sex taboos — are usually very arbitrary, yet we feel them so deeply that they are often mistaken for natural, universal truths.

We might think of this innovation in similar terms to the early history of computing. Early computers, or Turing machines, were made to perform a specific task. The innovations of von Neumann, Simon and others led to computers that were made to run arbitrary programs. Most animals have a much larger repository of instincts than we do, and learn much less. This leads to species-wide behavior patterns. Humans, on the other hand, owe much more of their behavior to culture than instinct. This means that culture can provide another layer of adaptation that can change much more quickly than evolution. It gives humans a competitive edge, by allowing us to adapt to any new environment with incredible speed and ease. When combined with our omnivorism opening a much wider array of possible foods, humans have thus become very possibly the most adaptable species on the planet.

Most animals, when confronted by fire, have a natural instinct to run away. At some point, long ago in our history, that instinct was stalled by our acculturation, and rather than run from it, some human actually went towards it, and brought it back under her own control. In time, we even learned how to start our own fires, yet the turning point of that first human to run *towards* the fire remains one of the most pivotal moments in our history. The Greeks immortalized that event in the myth of Prometheus, and the mythology of the San point to it as the turning point of our species:

Kaang gathered all the people and animals about him. He instructed them to live together peacefully. Then he turned to the men and women and warned them not to build any fires or a great evil would befall them. They gave their word and Kaang left to where he could watch his world secretly.

As evening approached the sun began to sink beneath the horizon. The people and animals stood watching this phenomenon, but when the sun disappeared fear entered the hearts of the people. They could no longer see each other as they lacked the eyes of the animals which were capable of seeing in the dark. They lacked the warm fur of the animals also and soon grew cold. In desperation one man suggested that they build a fire to keep warm. Forgetting Kaang's warning they disobeyed him. They soon grew warm and were once again able to see each other.

However the fire frightened the animals. They fled to the caves and mountains and ever since the people broke Kaang's command people have not been able to communicate with animals. Now fear has replaced the seat friendship once held between the two groups.

Humans spread out of Africa, into Asia and Europe. The ice age lowered the water levels, revealing the Bering Land Bridge, which humans followed into the Americas. The lower water levels made the islands of Indonesia and Micronesia larger, and the water between them smaller. Humans hopped from island to island in ancient canoes, until eventually they reached Australia. In these new environments, humans often relied more heavily on meat, at least at first, as they learned the new flora of these strange lands, what was safe to eat, and what was poisonous.

Until recently, the term "Holocene Extinction" referred to a rather minor spate of extinction which took place at the beginning of the Holocene, with the end of the megafauna — woolly mammoths, North American horses, sabertooth cats, and other large mammals. This occured at the beginning of the Holocene, as humans were first moving into many new environments, like the Americas and Australia. This has led to a long-standing debate between "overkill" and "overchill." Were the megafauna wiped out by climate change? Or by rapacious, brutal bands of overhunting human foragers? Both sides have their evidence, of course.

Nor is this merely an academic argument without reprecussion for the present. The "overkill" theory is routinely cited by some groups as if it were already a proven fact, and used as evidence that humans are an inherently destructive species. So we needn't worry ourselves with the environmental destruction we wreak. We can't help it. It's our nature.

As you might expect, the truth lies somewhere between overkill and overchill. Human populations were almost certainly too small to wreak such havok all by themselves, and the same climate changes that opened the way for humans into Australia and the Americas also had to affect the other large mammals living across the globe. Even more instructive, however, is the modern case of the wolves of Yellowstone. Alpha predators — like wolves, and like humans — play important, keystone roles in any ecology. The introduction of a new alpha predator can have dramatic effects, even causing cascades of extinction. This is not necessarily because the alpha predators overhunt or are even in the least bit maladaptive; this is simply the nature of alpha predators and how they relate in any given ecology. When humans came to Australia and the Americas, they were as harmless as wolves, lions, or any other big mammalian predator. Their presence caused cascades of changes throughout the ecosystem. Given that it was also a period of major climate change, a great number of species that were already under stress adapting to the new climate were tipped over the edge into extinction by the further ecological changes created by the adaptation of a new alpha predator. Our ancestors were hardly noble savages; but neither were they bloodthirsty killers bent on the destruction of all life on earth. They were animals, like any other.

* * *

In the Upper Paleolithic, we see a "revolution" leading to what paleoanthropologists sometimes refer to as "behavioral modernity." There is a good deal of misinformation all around on this point, so let me first address this concept of "modernity." Like the waste-basket of *Homo erectus*, paleoanthropologists have shoe-horned many different species into the category of "anatomically modern *Homo sapiens*" not based on fossil evidence, but because of their age. The alternative would be to recognize that human evolution was not a process of unilineal evolution — that it was not a tree, but a "bush." Though this conclusion has become inescapable to most paleoanthropologists today, the categorizations of their predecessors who were not so enlightened often remain.

This has led to some startlement among paleoanthropologists, as we see "anatomically modern" humans, but without evincing any sign of the things we define ourselves by: art, religion, philosophy, etc. So, many have split "modernity" into anatomical and behavioral aspects. This is a false dilemma born not only of the rough shoe-horning of evidence already discussed, but also of the "revolution" idea born of Eurocentrism.

In Europe, the Upper Paleolithic truly is a "revolution." We have cave art, sculptures, musical instruments, evidence of arithmetic and astronomy all appearing at once. This led many paleoanthropologists to think that "modern behavior" was a package deal, that there was some kind of genetic switch that allowed them all to fllower at once.

In Africa, however, we see each of these various elements accrue over time. They do not appear all at once, as in Europe. The conclusion is simple, and straightforward: "behaviorally modern" humans came out of Africa. This is the same "out of Africa" hypothesis that has won almost unanimous support over the multiregional hypothesis that has so long been the bulwark of racists and pseudo-scientists. If we look only at the European evidence, then, we have a "revolution" — but only because these new, African tribes arrived at a given time, practicing all of their culture at once.

Yet, all of these cultural phenomena that we define ourselves by *do* have a common origin, in shamanism. David Lewis-Williams is at his most convincing when he shows the underpinnings of shamanism in human neurology and psychology, and how rock art is an expression of that. Michael Winkelman has written a great deal on the evolutionary adaptations of shamanism. Both show how important shamanism was as an adaptation to the Pleistocene environment we evolved in, not only to reconcile the workings of our inner worlds to the world we live in, but also as a touchstone of community life and social function, an integrative function for the psychologically aberrant, and a healing function for the individual and the community.

Shamans most often induced altered states of consciousness through repetitive sound and motion — song and dance. Their visions provided the philosophy and world-view of their tribes, giving rise to the first religion and philosophy. Often, shamanic rituals were tied to the motions of the celestial bodies — and the first evidence we have of arithmetic is a "counting stick" cut off in sets of 28, most likely tracking the phases of the moon. Shamans were ethnobotanists of the highest order, and were willing to experiment even with the spirit world, so in some sense, we might even trace the first glimmerings of science to them, as well. "Behavioral modernity" goes back to the Upper Paleolithic, a gift from the shaman, and that unique adaptation to the Pleistocene that first tried to map the universe in our own minds.

* * *

The Pleistocene lasted for two million years — the same two million years that saw the rise of our genus. Like all animals, we are products of evolution, adapted to a specific niche. Our niche was the Pleistocene. The Holocene has been far too short for any significant amount of adaptation to occur, and how maladapted we are to our current lifestyle should be obvious. The effects of not walking as often on our health has already been touched upon. The loss of the shaman's role has led to the marginalization of people once well integrated into society, and the loss of tribal society has been catastrophic in other ways which we will explore in future theses. For the moment, I would like to turn to just one arena in which the Holocene has proven the bane of our species: health.

The Agricultural Revolution was a massive change in diet. Where once we had gained the majority of our energy from animal proteins, and our food came from hundreds of different species, the Neolithic saw an utter reliance on less than a dozen different species, with the majority of our energy now coming from carbohydrates. Even today, more than 50% of the American diet comes from just three plants — wheat, rice and potatoes.

Ben Balzer's introduction to the "Paleolithic Diet" provides a great deal of wonderful information on the nutritional deficits that agriculture has given us, but for now I will simply quote his analysis of grains:

« These advantages made it much easier to store and transport food. We could more easily store food for winter, and for nomads and travelers to carry supplies. Food storage also enabled surpluses to be stored, and this in turn made it possible to free some people from food gathering to become specialists in other activities, such as builders, warriors and rulers. This in turn set us on the course to modern day civilization. Despite these advantages, our genes were never developed with grains, beans and potatoes and were not in tune with them, and still are not. Man soon improved further on these advances — by farming plants and animals. »

As Belzar points out, grains are powerful packets of energy. The plants wrap their seeds in carbohydrates, to give them the energy to grow. Co-evolution has struck a balance between the needs of plants and animals: animals eat seeds and fruits, and in return, they help spread the seeds. Key here, from the plant's point of view, is that the seed not be destroyed, or else its part of the deal has been eliminated. Animals adapted to certain plant types will be able to gain nutrition from the wrapping around the seed, and those plants will generally not become toxic to those animals (or else their seeds won't travel very far). However, the seed itself is often quite toxic, to make sure the animals don't eat them.

Humans are very well adapted to eating any number of such fruits, nuts and so forth. Grains, however, are not on that list. Hominids have experimented with eating grains in the past. The only hominids ever adapted to that diet were the genus *Paranthropus*, once classified as the "robust" branch of the Australopithecines. These are, at best, distantly related great-uncles to our own species. We are not descended from them, and have not inherited the various enzymes and chemicals they required to make use of grains.

Grains are quite toxic when eaten raw, but cooking can render them edible. Even then, they are of substantially lower nutritional quality than almost any other edible plant. They contain little more than carbohydrates — an energy source our body can surely make use of, but it is not our bodies' favored source of energy. We are better adapted to the use of protein for energy. Grains also include a number of "anti-nutrients," such as lectins, which can have as wide-spread an effect through the body as hormones, but because they are foreign (and maladapted) to the human body, cause effects that are unpredictable and often deleterious. It may well be because of lectins that the first study of correlative cancer causes, performed by Stanislaw Tanchou in 1843, remains the most accurate. This page from *paleodiet.com* reviews much of the evidence for grains' implication in cancer. It includes:

Stanislaw Tanchou "....gave the first formula for predicting cancer risk. It was based on grain consumption and was found to accurately calculate cancer rates in major European cities. The more grain consumed, the greater the rate of cancer." Tanchou's paper was delivered to the Paris Medical Society in 1843. He also postulated that cancer would likewise never be found in hunter-gatherer populations. This began a search among the populations of hunter-gatherers known to missionary doctors and explorers. This search continued until WWII when the last wild humans were "civilized" in the Arctic and Australia. No cases of cancer were ever found within these populations, although after they adopted the diet of civilization, it became common.

The mechanism is not difficult to imagine. Cancer cells appear in every healthy human body with some frequency, but the immune system idenfities them as foreign and destroys them. Lectins — and generally poor nutrition — suppress the immune response, allowing more cancer cells to survive and become tumors.

Grains, beans and potatoes also have many enzyme blockers that shut down significant parts of the human digestive system. The most common type are protease inhibitors, which block the enzyme protease, which is required in the digestion of protein. Most of these are broken down in cooking, but not all.

Beyond the negative health effects of these "Neolithic foods," they are incredibly poor in the various other nutrients humans need, which were provided in abundance by our forager lifestyle. This is the very reason that humans in industrialized societies so often need dietary and vitamin supplements — our diet does not provide the nutrition we need, the nutrition our bodies evolved to expect.

Why then is bread called "the staff of life"? Simply because it is a staple food. Eaten in sufficient quantities, it can keep us alive — as it has kept generations of civilized people alive. It will keep us alive, for a short, sickly life. The finds at Dickson's Mounds showed the effects of agriculture. The literal children of six foot tall foragers that lived into their 60s or 70s with perfect health, would die of malnutrition or disease in their 20s or 30s, barely reaching five feet. The concentrated populations, proximity to animals (allowing germs to jump the species barrier), and heavy trade of agricultural life allowed for the rise of disease as we know it — this was one of Jared Diamond's main points in his indictment of agriculture as "the worst mistake in the history of the human race." But malnutrition and starvation also became fixtures of human life then. As a general rule, only farmers ever starve.

Realizing this, some have now started calling bread "the staff of death." Steve Brill calls the average American "overfed and malnourished," an idea that evokes the scientific idea of "affluent malnutrition." We maintain our lives — and even our obesity — by eating enormous quantities, but what we eat is so nutritionally bankrupt that even then we are only barely getting the basic requirements for survival.

Our civilization does need the Holocene. The grains it is so utterly dependent on are tempermental crops that can only tolerate the most minute climatic fluctuations. Humans, however, are animals of the Pleistocene. The Pleistocene was our home, it is what we are adapted to. The short 10 millennia of the Holocene has not given us sufficient time to adapt to our modern lives. Those lives are very nearly contradictions of the environment we evolved in: hierarchical, rather than egalitarian; carbohydrate-based, rather than protein-based; sedentary, rather than nomadic; plant-based, rather than animal-based; specialized, rather than generalized; regimented, rather than free-form; marginalized, rather than integrated. It is the very definition of dehumanizing.

There is a glimmer of hope, though. The Holocene is not the geological epoch we glorified it as. It is merely an interglacial; an interglacial due to end any time now. The Pleistocene will return. It's almost time to go home.

Thesis #7: Humans are best adapted to band life.

As we saw in the previous thesis, the division between our genus, *Homo*, and the Australopithecines occurred two million years ago, with *H. habilis* and his freakishly large brain. All primates have brain-to-body mass ratios that are much higher than normal, but the human ratio is remarkable even among primates. According to a study from the University of Liverpool, that disproportionately high brain-to-body mass ratio is determined by the size and complexity of their social groups.

Society has ever been the most powerful strategy that primates employ. We discussed the benefits of risk-sharing in the previous thesis, boiling down essentially to this example, using hunting:

But hunting is never a sure thing. Sometimes you bag yourself a big, juicy kill, and sometimes you come home empty-handed. Skill has a lot to do with it — but so does luck. Among foragers, it's been calculated that on any given hunt, a hunter only has a 25% chance of making a kill. Yet our ancestors not only derived most of their protein from meat, they derived most of their daily energy from meat, as well. How did they do this, if they only ate one day out of four? While the probability that one hunter will fail on a given day might be 0.75, the probability that four hunters that all go out on the same day will all fail to catch something is 0.316. In other words, if four hunters all agree to share whatever they kill between them, then there is generally a 68% chance that all four of them will eat that day — where alone, their chances drop to 25%.

Sharing amongst a group thus ensures food for everyone. It also helps guarantee safety from predation. Cooperation helped primates increase the food they obtained, and decrease the occurence of *becoming* food themselves.

The shift from scavenging and the occasional opportunistic hunt very likely had a good deal to do with another defining characteristic of our species: egalitarianism. Most social primates are strictly hierarchical, like chimpanzees. But, when troops of young, male chimpanzees go on hunting expeditions, that hierarchy often begins to break down. Hunting is a cooperative effort — trying to maintain hierarchy in that situation simply imperils the hunt. As humans began to look to meat for the bulk of its nutritional needs, cooperation became more important, and hierarchy became a luxury our ancestors could not afford.

Egalitarian societies built on sharing and cooperation and guided by consensus were much more adapted to the niche humans exploited than the hierarchical troops of other primates. This egalitarianism even became part of our very bodies — humans have some of the lowest sexual dimorphism in the entire animal kingdom, on par with penguins. Compare this to, say, the baboon, where males may be up to three times the size of females. In some animals, the genders look like entirely different *species* to the untrained eye. The kind of low sexual dimorphism found in humans is not unheard of in the animal kingdom, but in every case, it points to shared parenting behaviors.

There is an inherent complexity in any social group. Not only must we remember the individuals who make up the group, we must also remember the relationships between them — and while the number of individuals increases arithmetically, the number of relationships grows exponentially. If we have 99 people, and add 1 more, we've only added one individual, but 99 new relationships. It seems that it was precisely that complexity that drove the growth of the primate brain. If that is true, then the seperation from Australopithecine to *Homo* was likely driven by a *social* evolution. This is the same time we start to see the first stone tools, and possibly the first evidence for hunting, rather than scavenging. Hierarchical troops make social groups less complex, by fitting all members into a strict hierarchy — chimpanzees can get by simply remembering the individuals and their rank. Rhizomatic societies — that is, egalitarian societies — have an exponential number of relationships, as each individual relates to every other individual in new and different ways. As humans became hunter-gatherers, the simple hierarchical model that served so many other primates ceased to suffice. We needed to become egalitarian to survive, and in order to do that, we needed bigger brains relative to our bodies.

The report on the Liverpool study mentioned above, includes Robin Dunbar's conclusions:

« *Humans are primates, too — so do they fit into the pattern established for monkeys and apes? This is the key question which Robin Dunbar sought to answer by using the same equations to predict human social group and clique size from neocortex volume. The results were... ~150 for social group size, and ~12 for the more intimate clique size. He subsequently discovered that modern humans operate on a hierarchy of group sizes. "Interestingly", he says, "the literature suggests that 150 is roughly to the number of people* you *could ask for a favour and expect to have it granted. Functionally, that's quite similar to apes' core social groups." »*

Interestingly, forager bands tend to hover around that mark of 12 people (with some significant variance), and the line between tribe-level and chiefdom-level society — the line between egalitarian and hierarchical society — is invariably drawn at 150.

This number of 150 continues to pop up in many different contexts. Malcolm Gladwell discusses Dunbar's findings and their implications in *The Tipping Point*. On a much more off-beat note, David Wong references it in "Inside the Monkeysphere":

« *Yes, the Monkeysphere. That's the group of people who each of us, using our monkeyish brains, are able to conceptualize as people. If the monkey scientists are monkey right, it's physically impossible for this to be a number larger than 150. Most of us do not have room in our Monkeysphere for our friendly neighborhood Sanitation Worker. So, we don't think of him as a person. We think of him The Thing That Makes The Trash Go Away.* »

Here we see the essential problem with any large-scale society: we cannot conceive of so many *people*. It speaks to the very heart of Stalin's cold truism: "One death is a tragedy, but a million deaths are a statistic." Thus, for any society much larger than 150 people, we become neurologically incapable of maintaining an egalitarian society. Hierarchy becomes necessary, yet the human animal is very much adapted to egalitarianism — and in no way adapted to hierarchy. Cross-culturally, we all have some expectations rooted in that egalitarian heritage. We expect freedom, and we expect to be treated as a human being rather than a stereotype. We all feel some negative feeling of stress when these expectations are not met — as they invariably are not met in any large, hierarchical society.

As Steve Thomas put it:

« *Well, now you know the details of my social life. What's the point? That I'm awesome and have a lot of friends. But other than that, if you look closely at the group I've described (which is not set up very differently from other social groups, as far as I can tell — except for those dependant upon the shared-workplace or the shared-suburb; i.e., upon hierarchy) you can see that it operates on the basic principles of tribalism. The structure is basically that of the hunter-gatherer band, or the loose network of rhizome, including the fluidity of the individual microbands; the lack of a fixed power structure; and the fission-fusion, congregation-dispersal pattern of group interaction. The economic interaction, too, is tribal: people voluntarily band together to provide one another with a basic human need (in this case, companionship) The only difference is that the traditional band provided the hunter-gatherer with ALL of her/his needs, whereas the vast majority of our needs — particularly the most important, i.e., physical ones — must be provided by hierarchy »*

We gravitate towards band-level society whenever we have the option. Our social circles will tend to have a band-like quality to them, as Steve Thomas highlighted. When resources grow thin and the luxury of hierarchy can no longer be afforded, we consistently see people turn to band-level groups. In the wake of Katrina, "tribes" formed in New Orleans' French Quarter. Daniel Quinn pointed to cults and gangs as responding to this same impulse towards the small, tightly-knit community — even if they often neglected the essential element of egalitarianism that defines rhizome.

We are well-adapted to such groups. We expect such groups, neurologically, and where they do not exist, we will create them. We *need* such groups. This should hardly surprise us, as our groups have been adapted to us, as well. It is a case of co-evolution between social structure and the animal it serves — just like the co-evolution of pack and wolf, hive and bee, school and fish, so, too, did band and human mutually shape one another.

Let's take "sharing" as an example. Our culture denigrates sharing. The recent innovations in "intellectual property" especially have tried to make sharing illegal, and induce in us all a feeling of shame when we share with others. Yet we still believe sharing to be a virtue. In our evolution as band-animals, sharing was not simply nice, it was the cornerstone of survival. The Ju/'Hoansi have no word for "thank you"; to thank someone suggests that their actions were out of the ordinary. Caring for others in band-level society was the expected norm; it was the most selfish act one could come up with. The most effective way to serve oneself was to serve others. Bands very effectively defeated violence, cheating, and other "immorality" not nearly so much by condemning it, as by removing the incentive. Compare this to our own, hierarchical "Cheating Culture." Our survival does not depend on sharing with our small, close-knit community. Not only do the people around us no longer register as "people," beyond our 150-person neurological capacity, neither does their survival affect us in any way. In short, there is *great* incentive to steal, cheat, lie or commit any of the other "immoral" acts which small, egalitarian groups need not concern themselves with. As a result, we must impose laws, to create artificial disincentives against what is otherwise a very clear endorsement of "immorality." Yet this is an artificial disincentive — laws can be gotten around, police eluded, and so forth. There is no disincentive in the act itself; only in being caught.

Most of our problems today can easily be traced to some manner in which we remain maladapted to our present life — to the struggle of a Pleistocene animal, to adapt to the bizarre, Holocene nightmare we have created. Our social structure is one such example. We evolved as band-animals. Our egalitarianism defines us; it is probably the single most defining trait in humanity. We evolved as egalitarian band-animals in the Pleistocene. Egalitarianism is our natural state, and our birthright. It is what we expect, down to our very bones. Yet today, it has become so rare that many humans doubt its very possibility. We have accepted the evils of hierarchy — the trauma of an animal maladapted to its current environment — as inevitable.

Humans are best adapted to small, egalitarian bands, in the same way that wolves are adapted to packs or bees to hives. Humans flourish in such a social structure, providing us not only with our material needs, but also our universal psychological needs of belonging to such a group, of personal freedom, and of acceptance for ourselves as individuals. Hierarchical society is a social structure we left behind when we became human. It may provide for our material needs, but it fails utterly to provide for any of our psychological needs. So, we invent small, band-like societies — social circles, clubs and the like — to compensate for all the failings of hierarchy. In short, egalitarianism is an essential requirement for healthy human life; hierarchy is an utter rejection of everything that makes us human.

Thesis #8: Human societies are defined by their food.

Yehudi Cohen's 1974 *Man in Adaptation* is the kind of classic that made its case so well, no one ever reads it. Most introductory anthropology textbooks will devote an entire chapter to Cohen's framework — a framework that modern anthropology simply takes for granted. Cohen divided the world's cultures into any one of five "adaptive strategies": foraging, horticulture, pastoralism, agriculture, and industrialism. Cohen noted the strong correlations these strategies had with the rest of their culture; so strong that, simply given a society's mode of subsistence, accurate predictions could often be made about their level of political complexity, their kinship patterns, their population size and density, their modes of warfare, and even their religious beliefs. The underlying fact that makes Cohen's typology so useful — and these correlations so strong — is that human society is, first and foremost, a strategy for acquiring food, and the manner in which that food is acquired defines the shape, scale, and kind of that society.

That may come as a shocking statement to the layman, but it is quite intuitive if we assume that the development of culture has a place in human evolution. All evolution is ultimately geared towards genetic reproduction, but to achieve that end, evolution works on two broad goals: the reproduction of life, and the maintenance of life (at least until reproduction has been achieved). These can be reduced with little violence to the truth to the essential drives for food, and sex. Most of the necessities humans require could be served by any social group. Any mixing of males and females will invariably lead to sexual relationships and the successful rearing of children. Protection from the elements is gained easily through any number of methods. That leaves food as the factor which society must spend most of its effort procuring. Not only is food a requirement which is needed on a much more regular basis than sex or protection from the elements, it is also a much riskier prospect than the others. Minimally, only a single sexual liason may result in offspring, and a single shelter can protect several individuals from the elements for an extended period of time — but most people must eat several times a day. In any social group with both males and females, sexual relationships will form, and protection from the elements can be easily attained in any environment — but famines often afflict whole bioregions for lengthy periods of time, and hunger and starvation can even become endemic to an entire population. Any form of society would suffice for our other basic needs. Culture develops primarily as a means of procuring food, and everything in a given culture serves that end.

51

Until very recently, all humans were foragers, or hunter-gatherers. The vast majority of cultural diversity in humans is accounted for by foragers. Inuit, Plains Indians, Ju/'Hoansi and Kwakiutl are all examples of foragers — totem poles, potlatching, "the Dreamtime," "counting coups," igloos, the cave art of Lascaux, and the *n/um* dance are all artifacts of forager cultures. There are foragers that rely primarily on nuts and honey, but most rely primarily on meat. Others rely on fishing. There have been equestrian foragers, pedestrian foragers, aquatic foragers — even sedentary, complex forager chiefdoms. Yet there are still some discernable and important features that correlate very strongly with foraging. For instance, egalitarianism is almost universal among foragers. Most exist at a band level. There is no exclusive occupational specialization, though there is often differences of emphasis. Everyone is at least familiar with how to do everything, though some individuals may devote more time to medicine, tool-making, or the arts than others. Everyone is involved in the procurement of food — even the most respected shaman is still expected to hunt. Most foragers are nomadic, usually traveling in wide circles and returning on a semi-annual basis to the same areas. Their populations tend to be low and sparse.

Foragers are almost invariably shamanistic animists. Their religion posits a world that is sacred and bursting with life. Details vary *widely*, but there is almost always a deep appreciation for non-human life, even sometimes on par with human life, as well as a conviction that humans are intimately bound into the natural world. Humans often enjoy a pride of place, even in forager mythology, but the divide between human and non-human life that is so prominent in agricultural mythology is almost always absent. This can easily be seen as a consequence of the forager lifestyle, of course. Tracking, hunting, gathering fishing and all other forms of foraging require not only an intimate knowledge of the food species being sought, but its relations with all other species. This kind of appreciation for other organisms as part of a complex "web of life" cannot help but be reflected in the forager's own ruminations on humanity's place in the world. By the same token, any forager who takes on the more prominent ideas among agriculturalists concerning humanity's separation from the natural world and position as ruler, or in the best case "steward," of the world would be very prone to over-exploiting her resources. Such a forager culture would be at a distinct disadvantage to a more animistic forager culture. Thus, natural selection favors shamanistic and animistic beliefs among foragers, and selects strongly against the memes found in civilizations.

There are two important exceptions to all of this that are worthy of note: the North American Kwakiutl along the northwest coast in what is now British Columbia, and the foragers discovered by archaeologists at Sungir. In both cases, regular, predictable abundance created a situation that allowed for the control of a surplus. These societies then became much more complex; in the case of the Kwakiutl, even developing a rigidly ranked chiefdom, with a sedentary society dependent on regular salmon runs and potlatching. It seems reasonable to think there might have been something similar at Sungir. These examples highlight that it is not foraging itself that guarantees the kind of simple, egalitarian, free society that humans are best adapted to, but the lack of a controllable surplus that foraging *usually* creates.

Though possessing an abundant surplus, neither of these forager groups were expansionistic — because the nature of their surplus precluded expansion. Sungir's abundance relied on the regular bison migration patterns through the area; they could not expand into areas where the bison did not so migrate. The Kwakiutl depended on regular salmon runs; they could not expand into areas where the salmon did not so run. This highlights another important point: where foragers *do* develop the odd abberation of a surplus, it is *always* geographically limited — which makes complex forager societies incapable of expansion and conquest. This allows pockets of complexity, without wiping out all possibility for simplicity in the process.

This limitation was broken with the innovation of food production some 10 to 15 millennia ago. Cohen breaks food production out into four subtypes: horticulture, agriculture, pastoralism, and industrialism. This does not translate into greater cultural diversity, though. All food producing cultures exist within a tight range of possibilities. While horticultural cultures have some amount of diversity (though nothing approaching that found among foragers), pastoralism is a relatively rare strategy, agriculture is incredibly restrictive with incredibly little diversity, and industrialism is very nearly incapable of allowing for any diversity whatsoever. Indeed, we can see at least these last three as differing aspects of the same phenomenon. This suggests that Cohen's typology may be slightly ethnocentrically flawed: in breaking out more types within our own adaptive strategy, the traditional typology tends to give pride of place to our own culture that may not be entirely deserved.

Horticulture was the first type of food production practiced. At its simplest, it is nothing more than basic techniques to favor the regrowth of preferred plants. Very low-intensity work can allow significant returns, as the beginning of the marginal return curve allows for significant ERoEI. This is what makes horticulture the most efficient adaptive strategy available. Horticulturalists tend to organize at the tribe level with a larger, denser population. The tribe is still egalitarian, but it involves a more complex organization, often involving groups like clans, clubs, guilds and secret societies that cut across tribal boundaries and provide multiple dimensions of power and influence to stabilize a larger egalitarian society. The size of the horticultural village tends to fix more around Dunbar's number of 150 (*see* thesis #7).

Horticulturalists occupy an ambiguous area, where they are held in place by the tension between the forager and agricultural modes of existence. Horticulturalists do not produce all of their food; they still rely on foraging to supplement their diet. This means that the maintenance of ample wilderness remains an important issue for them. At the same time, shifting cultivation — especially slash-and-burn or swidden agriculture — often entails a very delicate balance of population and resources that can easily shift out of hand, resulting in massive ecological devastation. Much of the deforestation currently threatening the Amazon is the result of horticultural practices under severe population pressure.

It is difficult to solidly differentiate horticulture and agriculture; the best criteria that most anthropologists find is that horticulture always involves a fallowing period. This has led to the idea since Cohen of a "cultivation continuum" ranging from horticulture to agriculture, depending on the intensification of any of the four main inputs: land, labor, capital and machinery. This suggests, to me, that there actually *is* a solid differentiation between horticulture and agriculture: the point of diminishing returns.

(The point of diminishing returns defines the difference between horticulture and agriculture.)

The concept of diminishing returns was first developed in the context of agriculture. After a certain point, simply applying more labor yielded less and less benefit. Even in agrarian societies, it takes more calories of work to farm a field, than is returned in calories of product. Among simpler agrarian societies, this shortfall is made up with the use of tools and animals. The plow uses the fundamental physics of a lever to lessen the workload. Animals can leverage energy sources humans cannot — by grazing in lands too rocky or infertile to be cultivated. In modern petroculture, fossil fuels make up the shortfall. Petroleum doesn't just power tractors, it also forms the basic ingredients for everything from fertilizer to packaging, and the fuel for transportation. We now burn between 4 and 10 calories — mostly in fossil fuels — for every 1 calorie of agricultural product we produce.

The slope becomes sharper as more labor is applied — the process becomes increasingly inefficient — but the absolute number of calories yielded always goes up by *some* amount per unit of labor. So, production can still be increased even past the point of diminishing returns by applying more labor. It just becomes increasingly inefficient to do so.

Forager populations are very dispersed, because their food is very dispersed. Foragers gather food from the wild, whether by hunting, fishing, gathering, or simple scavenging. These resources are not collected in any one space, so every forager band requires a significant range of territory. This makes forager society very sparsely populated. This also means that the maintenance of wilderness is essential to their survival. Foragers do not seek to maintain wilderness only for religious conviction, but also for practical necessity.

By comparison, cultivation converts a specific area of biomass into human food, raising the edible ratio of that area to 100%. In swidden (a.k.a., "slash-and-burn") horticulture, for example, an area of rain forest is cut down and burned, and a garden is planted in the ashes. This is the only way to practice cultivation in the rain forest, as the ground is about as fertile as cement — all of the nutrients are locked in the trees. This very clearly illustrates the conversion from biomass into human food, as the biodiversity of some area of rain forest becomes fertilizer to grow a horticultural garden. This is the essence of all cultivation.

For agriculturalists, who depend entirely on their crops for food, the wilderness is no longer a resource, but a nuisance. Not only is it land "going to waste" (and very often put into just such explicit terms), it also harbors all manner of pests and vermin who threaten the agricultural way of life. Living beyond the point of diminishing returns is difficult and dangerous. It implies a constant threat of starvation. Any loss of crops to wild animals represents a direct threat to the agriculturalist's survival. This is why agriculturalists have innovated techniques of protecting their food from wild animals in a "program" that led Daniel Quinn to invent the term "totalitarian agriculture" for this adaptive strategy. Everything from scarecrows to fences, to the domestication of cats to hunt rats in grain silos, to modern pesticides fit under this rubric.

Agriculturalists are also inherently expansionistic. Agriculturalists must maintain very high birth rates to offset their high mortality rates from disease and starvation. Moreover, their intense cultivation drains the land's ability to support their practices further. The Fertile Crescent was not always a cruel joke — once upon a time, it was truly fertile. The blasted wasteland we see today is the result of 10,000 years of agriculture. It took only a few centuries to turn the American Great Plains into a dust bowl that is now supported almost solely by petrochemicals. While the rare technological innovation may allow agriculturalists to find new land to replace those they have made infertile — to say nothing of their need to feed their growing population in the "Food Race" — these innovations are few and far between, proving that innovations do not always occur simply because we need them. More often, this requires an expansion of the land under cultivation. This can often mean military conquest of one's neighbors — the conquests of Rome often listed the need for more agricultural land as the primary motivation quite explicitly — or, it can mean the destruction of wilderness. The destruction of wilderness is especially tempting, because not only does it bring more land under cultivation, it also destroys the habitat of those animals that threaten the agriculturalist's survival.

This is why agriculturalist belief systems so often posit some theme of "man vs. nature," or more often, divine permission to use nature as man sees fit. This relationship is necessary to allow for the actions agriculture requires. Agriculture requires the exercise of force against the natural world, and so, agriculturalist religion must find some way to justify that. The adoption of more forager-like religious beliefs about humanity's place in nature can only be held on any significant scale by those specialists that agricultural production allows to be far-removed from the day-to-day realities of subsistence.

Pastoralism is a very rare adaptive strategy, that always occurs alongside agriculture. I tend to think of it as a special case of agriculture, but little more, as it seems incapable of appearing independently.

Finally, industrialism is our own adaptive strategy. Many see the Industrial Revolution as the source of all our current woes, but in fact, industrialism merely represents an exponential increase in agriculture's scale — such that previously ignorable problems become very noticeable. Industrialism allows for the modern city, worldwide populations measured in the billions, and the kind of ecological devastation it takes to create the worst mass extinction in history. At the same time, industrialism allows the vast majority of the population to become specialists. These specialists are then able to dabble in things maladapted to their subsistence strategy, such as believing themselves to be part of the natural world, as foragers do. Interestingly, at this extreme, two forager correlates — the nuclear family, and the Inuit kinship system — return to the fore. The complexity of industrialism reduces the ROI of child-bearing while also lowering the death rate and extending the expected lifespan to very near forager levels. Europeans only reached the stature of their Mesolithic ancestors once again in about 1950, for example, thanks to "affluent malnutrition" — the state of nutrition that Steve Brill characterized as "overfed and malnourished." This results in a significantly lower birthrate for industrialized counties.

Unfortunately, like pastoralism, industrialism is also incapable of existing on its own. This extreme level of complexity is very costly, and can only be maintained by externalizing costs. This generally requires a less complex area — an agricultural region — that can serve to pay those costs. Despotic regimes in the Middle East (like the House of Sa'ud) maintain low energy prices for industrial society. Industrial consumer goods are manufactured in sweatshops. Industrial lifestyles — the size of our ecological footprint, and our concomittant low birth rate — rely on the poverty of agricultural areas (i.e., their small ecological footprint) and their concomittant high birth rate. During the Cold War, the face-off of two industrialized societies created the "First" and "Second" Worlds. The "Third World" was the un-industrialized rest of the world. The collapse of the U.S.S.R. has left only the First and Third Worlds. The Third World is where the First World externalizes its costs. Foreign aid and military support to various Third World dictatorships have maintained them in situations where they would otherwise have fallen to popular revolt. The Third World debt crisis is "a symptom of an international economic system that tolerates growing and abysmal poverty as a normal condition." Through the World Bank, the IMF, and outright military support, we have shown that we will go to great lengths to keep things as they are in the Third World, because these conditions maintain First World prosperity. We maintain conditions where sweatshops are the best alternative available, and where it's better to grow cash crops for First World consumption than food for your starving family.

In *The Historical Jesus*, John Dominic Crossan provided a brilliant sociological analysis of the early Roman Empire. In it, he shows that the *Pax Romana* was peaceful and prosperous only for the heart of the empire. Its peripheries suffered constant war and poverty. This was, in fact, by design.

The overall level of turmoil could not be lessened, but Italy could enjoy such a *Pax Romana* by exporting its ills to the provinces.

So, if the Third World *does* succeed in becoming like us, who will grow the cotton we clothe ourselves with? Who will grow the coffee beans? If democracy comes to power in the Arabian Penninsula, what happens if they decide their national interests are best served by charging us the *actual* cost of their oil, rather than externalizing our costs in the form of oppression and terrorism?

Thus, we see that industrialism cannot exist on its own. It can only exist on top of an agricultural system, by exploiting the lesser complexity of that system to offset its own costs. The First World needs the Third World — and so, industrialism can never succeed in replacing or eliminating agriculturalism. Industrialism and greater complexity are no solution to the current crisis of the diminishing returns on complexity.

Thesis #9: Agriculture is difficult, dangerous and unhealthy.

The previous thesis glossed over a number of significant points, which we must now go back and revisit in greater detail. The most glaring of these glosses is probably the assertion that agriculture is a risky, marginal and difficult means of acquiring food. Many readers would certainly object that agriculture provides a stable, secure and reliable source of food. After all, it was the bounty of agriculture that allowed us to give up hunting and gathering, constantly wandering and wondering where our next meal would come from, giving us the time to build civilization. That is the common picture we've all been told, but it is also the opposite of truth. In fact, the Neolithic Revolution was, to use Jared Diamond's turn of phrase, "the worst mistake in the history of the human race."

It is taken for granted in our culture that agriculture is the path of least resistance, an immediately obvious advantage over any other subsistence technology. Agriculturalist philosophers such as Thomas Hobbes assure us — without any empirical validation — that any other way of life is "solitary, nasty, brutish and short." Before agriculture, humans lived like animals, constantly in search of food, always on the brink of starvation. With agriculture came ease and security, and a better way of life. How can we ask *why* the Agricultural Revolution occurred? The question is *how*, not why; once agriculture appeared, its superiority would be so obvious, and it would be adopted by all.

This view of agriculture has no grounding in reality, but it is a necessary myth for our civilization to hold. We would not be agriculturalists today if we did not. This idea is a necessary meme for the functioning of an agriculturalist society, in order to maintain itself over generations. The traditional view can be broken down into four myths, which we must address in turn:

1. Agriculture is the path of least resistance.
2. Agriculture creates a more stable and secure food supply.
3. Agriculture leads to greater health and nutrition.
4. Agriculture allows more leisure time and a generally higher quality of life.

Myth #1: Agriculture is the path of least resistance.

That agriculture represents the easiest or simplest way of attaining one's food cannot be supported logically or empirically. Whereas hunter-gatherers must only accomplish the work equivalent to harvesting, and that on a low-intensity, rolling basis, an agriculturalist must also plant and tend to their crops. Agriculture is the most intensive form of cultivation, often requiring massive projects such as irrigation or terracing. This is borne out by empirical data. Due to the law of diminishing returns, though agriculture produces the most food absolutely, the ratio of food per unit of labor is in fact higher than any other subsistence technology. Agriculturalists must work harder for their food than anyone else. (Harris, 1993) In modern "petroculture," 10 calories of fossil fuels are burned for every 1 calorie of food produced. Horticulturalists have the most efficient lifestyle; foragers have the easiest lifestyle. Ours produces the most calories, but is also the most grossly inefficient.

Myth #2: Agriculture creates a more stable and secure food supply.

If agriculture is a more difficult means of attaining food, at least it is more secure, no? Where a forager won't know if they will eat today or not, an agriculturalist can be assured she'll have food for the day. This, as it turns out, is also a false statement. In all but the most marginal environments, a gatherer has a near 100% chance of finding *some* form of plant food, whereas the probability of a hunter's success lies closer to 25%. This has led to an emphasis on sharing in many forager societies, allowing them to take advantage of multiplicative probability. Whereas the chance of a single hunter retrieving nothing on a given day is 75%, the chances that ten will come back with nothing is $0.75 \times 10 = 5.63\%$. If even one hunter makes a kill on a given day, then the band will eat. (Lee, 2000)

On the other hand, few organisms are domesticable compared to the diversity of all wild species available for food. Moreover, those species which *are* domesticable are very closely related to each other. Inclement conditions for one domesticate, then, are all the more likely to affect *all* of the staples, leading to a severe famine. Agriculturalists are forced to depend on a very narrow selection of closely related plants and animals for food, and this makes them highly susceptible to famine. There are also wars and political pressures which are more often the causes of famine than natural conditions. These are the results of the complex political structures which often require agriculture in order to exist. When Lee studied the Ju/'Hoansi in the Kalahari desert (2000), the region was in the midst of a severe draught. The neighboring Bantu farmers and pastoralists were dying by the thousands of starvation; the Ju/'Hoansi, however, were able to subsist very healthily on an average of two hours of foraging a day.

Myth #3: Agriculture leads to greater health and nutrition.

There is mounting evidence that agriculture may be very unhealthy. Of course, it is well known that most epidemic diseases would not exist if not for agriculture (Diamond, 1987). Most epidemic diseases are not "native" to the human system — this should be evident from their virulence, as it is generally maladaptive for an organism to kill or even hinder its host's survival. Chicken pox, cholera, and plague, for example, were all animal diseases which had the chance to jump the species barrier due to the newfound proximity of humans and other animals which followed domestication. Others, such as malaria, were spread by agricultural practices (malaria only became so virulent when slash-and-burn agriculture attracted mosquitoes to human population centers). (Diamond, 1997). Even so, these diseases and others might not have ever achieved their impact if not for the large, dense populations which agriculture created. Whereas an epidemic disease among foragers may destroy at most a single band of 25, with the advent of cities and extended trade networks, the threat of such diseases became global for the first time.

This is, of course, a long-term impact of agriculture. The immediate effects are little better. Excavations at Dickson's Mounds show a sharp drop in all the customary benchmarks of health and nutrition, and also signs of immediate malnutrition. They evidence a catastrophically shorter life expectancy and smaller stature (indicating greater malnutrition). (Goodman & Armelagos, 2000) It is only in the past fifty years that the heights of Western Americans and Europeans, with the modern "affluent malnutrition," have come to match those of their Mesolithic forager ancestors. Greeks and Turks still have not attained the full stature of their Mesolithic ancestors.

Myth #4: Agriculture allows more leisure time and a generally higher quality of life.

Does agriculture at least provide more leisure time, and a generally higher quality of life? As we have already seen, agriculturalists must work much harder for their food than foragers; obviously, the argument that agriculture allows more leisure time is based on the untenable, ultimately philosophical, contention that agriculture is the "path of least resistance." Some argue that by providing for specialists, agriculture provides greater leisure time. However, such specialists must work comparable hours to farmers to offset the gross inefficiencies of agriculture. Whether by plowing the earth, making pots, or writing software, all agriculturalists must spend the majority of their life working for their food — whether directly, or trading their labor for various tokens that can be exchanged for food. Only the elites — what Thorstein Veblen called "the leisure class" — have greater leisure time. This class has an unprecedented amount of leisure, being able to shed even the few hours of walking that a forager must put in every day.

If by quality of life we mean health, then, as discussed above, agriculture is still a bad idea. To agriculture we owe disease, malnutrition and famine: things nearly unheard of to our Mesolithic ancestors (save perhaps for some foragers living in the most marginal areas, like the Arctic Circle), things we take for granted now as necessary and eternal evils. Even today, among the elites of the West, we have only achieved what some researchers have termed "affluent malnutrition." We eat large quantities of food, yes; but they are so poorly mismatched to the evolutionary needs of our species as to constitute outright malnutrition in its own right. Though we alone of all the agricultural peoples in history have the affluence to eat truly healthy foods (and even among us, the lower — and often, even the middle — class cannot afford such luxuries as healthy food), we are still sickly and in poor health because of agriculture, combining a sedentary lifestyle and a high-carbohydrate diet lacking in other essential nutrients.

Perhaps we should define "quality of life" in more abstract terms? This is precisely what makes it such a slippery concept, because it becomes impossible to gauge empirically. It may be offered as counter-point that "refined" or "high" culture — art, music, etc. — owes itself to agriculture. The music of Bach no doubt does; however, we have archaeological evidence of musical instruments predating the Agricultural Revolution. The polyphonic complexity of Pygmy songs was matched in Europe only in the 14th century. Without agriculture, Michelangelo would no doubt have painted something else. Art itself, though, dates back to the Upper Paleolithic. Those elements so often referred to as "civilized" in fact have nothing to do with civilization; religion, music, art, and other such abstract cultural elements existed before agriculture, and are to be found in all forager societies. They are universals of human culture, however we get our food.

The caves of Lascaux stand as an excellent counter-point to the contention that fine art can only develop from an agricultural society.

By any definition of "quality of life," we cannot say that agriculture increased it in any way.

Agriculture is not entirely without benefit, though. There are certain advantages to an agricultural system, and these are quite telling. Agriculture allows for sedentism. While not impossible, it is difficult for a forager group to remain sedentary over long periods of time. Whereas an acre of wild land will have a fraction of its biomass consisting of edible human food, an acre of farmland is entirely human food. This denser concentration of food allows a denser concentration of population. Whereas a forager will eventually begin to drain the resources of the surrounding country and have to move on, an agriculturalist must remain in one place, as agriculture represents a heavy investment into the location of the settlement. (Gilman, 1981) Agriculture also allows two things to be accomplished, and in fact, forces them: the creation of a higher population, and the production of a surplus.

The creation of a higher population, of course, is neither good nor bad to the general population itself. Nor is the creation of a surplus which is, by definition, unnecessary. While perhaps needed by populations facing periodic famine, as we have seen, this is an affliction of agriculturalists, not foragers. Sedentism, also, cannot be considered an advantage. In fact, it is the sedentary lifestyle of the West which leads to so much of our health problems (cf. Gladwell, 2000) However, as neutral as these are, there is one element of society to whom they are clear advantages: the elites. Before the modern era, elites were those able to control *human* capital more often than physical resources directly. (Hirth, 1992) They brokered more in esteem, opinion and influence than tangible wealth. A larger population, then, was advantageous to prehistoric, emergent elites, just as a larger treasury is advantageous to modern elites. Sedentism makes populations easier to control. It was nearly impossible for the Czar to control the Steppes nomads until they were co-opted as the Cossocks, for example. The surplus is no doubt the most important aspect, and, I believe, what drove the adoption of agriculture in the first place. With a surplus, specialists were able to develop, including elites themselves. However, emergent elites — "Big Men" — require surpluses for the competitive feasting which creates their power, by bolstering their influence.

Agriculture helps the elites by making most of humanity suffer. It is, as Jared Diamond put it, a mistake we are still trying to recover from. As he ends his famous article:

Hunter-gatherers practiced the most successful and logest-lasting life style in human history. In contrast, we're still struggling with the mess into which agriculture has tumbled us, and it's unclear whether we can solve it. Suppose that an archaeologist who had visited from outer space were trying to explain human history to his fellow spacelings. He might illustrate the results of his digs by a 24-hour clock on which one hour represents 100,000 years of real past time. If the history of the human race began at midnight, then we would now be almost at the end of our first day. We lived as hunter-gatherers for nearly the whole of that day, from midnight through dawn, noon, and sunset. Finally, at 11:54 p. m. we adopted agriculture. As our second midnight approaches, will the plight of famine-stricken peasants gradually spread to engulf us all? Or will we somehow achieve those seductive blessings that we imagine behind agriculture's glittering façade, and that have so far eluded us?

Bibliography

- Diamond, J.

  1987 "The worst mistake in the history of the human race". In: *Discover*, May 1987

  1997 *Guns, germs and steel: the fate of human societies*. London: Random House.

- Gilman, A.

  1981 "The development of social stratification in Bronze Age Europe". In: *Current Anthropology* 22(1) pp. 1–23

- Gladwell, M.

  2000 "The Pima paradox". In: Goodman, A.H., Dufour, D.L. & Pelto, G.H., *Nutritional anthropology: biocultural perspectives on food and nutrition*. Mountain View: Mayfield Publishing Company.

- Goodman, A. and Armelagos, G.

2000 "Disease and death at Dr. Dickson's mounds". In: Goodman, A.H., Dufour, D.L. & Pelto, G.H., *Nutritional anthropology: biocultural perspectives on food and nutrition*. Mountain View: Mayfield Publishing Company.

- Harris, M.

1993 *Culture, people, nature: an introduction to general anthropology*, 6th edition. New York: Harper Collins College Publishers.

- Hirth, K.

1992 "Interregional exchange as elite behavior: an evolutionary perspective". In: Chase, D.Z. and Chase, A.F., *Mesoamerican elites: an archaeological assessment*. Norman: University of Oklahoma Press.

- Lee, R.

2000 "What hunters do for a living, or, how to make out on scarce resources". In: Goodman, A.H., Dufour, D.L. &

- Pelto, G.H., *Nutritional anthropology: biocultural perspectives on food and nutrition*. Mountain View: Mayfield Publishing Company.

Thesis #10: Emergent elites led the Agricultural Revolution.

How the Agricultural Revolution happened is well understood. It is perhaps best explained by David Rindos' Selectionist Hypothesis, which Jared Diamond explained succinctly in *Guns, Germs and Steel* as a specific case of co-evolution. We could domesticate large herd mammals by identifying the leader; we could domesticate cereal grains because they were prone to harvesting. In the wild, a pea pod that doesn't explode will simply die off, but to a human gatherer, such a pod filled with delicious peas is much more desirable than picking individual peas off the ground. Even without conscious management, simply dropping a few peas by accident will leave even more of the mutant non-exploding pea plants near the traditional camp site when the band returns next year. Followed over centuries, this process will eventually create non-toxic almonds, turn aurochs into cows, and give rise to domesticated forms of wild organisms bred to better serve human interests. *How* this all happened is not the question. The question is *why*.

Theories of why the Agricultural Revolution happened have traditionally been divided between "push" and "pull" theories. Childe's "Oasis Hypothesis," Braidwood's Natural Habitat Hypothesis and the Population Pressure Hypothesis are all examples of "push" theories, where something forces a population into agriculture. Most "push" theories make no attempt to answer why agriculture was adopted, only how. Both Childe's Oasis Hypothesis and Braidwood's Natural Habitat Hypothesis explain how agriculture might have been made possible, but neither even attempts to explain why it happened. For both, "why" is an absurd question; the superiority of agriculture should be self-evident. As we have already seen, though, this is a severely flawed assumption.

By far, however, the Population Pressure Hypothesis is the most important of the push models. It is nearly taken for granted in many circles. The hypothesis states that agriculture *had* to be adopted because of rising populations through the Mesolithic. Yet, for any given grain of wheat, there is a decision to be made. One can either eat it, or plant it, but never both. Planting wheat is an investment of food; it's sacrificing food now, in order to have more food in the future. Investment is not an activity engaged in by people lacking resources; it's something only people with resources to spare indulge in. Poor people aren't very big in the stock market, and starving people who buried all their rice would never survive long enough to reap the harvest. We take it nearly without argument that the Neolithic began with increasing, hungry populations, but there are two questions left unanswered:

1. Since human population is a function of food supply, where did this population come from? and
2. Why did starving populations bury their wheat, instead of eat it?

Human populations, like all animal populations, are controlled by food supply, so what made those populations begin to grow in the first place? As the first foragers began to experiment with horticulture, the structural barriers against agriculture would have disappeared, and a gradual slide into agriculture would have begun. Yet there remains a pivotal moment here, as well: when those first foragers settled down in horticultural villages, and decided that from now on they would grow their food in gardens (and hunt to supplement), instead of hunting for it (and gardening to supplement) — a *huge* difference.

By contrast to "push" scenarios, "pull" models discuss factors which enticed populations and pulled them into agriculture. The Selectionist Hypothesis mentioned above is the most widely accepted of these models, where co-evolution "pulled" human societies towards agriculture by providing domesticates. Of course, this cannot be the full story. The availability of domesticates hardly demands such gross inefficiency in their harvesting, and though no species evolves in a vaccuum, not many squirrels are known for their agricultural techniques.

Perhaps the most compelling of all these theories, though, is a "pull" model: Bender & Hayden's Social Hypothesis. In this hypothesis, food production is taken up in all its deadly earnest to generate the surpluses required by "Big Men" for competitive feasting.

The term "Big Man" was first used in Melanesia (Van Bakel et al, 1986), where it was used to describe leaders who could not accurately be described as "chiefs," as they lacked any ascribed position. While sometimes denounced as a vacuous term when applied outside the realm of Melanesian ethnography, it is nonetheless often used of a type of leader, who gains prestige — and with it, influence — not through ascribed political institutions, but through achieved status. "Big Men" rarely control material resources, so much as social ones. Their prestige gives them great influence over others, but they cannot enforce their will. Rather, "Big Men" primarily spend their time trying to convince, cajole, and persuade their followers to intensify production. (Harris, 1993) The essential function of most "Big Men" is as competitors for prestigate in an ever-escalating, high stakes game of competitive feasting. Typified by the Kwakuitl potlatch or the New

Guinea moka, it is from these extravagant displays of generosity that "Big Men" derive their prestige, and thus, their power. Through an elaborate system of loans, "Big Men" are able to collect large amounts of food together at a single time for competitive feasting. New Guinea Big Men, for example, could never raise a sufficient number of pigs for an acceptable moka. They do keep significant herds of their own, but they constantly lend those pigs to others, as well as lending their time and labor. Then, when the time comes for a moka, they collect on all of those debts at once, amassing an amount of resources they never could have gathered themselves. In this way, "Big Men" use generosity and gratitude to co-opt an entire community for their own purposes.

Rather than accumulating wealth, "Big Men" might rather be seen as a conduit of wealth, as the "Big Man" economy becomes, essentially, redistributive. Wealth is extracted by them from their followers, and flows quickly out from them to the population as a whole. This is essentially the same economy which chiefdoms formalize. The primary activity of the "Big Man" is increasing the intensity of production, in order to create a surplus of food which can be distributed for competitive feasting. (Harris, 1993) This is precisely what occurred in the Agricultural Revolution. Hayden & Bender have argued that competition between groups is fiercest in periods of scarcity or abundance, but especially so in a period of abundance which follows a period of scarcity.

This is precisely what occurred at the beginning of the Neolithic, with the end of the Pleistocene. The chaos of the Younger Dryas created alternating seasons of famine and plenty, and such inter-group competition can act as a form of insurance against periodic shortfall of resources. Famines are characteristic of agriculture, not foragers; but there is evidence for inclement conditions at the time of the Agricultural Revolution. It is doubtful these conditions would have led to famines — we know of no foraging group to have ever faced such conditions, archaeological evidence for widespread malnutrition before the rise of agriculture is generally lacking, and even a desert like the Kalahari can be abundant for a forager — however we can easily imagine a scenario of periods of less prosperity than usual. This would have been precisely the conditions to foster competitive feasting.

Generally, neighboring groups are invited to the lavish feasts the "Big Men" provide. The shame of being so outdone requires the other group to reciprocate in a few years' time. This can be seen as somewhat like the foragers' sharing within the group, only on a larger scale. When one group

68

is fortunate enough to have a surplus, they share it in these competitive feasts — albeit for self gain — with those who might not be so well-off. In time, when the situation is reversed, they may be treated to such a feast — out of vengeance, for those giving it. The competitive nature of this feasting gives it a self-serving motivation, so that it does not rely on such a shaky foundation as altruism. With personal motivation, this system could have greatly aided the survival of forager groups facing the inclement conditions of the early Holocene. With this new emphasis on competitive feasting, the prominence of the "Big Man" would have increased accordingly. As an adaptation to inclement climate, "Big Men" rose to power, and required ever larger surpluses to maintain that power. Every feast must be larger than the last one; one's rival must provide a larger feast than you did, which obliges you to provide an even larger feast than that. The only resource "Big Men" could truly control was labor, and that only through persuasion. The natural response of "Big Men" to this sort of pressure would be to intensify cultivation — that is, to begin practicing agriculture.

As mentioned above, the prototype of the chiefdom-level redistributive economy can easily be recognized in the swift flow of wealth through the "Big Man." Why, though, would egalitarian groups allow "Big Men" to solidify their power, so as to develop ascribed institutions? The usual forager response to individuals grabbing for power is fission of the group — the unsatisfied dissidents simply leave. However, where there are significant, immobile resources, this may not be possible. (Gilman, 1981) Surprisingly, recent archaeological discoveries have revealed that, contrary to usual thinking, sedentism *preceded* agriculture. Most likely, an increasing reliance on cereal grains required the use of large, immobile processing units. With such stationary assets, villages would develop, as the group could no longer easily move about. (Harris, 1993) This is precisely the sort of situation Gilman describes (1981) for how "Big Men" might be able to attain ascribed position for themselves and exert their dominance.

Such pre-agricultural villages may also help to explain the nutritional crisis faced by these groups. Famine still seems unlikely, as reliance on cereal grains would most likely not have occurred, and the groups have simply moved elsewhere, had they not been able to support a relatively sedentary foraging population in the first place. However, periodic shortfall would most likely have been a rather common occurrence. Trade, like competitive feasting, can be a sort of insurance against such shortfalls (Hirth, 1992; Gilman, 1981). Here, again, the primary figures are the elites. The trade in question is primarily of elite goods, conducted between elites of different groups. In so doing, fledgling elites extend the social network under their influence over a much wider area than their own group. While aiding in the nutrition and survival of their group, it also serves to reinforce the primacy of the elite. And, with significant investments of labor, time and resources into a specific location, simply leaving an area may not be a viable means of dealing with a power-hungry despot. Do you up and leave the land your family has farmed for generations, simply because the village headman wants his son to succeed him?

It has been argued that the chiefdom is a transitional form, which ultimately becomes a state. (Kottak, 2000) However, its relation to the "Big Man" systems found in egalitarian societies should also be fairly obvious. The transition from egalitarian society to state-level society should be fairly easy to see here. It is a transition driven primarily by competitive feasting, leading to the need for greater intensity in cultivation, the need for a surplus, the inability to meet those needs by transhumance, and the resulting elites who arise from those factors.

The most complex, hierarchical political structure is the state; "civilization" is, in anthropological terms, synonymous with that level of society. Even in archaic states, the primary asset of the political structure was not material, but social (Hirth, 1992). The state controlled human labor, and material goods indirectly through that medium. Civilization rests heavily on specialization: specialists in crafts, specialists in religion, specialists in defense, even specialists in bureaucracy — the elites themselves. These specialists are supported by the surplus of agriculture; without agriculture, civilization could not exist. It is the foundation, the absolute minimum prerequisite of state-level society. Another possible explanation for agriculture is that the surpluses were needed to feed specialists, such as artisans. Of course, the need for artisans would only arise from trade. If trade became the primary means of safeguarding against starvation, artisans may become important in order to produce goods to be traded. Once again, it is an elite activity — trade — which drives agriculture. In many formulations of the Social Hypothesis, it is trade specifically which is cited as the cause of agriculture: a society must have extensive trade networks, and the elites required to administrate them, as a prerequisite to agriculture.

We have archaeological attestation of sedentary foragers in the Middle East and Mesoamerica just prior to the inception of agriculture (Harris, 1993). These forager villages were most likely created because of the large mills and other equipment required to extract food from cereal grains. With these stationary assets, the ability of the foragers to move was reduced, and permanent housing was developed at the site. At first, this did not interfere with foraging as their subsistence base. (Harris, 1993)

With the end of the Pleistocene, conditions became warmer and drier in general (Harris, 1993). This change in climate may have made the foraging lifestyle of these village-dwellers more difficult to maintain, with periodic hunger becoming more and more common. Two mechanisms for dealing with this have been discussed: competitive feasting, and trade. Both operate as safeguards by indebting neighboring groups or otherwise expanding social influence beyond the local group. Both also require elites — "Big Men" and/or chiefs — to administrate. Both require the production of a surplus. Elites need ever larger surpluses to maintain their power in the ever-escalating cycle of competitive feasting, and the artisans employed by the elites require food to create goods for trade. Both activities create and solidify elite dominance, and both require a surplus. None of the other hypotheses examined adequately explain why such a surplus would be desirable, as a surplus is, by definition, unnecessary, and as we have seen, the costs of agriculture are sufficiently high to demand a very good reason for the desirability of such a surplus. In this scenario, two closely interrelated factors — the dominance of the elites and the food security of the group — demand this surplus.

The primary ability of "Big Men" is to intensify production. The selectionist argument assures us that at least semi-domesticated plants were already available from the local environment, due to millennia of evolutionary interaction. Furthermore, active intervention to favor the regrowth of favored crops is not unknown among foragers. More intensive work may well have been a high priority of "Big Men" in the area. Whereas agriculture would be a terrible idea for an overly-large population, or a group otherwise facing frank malnutrition, such an investment of food for the future would be quite reasonable for a group in the midst of a temporary time of plenty — particularly when inclement conditions assured such prosperity would not last.

With agricultural intensification, the investment placed into a specific geographic location increased drastically. Already sedentary due to the immobility of the processing equipment an emphasis on cereal grains required, the Agricultural Revolution required the clearing of fields, irrigation, terracing, and other large initial investments of labor that made

71

simply moving away a difficult prospect. This changed the dynamics of human politics; whereas the primary means foragers use of settling disputes is to simply go somewhere else, this was no longer an option. The difficulty of group fission allowed "Big Men" to become chiefs with permanent, ascribed position and title (Gilman, 1981).

War, rather than being a strategy for maintaining the band's freedom and autonomy, became a tool for economic expansion (Godesky, 2000), leading directly to the intensification of conflict found among agricultural societies (Eckhardt, 1992; Harris, 1993). Further bolstered by intensified conflict, elites became administrators of defense as well (Gilman, 1981), and were able to create permanent power structures for themselves. Without recourse to group fission due to the huge investments placed into the specific region, groups had no choice but to capitulate to the rulers thus created.

Transporting food over significant distances was generally difficult in the ancient world. The Roman Empire exercised sufficient control to feed the Eastern Empire with grain from Egypt, and the West from Britain, but this was a feat of administrative and logistical prowess which even the Romans could not sustain forever. Their inability to continue such Herculean feats was one of the primary reasons for the end of the Western Empire.

More generally, one had to be relatively close to one's food. Every city was surrounded by a hinterland that fed that city; this was the ancient city-state, whether that city-state be Greek or Teotihuacani. The Roman Empire itself was primarily a patch-work of various *civitates*, or city-states, that paid tribute to the central city of Rome — the perfect model of inter-community trade, so far as any one community might be concerned.

As Hirth points out, every agricultural society faces a dilemna of whether to specialize to create a greater surplus, or diversify to offset the danger of a bad harvest. It is a classic dilemna in economics, and the classic answer has always been trade; I specialize in A, you specialize in B, and if we trade, then we can both have more of A *and* B.

But trading food was difficult. Most foods spoil, so they can't be taken very far. They're heavy, and the profits are not usually very high. It is generally more economical to trade light-weight, expensive luxury items. We have significant evidence that, prior to the Neolithic Revolution, trans-continental trade of lightweight luxury items occurred both in North America and Europe, if not elsewhere.

But if trading food is difficult, why does trade help anything? Because trading food is *difficult* — not impossible. The trade of luxury items and prestige goods helped create a marked upper-class: those who controlled this exotic trade with other groups. These would be the same "Big Men" who emerged in competitive feasting. Such goods helped demarcate their power and status, and were major assets in reinforcing their power. Like the kings of medieval Europe who would universally condemn peasant revolts, even against their enemies, the Big Men knew when to stick together. They needed one another for the trade on which their power and position relied, and if one of their primary trading partners fell on hard times, they could marshal their resources to rescue their ailing neighbors in the most ancient form of foreign aid.

So we have a clearer picture of the late Mesolithic coming together. The end of the Pleistocene fluctuates the climate, alternating between times of plenty and times of want. While starvation is rare and it would be a stretch to call the bad times "famine," some years are undeniably harder than others.

In such uncertain times, "Big Men" emerge, providing some level of stability. In fat years, their lavish potlatches and mokas increase their own prestige and indebt neighboring groups — providing insurance against the hard years that will follow. These Big Men further bolster their position within the group, and cultivate a reciprocity network *beyond* the group, by using their power and influence to engage in long-distance trade. As a last resort, when all other possibilities are gone, they can call on neighboring Big Men to provide food.

These late Mesolithic foragers spend more and more time cultivating at more intensive levels, to produce enough food for the escalating competition of the Big Men's feasts. It is hard, and they must sacrifice the freedom and liesure of their former life, but at least they have some security. Eventually, those Big Men have sufficient influence to make their followers stop thinking of themselves as hunters who farm, and begin thinking of themselves as farmers who hunt.

Big Men become chiefs, chiefs become kings, populations explode and civilization moves inexorably from that beginning to the present crisis.

In the years since 9/11, a quote from Benjamin Franklin has enjoyed renewed popularity in certain circles: "They that can give up essential liberty to obtain a little temporary safety deserve neither liberty nor safety." The loss of civil liberties and freedoms suffered by the United States' citizenry under the second Bush regime, though significant, remain small when compared to the freedoms lost 10,000 years ago when our forebears (memetically, if not genetically) took up civilization. Agriculture is a hard life, as we have already seen. Malnutrition and disease followed almost immediately; war, tyranny and poverty followed inexorably. By relying solely on domesticated crops, intensive agriculture becomes the only subsistence technology that is truly susceptible to *real* famine. The safety the Big Men offered was illusory; in fact, that ancient bargain put us in a more precarious position than we had ever known — or will likely ever know again.

Ten thousand years ago, our ancestors traded the bulk of that very real freedom that is our species' birthright, for a little temporary safety. If there is an original sin, a fall of man, that was it. From that day to this, we have not deserved — nor have we had — either one.

Bibliography

- Eckhardt, W.

  1992. *Civilizations, empires and wars: a quantitative history of war.* New York: McFarland & Co., Inc.

- Gilman, A.

  1981 "The development of social stratification" *Anthropology* 22(1) pp. 1–23

- Harris, M.

  1993. *Culture, people, nature: an introduction to general anthropology,* 6th edition. New York: Harper Collins College Publishers.

- Godesky, J.

  2000. "War and Society." Published online: *media.anthropik.com*

- Hirth, K.

1992. "Interregional exchange as elite behavior: an evolutionary perspective." In: Chase, D.Z. and Chase, A.F., *Mesoamerican elites: an archaeological assessment*. Norman: University of Oklahoma Press.

• Kottak, C.

2000. *Cultural anthropology*, 8th edition. Boston: McGraw-Hill.

• Van Bakel, M., Hagesteijn, R. and Van de Velde, P.

1986. *Private politics: a multi-disciplinary approach to 'Big Man' systems*. Leiden: E.J. Brill

Thesis #11: Hierarchy is an unnecessary evil.

Egalitarianism is an essential part of human nature; it is the very thing that led to our humanity, and remains an undeniable yearning in the human spirit that continues to shape our political fortunes (*see* thesis #7). Hierarchy is the antithesis of that, and thus, we cannot avoid the inescapable conclusion that hierarchy itself is dehumanizing and maladapted to the human condition. It appears to suit many of our closest primate relatives just fine (chimpanzees, for example), but it denies the very thing that created us as a unique species — our egalitarianism. It squashes the vast diversity of possible social interactions into a rigidly defined structure, and thus, violates the principle set forth in thesis #1 — making hierarchy "evil." The question is, is hieracy a *necessary* "evil"?

First, you will recall that we defined "hierarchy" and "egalitarianism" in thesis #7 in terms of graph theory. Individuals are nodes in a social graph, and edges are power relationships between them; the graph as a whole becomes a depiction of a society. Power is an inescapable fact of life; even in egalitarian society, some individuals have influence over others. What defines an egalitarian society is that this graph has no particular structure. It can take any shape. The possible diversity of egalitarian social structures is limitless. The result of such chaos is that there is no single, dominant indivdual across every dimension of power. Hierarchy, then, is a very specific case, in that hierarchy is a kind of society with a very specific shape — a triangle. Hierarchy is when the graph of a society is triangular; egalitarianism is when the graph of a society is any other shape than triangular.

We can also speak of a continuum of hierarchy, as few societies have ever formed a perfect triangle with all power culminating into a single, apex individual. Contemporary American society is undeniably hierarchical, but its zenith is not a single individual, but a small, tightly-knit circle.

By itself, a hierarchical society would be another point in the diversity of social structures — and thus, good. The problem is when *all* societies are hierarchical. Hierarchy's need to crush all alternatives is what makes it "evil," because it is driven to wipe out all diversity besides itself. The ultimate driving force behind this is the simple fact that hierarchy does not work well for people. They must be somehow "forced" into it — meaning that all alternatives must be systematically eradicated, or hierarchy will be abandoned by the lowest ranks, the ones that are, simultaneously, most needed by hierarchy, and have the least to gain from it. Daniel Quinn raises the phenomenon of children running away to join the circus as a proverbial expression of this abandonment. Ancient Roman apprehension about the Cynics is another expression, as was much of the fervor generated in the 1960s against the hippie countercultural movement.

Baboons can be instructive to us on the effects of hierarchy on humans, so long as we keep in mind that we are dealing with a key difference between the two. Baboon males are roughly three times larger than females; human sexual dimorphism is nearly non-existent, one of the lowest in the entire animal kingdom. Baboons are well adapted to hierarchy; as we have seen, it was the rejection of such hierarchical lifestyles and the adoption of egalitarianism that created humans in the first place. But even baboons, as adapted to hierarchy as they are, are stressed by it. Robert Sapolsky, one of the world's foremost authorities on baboon society, put it this way:

« *[M]y initial assumption that I sort of squandered my first 15 years on with them was dominance rank. That's the thing. If you're a low-ranking baboon you're gonna have the stress-related diseases. And what I've learned since then is, yeah, rank's important. Far more important is what sort of society you have that rank in. Is it a troop that treats its low-ranking animals miserably? Is it a troop whose hierarchy is unstable? Those are both much more stressful situations. And then even more important than your rank in the sort of society in which it occurs is your personality. Which is basically saying, What's your filters with which you see the world around you?* »

This is very reasonable, particularly for baboons, who have millions of years of evolution adapting them to hierarchical social structures. We would expect hierarchy to stress them less than humans. That said, even among humans, we can understand the importance of personality types and the type of hierarchy on the level of stress we experience in that hierarchy — what we might call the perception of oppression. Some personality types can accept their circumstances more easily than others, and some hierarchies are much worse to be at the bottom of than others. This is why no hierarchy can ever succeed being *purely* exploitative. The most coercive regimes collapse almost immediately, e.g., the trend of fascism in 1930s Europe. Rome was incredibly exploitative, but succeeded by tempering that exploitation with the myth of legitimacy. Caracalla's move to open citizenship to the provinces was key to Roman success, by making the exploited feel like they had a vested stake in the empire. It created legitimacy, and removed the perception of oppression.

So we see that not all hierarchies are created equal. Some hierarchies are more "evil" than others. The contemporary United States, for instance, is a case study in the attempt to create the least evil hierarchy possible — the playing out of what happens when the mutually exclusive concepts of "freedom" and "the state" are combined. And yet, even in the contemporary United States — the historical peak of prosperity and freedom within hierarchy — we cannot deny the chafing restrictions and insult to human dignity imposed by subjection to another human being.

In essence, we are dealing with shifting the mean of a bell curve. The distribution of personality types would naturally create a bell curve — some are very stressed out, and some are very relaxed, but most will cluster about the mean. Across this distribution, we can draw a line of the perception of hierarchy. Above this line, more stressed individuals notice the imposition of hierarchy; below it, the less stressed individuals do not. The more hierarchical a society is, the more that line shifts to the left — enveloping more of the area under the bell curve on the "oppressed," right side of the line. There will always be individuals who are able to cope with any level of hierarchy — and there will always be individuals who chafe under even the lightest power relation. That is not important. What is important is the overall level of human suffering caused by subjecting increasing populations to the dehumanizing ordeal of hierarchy.

At this point, we should be able to clearly say that hierarchy is, indeed, "evil" — but that it also is a measure of degree, rather than kind. We can characterize a society as "hierarchical," but we must understand that this means that it bears a greater resemblance to the hierarchical ideal than the egalitarian ideal, rather than to say that it is a perfect image of the hierarchical ideal. We might characterize such a society as "78% hierarchical," for instance.

Jeff Vail has done an excellent job charting the gross inefficiencies of hierarchy. In perhaps his very best argument on this, Vail highlighted the complete inability of hierarchy to effectively process information in perhaps hierarchy's single greatest achievement in this regard: the United States Air Force. Vail writes:

« *"Span of Control" is one term for the management concept that one person can only effectively control a limited number of subordinates. As a hierarchal organization grows, more and more intermediary layers must be created to keep this span of control within reasonable bounds. Let's explore the (quite obvious) ramifications of this, as a means of better understanding R.A. Wilson's SNAFU principle: As hierarchy grows, the increasing number of relays that information must cross, and the self-interested distortion of information at each relay ensures the inefficiency of information processing within hierarchy. »*

...

In reality, the number of staff tiers keeps increasing (for example, I've never seen an Air Force "wing" with only 12 wing-staff personnel, as the two-tiered staff formula would suggest). Wilson's SNAFU principle would suggest that as the number of layers (and hence relays) increases, the number of personnel involved in information processing functions will keep increasing beyond the 76% suggested in the 6-layer organization above. In reality, this does in fact happen, as at each higher level there are additional staff functions that must be added (e.g. at the Flight level, the staff doesn't include medical, but at the Wing level it may include an entire hospital). Additionally, the degree of autonomy is increased from the Group to Wing level, as necessitated by the sheer impossibility of maintaining effective communications through 5 hierarchal relays.

The "SNAFU principle" Vail refers to is the effect of message corruption through multiple relays in a self-interested system. It is exemplified by this "fable" from the hacker culture, which dates back to the 1960s:

In the beginning was the plan, and then the specification; And the plan was without form, and the specification was void.

And darkness was on the faces of the implementors thereof;

And they spake unto their leader, saying: "It is a crock of shit, and smells as of a sewer." And the leader took pity on them, and spoke to the project leader: "It is a crock of excrement, and none may abide the odor thereof." And the project leader spake unto his section head, saying: "It is a container of excrement, and it is very strong, such that none may abide it."

The section head then hurried to his department manager, and informed him thus: "It is a vessel of fertilizer, and none may abide its strength."

The department manager carried these words to his general manager, and spoke unto him saying:

"It containeth that which aideth the growth of plants, and it is very strong."

And so it was that the general manager rejoiced and delivered the good news unto the Vice President. "It promoteth growth, and it is very powerful." The Vice President rushed to the President's side, and joyously exclaimed: "This powerful new software product will promote the growth of the company!" And the President looked upon the product, and saw that it was very good.

This litte piece whimsically illustrates a very serious problem in hierarchy. The span of control limits how many subordinates a single hierarch can control through the same neurological limitations from which we derive Dunbar's number (~150). Because of that span of control, hierarchy must create more levels to accomodate larger populations. However, more levels means more transmissions from the bottom of the hierarchy to the top. This is why we note the greater efficiency of smaller corporations over larger ones, or the eternal litany against government bureaucracy. Elsewhere, Vail has discussed the superior information processing capabilities of an "open source," rhizomatic network:

« *Rhizome processes information entirely differently than hierarchy. It depends on the fusion of a regular network of local links between peers along with occasional, distant and weak contacts with a broad and diverse set of contacts. This "weak network" theory, and how rhizome can use it to process information more efficiently than hierarchy, is well illustrated by the classic example of the job search: in a traditional communications model (as used by hierarchy), you ask your 10 close friends for leads on jobs, and they each ask 10 close friends. The result — you don't span a very large social network in your search. In the "weak network" model you ask 10 distant friends, and they in turn each ask 10 distant friends. With such a method you can span a far wider social network, and are more likely to locate a job prospect. Rhizome is defined by the non-hierarchal cooperation between peer entities, and this cooperation — the fundamental economic activity in rhizome — depends entirely on such effective forms of communication.* »

So, we must now return to the original question — is hierarchy a *necessary* evil? Must we adapt to this evil in all its gross inefficiency and learn to cope with it, as so many of our primate cousins have? Or is it unnecessary — and therefore, something we should work to reject once again, even as our first human ancestors did?

In thesis #7, we also touched on *why* hierarchy becomes necessary. After a discussion of Dunbar's number, and the reflection of egalitarianism in the evolution of the human brain, I noted:

Here we see the essential problem with any large-scale society: we cannot conceive of so many *people*. It speaks to the very heart of Stalin's cold truism: "One death is a tragedy, but a million deaths are a statistic." Thus, for any society much larger than 150 people, we become neurologically incapable of maintaining an egalitarian society. Hierarchy becomes necessary, yet the human animal is very much adapted to egalitarianism — and in no way adapted to hierarchy. Cross-culturally, we all have some expectations rooted in that egalitarian heritage. We expect freedom, and we expect to be treated as a human being rather than a stereotype. We all feel some negative feeling of stress when these expectations are not met — as they invariably are not met in any large, hierarchical society.

Hierarchy eases the burden on our brain by dividing the world into neatly stereotyped classes. We do not need to know the bum on the street personally, because we know that he is "homeless," and we know what "the homeless" are. We do not need to know our given Congressman personally because he is a "politician" and we know what "politicians" are. Hierarchy helps simplify the world, allowing our brains to function in a society of 6.5 billion. We may be academically aware that this is an abstraction and far removed from the actual complexity of our society, but we are neurologically incapable of actually understanding such complexity. Hierarchy provides us a model of a simplified world that is easier to understand than a complex world of 6.5 billion persons.

There are two elements here that make hierarchy necessary, and population is only the first. However, even a large population would not require hierarchy if it accepted *fissioning*. This is common among many primitive societies, and nearly universal among hunter-gatherers. When groups become too large (or often, when an individual aspires to power), the group fissions. The Bible contains a memory of this process in Genesis 13, with the fissioning of Abram's and Lot's groups. Tribalism, Balkanism, whatever we call it, even a large population can eschew hierarchy if it is prepared to break down into a sufficient number of small, autonomous groups.

However, this is possible only under certain energy distribution schemes — and agriculture is not one of them. Agriculture requires significant investment in a given piece of developed land, often requiring terracing or irrigation. This makes fissioning geographically difficult. As a more general principle, it concerns the distribution of energy. Vail writes:

Historically, patterns of energy useage can effectively predict, and are a useful tool in understanding societal structure and hierarchy. Ancient China and Egypt, home to the earliest and most centralized/despotic civilizations, can be explained in terms of an energy-dependence dynamic. The energy that drove both these systems was control of the periodic flooding of the nile and yellow rivers, used to irrigate the agricultural systems of the respective societies. The individual land control of farmers in both societies has mystified many historians as to why such despotic political systems were allowed to develop. This can, however, be easily explained by the fact that it required huge, often 100,000+ man work details to keep these "hydraulic" (see Wittfogel) agriculture systems functioning — something that could only be accomplished by a powerful, centralized authority.

Conversely, tribal political structures, epitomized by autonomy and individual freedom (if not material wealth) are examples of highly de-centralized energy systems — mainly firewood gathered by individuals at a sustainable rate.

Taking advantage of the distant mirror of history to examine our own society, it is clear that our dependence on petroleum-derived energy has led to a complete dependence on a despotic government-corporate complex that controls and ensures our supply of petroleum. Our society of "freedom and empowerment", our vaunted democracy might, to those in a removed vantage point, look like the same superficial good deal as the pharoh's providing and maintaining a complex hydraulic-irrigation network must have looked like a good deal to the ancient egyptian peasantry.

Thus, the question, "Is hierarchy necessary?" is actually two questions — "Is a large population necessary? And must this population depend on centralized energy sources?" It seems that centralized energy sources may be a prerequisite for such large populations, but the size of such populations are deeply ambiguous. There is no inherent value in having a large population. We don't need to have a large population; we did well with a much smaller population for millions of years. Large populations must make frightening cuts into the ecology they depend on, placing them in a permanently precarious position.

In fact, the only thing that necessitates a large population is hierarchy itself. Hierarchy requires large pools of labor to provide for the nobility, and large populations that can be levied into large armies with which hierarchy can expand.

Therefore, hierarchy is only necessary *for hierarchy*. We gain nothing from it, but lose much to it. The only one who benefits from hierarchy is the hierarch himself. This makes hierarchy an unnecessary evil.

Thesis #12: Civilization must always grow.

Two suspects A, B are arrested by the police. The police have insufficient evidence for a conviction, and having separated both prisoners, visit each of them and offer the same deal: if one testifies for the prosecution (turns King's Evidence) against the other and the other remains silent, the silent accomplice receives the full 10-year sentence and the betrayer goes free. If both stay silent, the police can only give both prisoners 6 months for a minor charge. If both betray each other, they receive a 2-year sentence each.

Such is the classical formulation of the Prisoner's Dilemma. It is one of the founding problems of game theory. The best case scenario would arise from cooperation: if both prisoners remain silent, both go free. However, not only does betraying the other mean you will go free immediately, but *not* betraying the other carries a 50% chance of bearing the maximum penalty alone. Altruistic cooperation is so rare in this game that it barely warrants any consideration whatsoever; nearly every game involves one, the other, or both, betraying his fellow.

The Prisoner's Dilemma provides the logical foundation of why civilization must always continue to grow. Each society faces a choice: do we continue to intensify production, adopt greater complexity, and increase the size or scale of our society, or do we happily accept the level we're already at? If you choose not to intensify, you will be out-competed by those who do — and your lower level of intensity and complexity will become a resource they can absorb to fuel their further acceleration, whether by outright conquest or more subtle forms of economic or cultural exploitation.

This is the underlying logic of Joseph Tainter's argument concerning collapse in peer polities in *The Collapse of Complex Societies*. If one peer polity does choose to collapse, that region becomes a resource that can be exploited by its neighbors. Whoever conquers it first will have an advantage over the others in the continuing race of escalation.

The same logic was successfully applied to the arms race between the United States and the Soviet Union during the Cold War. The growth of civilization can be seen in similar terms. Even when the problems of unrestrained growth are recognized by a society — even when all can plainly see that a smaller-scale, less complex society would be preferable — there is no option to make use of that knowledge. Ultimately, it is an application of Tainter's principle that no single polity can collapse in a peer polity system (even if that collapse is merely trying to stand still). To do so means becoming less complex than one's neighbors, to exploit one's resources less intensively, to have smaller populations, smaller armies, equipped with less material (and less complex material). Such a region will be absorbed by some other, more complex entity — whether directly and military, or indirectly and economically is a trivial distinction, for they both end with the same result, whether *de juris* or *de facto*.

Civilization itself is a Prisoner's Dilemna driving ever greater intensification, complexity and growth. Garrett Hardin compared the "Tragedy of the Commons" quite explicitly to the nuclear arms race; Daniel Quinn, similarly, compared his "Food Race" directly to the arms race. Both illustrate the arms race itself as a single, minor aspect of a much larger phenomenon that in fact defines all of our recorded history: civilization's need to continue growing, no matter the cost.

Our entire economy is based on the principle of continual and unrestrained growth. The Great Depression did not see a contracting economy — it did not even see the economy ceasing to grow. Instead, the Great Depression was the result of the economy growing *only* at 75% of its capacity. Not only must our economy continue to grow; it must continue to grow as quickly as possible. In *A Theory of Power* (ch. 7), Jeff Vail explains:

«*Misplaced faith in perpetual growth exists as a by-product of the intensifying, hierarchal master pattern that underlies most aspects of human society. Despite the clear reality that we live within a system limited by finite resources, our entire economy rests on the need for continual growth.* »

The publicly owned corporation serves as an example of a pervasive pattern that cannot accept stability; if it does not provide a regular, growth-based return to its investors, it will find itself quickly dissolved. The press, politicians and the general public often rush to express surprise at the corporate decision making process. Why won't corporations act as more responsible citizens, help protect the environment, or take better care of their employees? Doing so may provide long-term benefits, not only for society, but also for the corporation's bottom line. Ultimately, however, the very structure of the corporation constrains it in its decision making process: it must respond to the short-term demand to increase shareholder value, resulting in the ubiquitous, shortsighted decision making of corporate America. Like the corporation, economists see serious trouble for a country's economy as a whole if it temporarily stops growing,(4) as the debt and inflation based finance structure cannot handle mere stability. Any entity, whether a small business or a national economy, that finances its operation by borrowing money at interest must continually grow in order to remain solvent due to the demands of repaying the time-value of money. No wonder, then, that with an institutionalized demand for continuous growth, our society seems willing to ignore the clear realities of finite resources. This process begs the question: should we view environmental overshoot as a possibility or as a foregone conclusion if we continue with our present economic structure?

Theoretically, let us consider a set of societies who have all agreed on the foreseen consequences of such unrestrained growth, and understand that such rampant growth inside of a finite universe is unsustainable and must ultimately end in collapse. They may adopt the "seventh generation" sustainability outlook that was expected of Iroquois chiefs, or some similar ideology. Regardless, they have the means of intensification, but they are expected all to forego that because of the catastrophe it would visit on all.

We have, in effect, a cartel. Cartels, like OPEC, agree to fix the price of a given commodity they control — usually higher, in order to create greater profits. However, this creates a Prisoner's Dilemma as well. The first one to defect from the cartel and price his goods lower will out-compete everyone else in the cartel and more than make up in volume what he lost in each unit. Ultimately, cartels always fail — as OPEC will eventually fail — because the incentive to defect is too strong. Eventually, one member of the cartel will defect, and because of its nature, it only takes one defection to bring it all down.

We have the same situations amongst our sustainable societies above. They have made a cartel, pledging not to grow, but to remain stationary. The first member who defects and decides to accelerate his growth will be in a very advantageous position over the rest of the cartel — tipping off the very same "growth race" we see today. The effects of one's actions to the seventh generation mean nothing if you face extinction at the hands of a more complex, intensive neighbor today.

Thus, civilizations must always grow. Failure to grow makes them vulnerable to other civilizations, and all are compelled to continue the self-reinforcing, positive feedback loop of continual growth, or die trying. Civilizations which fail to grow mark themselves for extinction. Constant growth is the only condition under which civilization can persist. It cannot continue in decline; it cannot continue standing still. In *Collapse*, Jared Diamond notes that a civilization's collapse very often swiftly follows its peak. In an article for *The New York Times* (1 January 2005), titled "The Ends of the World as We Know Them," he remarks:

« History warns us that when once-powerful societies collapse, they tend to do so quickly and unexpectedly. That shouldn't come as much of a surprise: peak power usually means peak population, peak needs, and hence peak vulnerability. »

In other words, collapse occurs not when those resources we require run out — it occurs when the acquisition of those resources stops continuing to grow, but not our need for them. When demand outstrips supply, the economy acts to correct the situation. Usually that means a higher price, extinguishing demand — but when the resource is necessary for life, other means may also be necessary. Ultimately, the market *always* finds a solution; the problem is that most people who trumpet that fact tend to suffer a lack of imagination where what such a solution might entail is concerned. As Joseph Tainter took such pains to point out in *The Collapse of Complex Societies*, collapse is, above all, an *economizing* process.

Thesis #13: Civilization always pursues complexity.

What is "**civilization**"? When asked this question directly, many people answer that a civilization is simply a synonym for "society" — that a civilization is simply a group of people living together. This definition is betrayed when you press the point with borderline examples. Are you comfortable with the phrase "Inuit Civilization"? Or "!Kung Civilization?" Or "Australian Aborigine Civilization"? Most people are not. There is no doubt as to whether the Inuit, !Kung or Aborigines constitute societies, but we waver on the question of their civilization. Obviously, then, the two words are not the synonyms some would claim.

WordNet provides four definitions for the word:

1. civilization, civilisation — (a society in an advanced state of social development (e.g., with complex legal and political and religious organizations); "the people slowly progressed from barbarism to civilization")
2. civilization, civilisation — (the social process whereby societies achieve civilization)
3. culture, civilization, civilisation — (a particular society at a particular time and place; "early Mayan civilization")
4. refinement, civilization, civilisation — (the quality of excellence in thought and manners and taste; "a man of intellectual refinement"; "he is remembered for his generosity and civilization")

The third definition is the synonym of society discussed previously (are not all societies in some particular time and place?). The other three all have a common root in nineteenth century ideas of unilineal cultural evolution. Fundamental to this idea is the notion of a society's progression from savagery to civilization: "the people slowly progressed from barbarism to civilization."

Progression, though, implies the reality of perfection. For societies to "progress," there must be some single goal to move towards. Every culture believes itself to be superior to all others, but even after centuries of philosophical theorizing on the subject, we have yet to develop any objective criteria that do not require us first to accept the superiority of our own culture. We can prove our superiority only when it is taken as a premise, making the entire argument moot. Given that such ethnocentrism is a universal among all human cultures, we should not count our own for anything more than that. Ethnocentrism once had its place: a smug sense of superiority could help keep people from wandering off by themselves and dying alone. Usefulness should not be mistaken for truth.

So we see that none of the four definitions provided are really meaningful. One fails to capture what we really mean by the word, and the other three are based on a deeply flawed premise.

Etymologically, the origins of the word "civilization" lay in the Latin word *civis*, often translated as "city," but perhaps more accurately translated as "city-state." The Roman Empire was a patchwork of *civitates*, fulfilling a role not terribly far removed from states in the U.S., though the Roman Empire was less influenced by notions of Cartesian space and more interested in spheres of influence. The Roman Empire was, in fact, a hierarchy of such smaller imperial dominions; the *Pater familias* was emperor of his family, and the magistrate was the emperor of his *civitas*. Strictly speaking, a *civis* was the "citizen" of such a *civitas*, but the word was also applied to the sense of "city-ness," as well as the city itself.

Etymology, then, gives us our first workable definition: "civilization" is a culture of cities. Working more along these lines, and trying to identify a set of defining criteria among those cultures we can comfortably call "civilized," Vere Gordon Childe defined a set of criteria still taught in introductory anthropology courses and widely accepted as *the* criteria for civilization:

Primary Criteria

1. Settlement of cities of 5,000 or more people.

2. Full-time labor specialization.

3. Concentration of surplus.

4. Class structure.

5. State-level political organization.

Secondary Criteria

6. Monumental architecture

7. Long-distance trade

8. Sophisticated art

9. Writing

10. Predictive sciences (math, astronomy, etc.)

The secondary criteria have a general correspondence with civilization, but are not definitive. There are plenty of civilizations that lack one or more of them (Teotihuacan most likely lacked a writing system), two out of five (predictive sciences and sophisticated art) are human universals, and two of the remaining items (monumental architecture and long-distance trade) are known among non-civilized societies.

The primary criteria, though, help us to begin to understand the true nature of civilization. These five criteria are, however, bound to one another through causation. Thus, they always appear together, and never without the others — forming a clearly defined cultural package that we can call "civilization." This should not be terribly surprising, because culture is a reflexive system, and changes to one part of that system will cascade throughout the whole. In thesis #8, we saw how formative subsistence strategy is for a culture, and how the precarious nature of food production limited cultivating societies to a very narrow range of possible diversity. We saw that Service's traditional breakdown may be somewhat biased to tease out greater distinction among those societies more like ourselves, while lumping together far greater diversity among foragers not like ourselves. The differences between industry and agriculture are differences of scale, not kind. The Industrial Revolution did not fundamentally change the nature of agricultural society, it merely accelerated it along previously defined lines. Also, pastoralism is an extremely unusual option, confined almost entirely to the Middle East and Africa. Moreover, such societies cannot exist independently of an agricultural society. I tend to think of them more as an unusual case of symbiosis with agricultural societies: a remora to agriculture's shark, if you will.

That leaves us with a simplified model of just three subsistence strategies: agriculture, horticulture and foraging. This can be simply explained by two, irrefutable bits. Either you grow plants to eat, or you do not. If you do not, you are a forager. If you do, you either work above or below the point of diminishing returns. If above, you are an agriculturalist; if below, you are a horticulturalist. Consider the graph below, where "utility" is the ratio of calories obtained versus calories spent, and "production" is simply the number of calories obtained:

The Point of Diminishing Returns in Cultivation defines Agriculture and Horticulture.

The concept of diminishing returns was first developed in the context of agriculture. After a certain point, simply applying more labor yielded less and less benefit. In fact, from a caloric viewpoint, *all* agriculture is beyond the point of diminishing returns. Even in agrarian societies, it takes more calories of work to farm a field, than is returned in calories of product. Among simpler agrarian societies, this shortfall is made up with the use of tools and animals. The plow uses the fundamental physics of a lever to lessen the workload. Animals can leverage energy sources humans cannot — by grazing in lands too rocky or infertile to be cultivated. In modern petroculture, fossil fuels make up the shortfall. Petroleum doesn't just power tractors, it also forms the basic ingredients for everything from fertilizer to packaging, and the fuel for transportation. We now burn between 4 and 10 calories — mostly in fossil fuels — for every 1 calorie of agricultural product we produce.

The slope becomes sharper as more labor is applied — the process becomes increasingly inefficient — but the absolute number of calories yielded always goes up by *some* amount per unit of labor. So, production can still be increased even past the point of diminishing returns by applying more labor. It just becomes increasingly inefficient to do so.

Forager populations are very dispersed, because their food is very dispersed. Foragers gather food from the wild, whether by hunting, fishing, gathering, or simple scavenging. These resources are not collected in any one space, so every forager band requires a significant range of territory. This makes forager society very sparsely populated.

By comparison, cultivation converts a specific area of biomass into human food, raising the edible ratio of that area to 100%. In swidden (a.k.a., "slash-and-burn") horticulture, for example, an area of rain forest is cut down and burned, and a garden is planted in the ashes. This is the only way to practice cultivation in the rain forest, as the ground is about as fertile as cement — all of the nutrients are locked in the trees. This very clearly illustrates the conversion from biomass into human food, as the biodiversity of some area of rain forest becomes fertilizer to grow a horticultural garden. This is the essence of all cultivation. With a denser food supply, cultures that depend on cultivation for their food can support much denser populations. Horticultural societies typically live in villages, even complex networks of villages. Agricultural societies practice even more intense cultivation, producing even more calories — and thus, producing an even larger population, because human population is a function of food supply (*see* thesis #4). These populations are even larger, and even denser — leading to cities, the first of Childe's five primary criteria.

Foragers enjoy a naturalistic social arrangement. Their life is sufficiently comfortable and easy to simply handle things naturally. Decisions are made by concensus. Infractions of social norms can be handled on a case-by-case basis, by the community as a whole. Circumstances and personalities can be fully considered, and rather than focusing on "punishment," such societies can instead address the harm done directly. Where most civilized societies simply ritualize a sanctioned form of vengeance and mob rule, these "primitives" enjoy true justice.

The number of infractions of social norms — "crimes" — is always some fraction of the total number of interactions between individuals. In a pairing of two individuals, there is only one interaction. Add a third individual, and there are three possible interactions. A fourth raises the number to six; five, to ten; six, to fifteen, and so on. As the number of individuals increases, the number of interactions increases exponentially, and as that number increases, so, too, do the number of infractions. Before long, the community is so large that individuals are no longer universally known, circumstances are not appreciated by all members of the community, and the number of such incidents is too great to be evaluated on a case-by-case basis. The essence of "law" is the abridgement of justice — to resolve cases more quickly, by compromising fairness. Most legal systems attempt to abrogate this essential fact, but it remains the basic truth of law. Justice is a luxury only the sparsely populated can afford.

Thus, large populations require a legal body, and judges to execute that law. The nature of agricultural production also demands defense. While ideas of property and ownership are essential to an agricultural society, they are alien to the rest of the world. The gross inefficiency of agricultural life puts the agricultural society in a very tenuous position. This is why only agricultural societies suffer famine. When Richard Lee made his famous study of the !Kung and calculated their average work per day to be three hours, the

Kalahari was suffering one of the worst draughts in living memory. The !Kung's Bantu neighbors — pastoralists — were dying of starvation, while the !Kung complained of having to work so hard — three whole hours — to gather their food. Humans are omnivores, and it would take nothing less than a mass extinction to threaten our survival as foragers. We risk starvation only when we culturally redefine "food" to a small number of closely related, domesticated species. Because of this, any agricultural society that does not protect its fields from animal predators — both human and otherwise — will not last very long. Even worse, the inefficiencies of agriculture require constant expansion in order to continue (*see* thesis #12).

The need of agricultural societies to defend, expand, and enforce law requires the formation of state-level political organization. So far, we have seen two of Childe's primary criteria — 1 and 5 — as unavoidable consequences of sufficiently intensive agricultural production.

Of course, standing armies and state-level political organization already demand the second criterion: full-time labor specialization. Soldiers in a standing army are, after all, specialists in combat. Politicians and rulers are specialists in administration; judges specialists in law, etc. Such complexity in labor division can easily be extended. Such specialists produce no food of their own, and so are dependent on others for their subsistence. This builds an innate inequality to all agricultural exchange, as one party posesses something needed, while the other merely posesses something desired. That inequality can be shifted through threats and coercion — either of physical violence on the part of a military-backed secular force, or of spiritual retribution on the part of a religious organization. This brings us Childe's third criterion — concentration of surplus — and its consequence, class structure, Childe's fourth criterion.

So we see that all five of Childe's primary criterion — cities, full-time specialization, concentration of surplus, class and the state — are all necessary consequences of sufficiently intensive food production. This kind of escalation is, itself, an example of a much more basic phenomenon: increasing complexity.

In his 1983 paper, "Breaking down cultural complexity: inequality and heterogeneity," (in *Advances in Archaeological Method and Theory*, vol 6), McGuire provides this definiton of complexity:

« Complexity is generally understood to refer to such things as the size of a society, the number and distinctiveness of its parts, the variety of specialized social roles that it incorporates, the number of distinct social personalities present, and the variety of mechanisms for organizing these into a coherent, functioning whole. Augmenting any of these dimensions increases the complexity of a society. Hunter-gatherer societies (by way of illustrating one contrast in complexity) contain no more than a few dozen distinct social personalities, while modern European censuses recognize 10,000 to 20,000 unique occupational roles, and industrial societies may contain overall more than 1,000,000 different kinds of social personalities ».

In "Complexity, Problem-Solving, and Sustanable Societies," Joseph Tainter reiterates a point he makes in greater detail in his 1988 classic study, *The Collapse of Complex Societies*:

« As a simple illustration of differences in complexity, Julian Steward pointed out the contrast between the native peoples of western North America, among whom early ethnographers documented 3,000 to 6,000 cultural elements, and the U.S. Army, which landed 500,000+ artifact types at Casablanca in World War 11 (Steward 1955). Complexity is quantifiable. »

...

The conventional view has been that human societies have a latent tendency towards greater complexity. Complexity was assumed to be a desirable thing, and the logical result of surplus food, leisure time, and human creativity. Although this scenario is popular, it is inadequate to explain the evolution of complexity. In the world of cultural complexity there is, to use a colloquial expression, no free lunch. More complex societies are costlier to maintain than simpler ones and require higher support levels per capita. A society that is more complex has more sub-groups and social roles, more networks among groups and individuals, more horizontal and vertical controls, higher flow of information, greater centralization of information, more specialization, and greater interdependence of parts. Increasing any of these dimensions requires biological, mechanical, or chemical energy. In the days before fossil fuel subsidies, increasing the complexity of a society usually meant that the majority of its population had to work harder.

Tainter recognizes five primary subcategories of a culture's complexity: subsistence methods, technology, conflict, sociopoltical organization, and research and development. Each area can be made more complex by an investment of energy; each can open up access to greater sources of energy by becoming more complex. Complexity is an investment that requires a given input, and makes a given return.

Civilization is a culture which adopts some key element of complexity for which more energy can be gained simply by intensifying input. Agriculture is the classic example: more intensive cultivation will yield more food. This is not necessarily true of foraging, which includes much more of a gamble. This creates a positive feedback loop by kicking off a game of Prisoner's Dilemna. Failing to intensify production puts one at risk from those who choose to do so. Thus, all civilizations become compelled to grow at all costs (*see* thesis #12). Because of this, civilizations are forced to constantly increase their complexity whenever possible, whether by refining bureaucratic or administrative functions, increasing agricultural yields, using miltiary force to secure new energy resources (whether this is expressed in Roman conquests explicitly made to acquire new farmland, or contemporary U.S. military involvement in the Middle East), inventing new technology, or any other form of complexity.

So, at last, we have a working definition of civilization. A civilization is any society which chooses to answer all stresses with an increase in complexity. As such, the seeds of collapse are sown in civilization's very nature, because complexity itself is subject to diminishing returns, and pursuing *any* one strategy as the response to *every* stress will suffer the same fate.

Thesis #14: Complexity is subject to diminishing returns.

Joseph Tainter's 1988 *The Collapse of Complex Societies* remains the definitive work in the field of collapse. Tainter reviews other explanations of collapse — including economics, invasion and environmental problems — and finds them all insufficient. While these factors certainly play their roles, these are also the very same stressors that complexity is *supposed* to deal with. Thus, while these might suffice as proximate causes, it only underlines the ultimate cause all the more. Why do complex societies become vulnerable to the very kinds of stress which, at an earlier time in its history, the society in question would simply shrug off?

Tainter's answer lies with complexity itself, and the law of diminishing returns. As a society becomes more complex, greater complexity becomes more costly. The escalation of complexity becomes increasingly difficult to maintain, until it finally becomes *impossible*.

It is well worth noting, as Tainter does, that complexity is a function of energy. He writes:

« Human societies and political organizations, like all living systems, are maintained by a continuous flow of energy. From the simplest familial unit to the most complex regional hierarchy, the institutions and patterned interactions that comprise a human society are dependent on energy. At the same time, the mechanisms by which human groups acquire and distribute basic resources are conditioned by, and integrated within, sociopolitical institutions. Energy flow and sociopolitical organization are opposites sides of an equation. Neither can exist, in a human group, without the other, nor can either undergo substantial change without altering both the opposite member and the balance of the equation. Energy flow and sociopolitical organization must evolve in harmony. »

Not only is energy flow required to maintain a sociopolitical system, but the amount of energy must be sufficient for the complexity of that system. Leslie White observed a number of years ago that cultural evolution was intricately linked to the quantities of energy harvested by a human population. The amounts of energy required per capita to maintain the simplest human institutions are incredibly small compared with those needed by the most complex. White once estimated that a cultural system activated primarily by human energy could generate only about 1/20 horsepower per capita per year. This contrasts sharply with the hundreds to thousands of horsepower at the command of members of industrial societies. Cultural complexity varies accordingly. Julian Steward pointed out the quantitative difference between the 3,000 to 6,000 cultural elements early anthropologists documented for the native populations of western North America, and the more than 500,000 artifact types that U.S. military forces landed at Casa Blanca in World War II.

More complex societies are more costly to maintain than simpler ones, requiring greater support levels per capita. As societies increase in complexity, more networks are created among individuals, more hierarchical controls are created to regulate these networks, more information is processed, there is more centralization of information flow, there is increasing need to support specialists not directly involved in resource production, and the like. All this complexity is dependent upon energy flow at a scale vastly greater than that characterizing small groups of self-sufficient foragers or agriculturalists. The result is that as a society evolves toward greater complexity, the support costs on each individual will also rise, so that the population as a whole must allocate increasing portions of its energy budget to maintaining organizational institutions. This is an immutable fact of societal evolution, and is not mitigated by type of energy source.

So, we see with the rise of complexity two distinct phenomena arising with relation to energy. First, greater complexity allows for more energy to be unlocked. Agriculture is more complex than foraging, and yields more calories than foraging; an oil rig is far more complex than a bow drill for making fire, and yields far more energy. At the same time, complexity also has an energy cost — a cost which grows greater the more complex a society is. Thus, complexity is an investment. It has a benefit, and it has a cost, both in terms of energy.

It is also worth noting that, for a variety of reasons, including the fact that human population is a function of food supply (thesis #4) and thus, energy, as well as the Prisoner's Dilemna that forces complex societies into a positive feedback loop of increasing investment in complexity (thesis #12), that societies are often compelled to make every investment into complexity that they are capable of making, due both to their own population pressures, as well as the threat of competition from those societies that *do* make such investments. As such, complexity becomes a function of energy flow, such that given information about a society's energy flow, its level of complexity can be accurately predicted.

However, Tainter has also highlighted the *cost* of complexity — a cost which, due to the law of diminishing returns, is constantly increasing, while the benefits of complexity are likewise diminishing. This provides a counter-force to the positive feedback loop of societal complexity. Eventually, further complexity becomes far too costly, making the positive feedback loop impossible to pursue any longer. When that occurs, as Tainter highlights, it means *collapse*.

Tainter discusses four aspects of complexity in his discussion of complexity's marginal returns:

1. Agriculture and resource production.
2. Information processing.
3. Sociopolitical control and specialization.
4. Overall economic productivity.

To this, I would like to add for the purposes of our current discussion:

5. Technological innovation.

It stands to reason that if each of these five elements of complexity are subject to diminishing returns, then we may also conclude that the thesis, "Complexity is subject to diminishing returns," is also reasonable.

Agriculture and resource production.

The Law of Diminishing Marginal Returns was originally formulated in the context of agricultural production. It was observed that adding more workers to a field would increase productivity. However, when this was pursued far enough, it became evident that the added productivity of any given worker was not strictly additive. Two workers could double the yield of just one, but eventually a point was reached where each additional worker meant less of an increase over the previous one. Each new worker still added some additional yield, but that additional yield began to approach zero. Meanwhile, the investment of one more worker remained the same. Thus, the marginal return — how much is returned per investment — went down. The point at which adding another unit of investment, such as another worker, ceased to have a simple additive effect on returns, is called the point of diminishing returns. Past that point, investment cost remains the same, but the benefits returned begin to approach zero.

When we abstract to any kind of subsistence technology, we see this is also tied to the "low-hanging fruit" problem — in this case, *literal* fruit. If a forager band picks the largest, sweetest, most nutritious, and easiest to acquire fruit first, then any expansion of harvesting *must*, necessarily, involve more effort (as they took the easiest to acquire fruit first, so the remaining fruit must be more difficult to obtain), for less reward (as they took the largest, sweetest and most nutritious fruit first, so the remaining fruit must be smaller, more bitter, and/or less nutritious). The same principle extends to horticulture and agriculture, as well. The first fields will be planted in the most fertile, easily tilled soil; further cultivation must, then, take place in less fertile and/or more difficult soil. Thus, either the cost will go up, the yield will go down, or — as is usually the case — both.

Information processing.

Jeff Vail has often written on the inefficiency of hierarchy's information processing capabilities. The span of control limits how many subordinates any hierarch can effectively administer (usually around 5), while the SNAFU principle and signal degradation limits how deep a hierarchy can go before suffering severe efficiency problems (*see* thesis #11). Thus, while hierarchy provides the only readily available alternative to simply working inside the limit of Dunbar's number imposed by human neurology, it has a set of limits all its own. To expand this hierarchy beyond those limits means either overwhelming each hierarch beyond the span of control, and/or creating a hierarchy too deep, such that signal degradation becomes an overwhelming concern. This seriously limits the effectiveness of each new investment to expand such a hierarchy, necessitating the use of a new class of specialists dedicated simply to information processing. This increases the cost of expanding a hierarchical information processing structure — costs which yield increasingly little benefit as signal degradation sets in. As an example, in "'Span of Control' and Inefficiency of Hierarchy," Vail writes:

The US Federal Government's National Incident Management System (NIMS) is based upon the Incident Control System (ICS) methodology developed by wildfire fighters to create a standard for command and control systems (hierarchy) as government agencies respond to incidents. NIMS and ICS both state that the maximum desirable span of control is 5, meaning that one supervisor should control no more than 5 subordinates. The US Military follows a similar formula: one commander controls three subordinate units, as well as a staff function, which results in a span of control of roughly 5. This military formula is virtually identical around the world — a time-tested formula for maximum span of control. The military formula, however, is more revealing, for while it uses a 5:1 span of control, the *operational* span of control is only 3:1 (that is, the number of subordinate units that actually carry out the fundamental mission of the organization). The remaining two (roughly) staff positions under each commander are actually information processing assistants necessary to make even the 3:1 span of control effective. Without getting in to two much details, those staff positions are normally broken down to an executive officer, who is in turn responsible for the commander's administrative staff, and a deputy commander, who is in turn responsible for the commander's non-administrative staff (Intelligence, Logistics, Human Resources, etc.). As a result of the executive officer and deputy commander concept, the non-operational tail actually extends down two layers from each "operational" commander at the higher levels.

Tainter discusses education and R&D under the heading of "information processing," and shows that each of them are also subject to diminishing returns, and both for much the same reason. Basic information is not only easily obtained, it is the foundation for all other information. By comparison, more advanced knowledge is more difficult to obtain, but is much more narrowly applicable — as it applies only to a specific field of research or learning. In education, one can look at how easily children learn to read, and how universally important that skill is, versus the extreme cost of a Ph.D., which is much more narrow in its usefulness. In science, research and development, we can note the low cost of a "paradigm shift" like evolution and how much such shifts have informed our knowledge, versus much costlier information that is much more esoteric in its application. Thus, we see a problem of "low-hanging fruit" applied to knowledge itself. The knowledge we come to first forms a basis of all other things we learn, making it by definition more widely applicable. The knowledge we gain based on that comes at a greater cost, but it is much more esoteric. It is worth noting that Tainter *does* discuss the role of a "paradigm shift" in essentially "resetting" a new marginal return curve for such fields.

Education especially faces an increasing burden as society becomes more complex, and there is simply more society that each individual is expected to be conversant in. An American child requires some two decades of education in order to become fully conversant in the various areas of mathematics, science and culture that is expected of any individual in contemporary America. By comparison, most forager cultures had taught their entire culture to their children by their sixth birthday, leaving plenty of time to learn up to 1,000 different species of wild, edible plants, as well as advanced hunting techniques, so that they could be fully self-sufficient by the age of 12.

Sociopolitical control and specialization.

The diminishing returns of sociopolitical complexity are the bread and butter of 24 hour news networks and any politican running on a platform of "reform." It is precisely the inefficiencies engendered by such diminishing returns that has so often been bemoaned in the political process — and it is precisely because this is an intractable feature of sociopolitical complexity that every politician's promise to "clean up government" ultimately fails. Tainter identifies six reasons for diminishing sociopolitical marginal returns:

1. Increasing size of bureaucracies.
2. Increasing specialization of bureaucracies.
3. The cumulative nature of organizational solutions.
4. Increasing taxation.
5. Increasing costs of legitimizing activities.
6. Increasing costs of internal control and external defense.

Very often, more efficient administration is an excellent response to some stress. After 9/11, noting the failure of information processing that allowed the attacks to take place, the Bush administration created the Department of Homeland Security in order to effect better information processing across many of the diverse federal agencies involved. Ultimately, however, this added several more levels of hierarchy — and thus, decreased the information processing capabilities of hierarchy (by introducing more signal degradation), while increasing the cost (by requiring more information processing personnel — more bureaucracy — to handle such inefficiencies). Thus we see that much of the reason for the diminishing returns on sociopolitical complexity, are the diminishing returns on information processing through a complex structure.

Sociopolitical structures must also undertake legitimizing activities in order to justify their existence. Ancient Rome had "bread and circuses" on a monumental scale; today, welfare programs take up the bulk of the non-military federal budget in the United States. Tainter explains:

The appeasement of urban mobs presents the classic illustration of this principle. Any level of activities undertaken to appease such populations —

the bread and circuses syndrome — eventually becomes the expected *minimum*. An increase in the cost of bread and circuses, which seems to have been required in Imperial Rome to legitimize such things as the acession of a new ruler or his continued reign, may bring no increased return beyond a state of non-revolt. Rewards to Roman military personnel would often follow the same pattern, particularly when bounties were granted upon a ruler's acession. Roman soldiers regarded such bounties as a right.

Though by far the greater expense, for both Rome and the United States, was the military. Tainter explains why this is also subject to diminishing returns:

If increased complexity develops to deal with internal unrest or external threats, this solution may yield no tangible benefit for much of the population. Arms races present a classic example. Increasing costs of military hardware, and military and civilian personnel, when undertaken to meet a competitor's like increases, yield no increased security for the added cost. Such increased costs are often undertaken merely to maintain the balance-of-power status quo. As a military apparatus increases in complexity its administrative costs increase disproportionately, as Parkinson's figures indicate, usually to little or no competitive advantage.

Overall economic productivity

Economics does not call many things "laws," but it has granted that honor to the Law of Diminishing Marginal Returns, because it governs nearly every facet of the economy — and thus, the economy itself.

As GNP rises, per capita rates of economic growth decline, so that as an economy expands, its rate of growth slows down. Many economists tie this to "using up" innovations, requiring that new innovations be made — thus, incurring the cost of further R&D, which is itself bound by diminishing marginal returns, as we have already discussed. Tainter hypothesizes that this may be but one application of a more abstract principle: as the marginal return curves of other areas of complexity require more and more resources simply to maintain the *status quo*, there is less and less capital available for investment in the future growth of the economy.

Technological innovation

One aspect of complexity which Tainter does not specifically address as such is that of technological innovation, the oft-cited counterbalance that makes no trend "inevitable." This faith in the messianic power of technology to save us from all ills is an irrational statement of religious belief. There is no rational, logical or scientific reason to believe this to be so. In fact, logic, science and reason more often present us with the *limitations* of technology. For instance, Einstein showed that no one can go faster than the speed of light for very real reasons. Science fiction authors often like to compare this to old pronouncements — made without any logic case — that the sound barrier could never be breached. The difference is not the type of claim, of course, but the evidence backing it up. Computational theory recognizes a large set of problems which are impossible for a computer to solve, and another class that can only be solved in exponential time, making them forever impractical, regardless of what innovations we make in computer hardware. Jevon's Paradox highlights the futility of more efficient technologies to limit the use of resources — by making the use of that resource more efficient, such a technology results in *greater* overall use, not less. We all know pronouncements like that falsely attributed to Charles H. Duell, U.S. Commissioner of Patents, in 1899, "Everything that can be invented has been invented." Such statements were wrong in the past, therefore, any similar statements made in the future must also be wrong. This is nearly as egregious a logical error as the belief that technology can solve all problems itself.

Yet, technology is, itself, subject to diminishing returns. Tainter explains:

« *Technical innovation, particularly the institutionalized variety we know today, is unusual in human history. It requires some level of investment in research and development. Such investment is difficult to capitalize in an agriculturally-based society that produces little surplus per capita. Technical innovation often responds to labor shortages, which in the ancient world were the exception. As a result, technical development in societies not based on a fossil fuel economy tends to be minimal. Where technical innovation in ancient societies did occur, it often tended actually to depress the productivity of labor.*

In industrial societies, technical innovation responds to market factors, particularly physical needs and economic distress. It is not, though, always the panacea that is imagined. In an input-output analysis of the U.S. economy from 1947–58, corrected for inflation, Carter found that 'technological change (or progress!) had actually added about $14 billion to the task of satisfying the same final [national] *demand.' Technological innovation, as discussed above, is subject to the law of diminishing returns,* *and this tends to reduce (but not eliminate) its long-term potential for resolving economic weakness. Using the data cited by Wolfle, Schrerer observes that if R&D expenditures must grow at 4–5 percent per year to boost productivity 2 percent, such a trend cannot be continued indefinitely or the day will come when we must all be scientists. He is accordingly pessimistic about the prospects for long-term productivity growth. Colin Renfrew correctly points out (in the context of discussing the development of civilization in the Aegean) that economic growth is itself susceptible to declining marginal productivity. »*

The lever is perhaps the simplest technology possible. It is cheap, virtually impossible to break, and highly effective for all manner of tasks. The lever is incorporated in many other kinds of technology. As a piece of technology becomes more complex, it becomes more prone to breaking. As any computer programmer knows, simplicity and robustness are usually the same thing, leading to the elegance of simplicity incorporated as an ideal in Eric Raymond's definition of the bazaar model. Many of our greatest technological achievements have been achieved so cheaply, they were actually accidents. Penicillin, perhaps our greatest medical achievement, was discovered by accident. Its total development cost approximately $20,000. Compare this to the usual R&D budget of contemporary drug companies, running well into the millions of dollars and more, and taking an average of about 20 years.

Ultimately, a new technology is another piece of complexity, and ultimately it is precisely that complexity, rather than any one crisis we presently face, that is the ultimate cause of collapse. Other crises may serve as a proximate cause, but it is the marginal return curve on complexity itself that seals the fate of any complex society. Thus, any "techno-fix" solution may succeed in solving any given proximate cause for collapse, only by contributing still more to the ultimate cause of collapse — complexity itself. Neither is this considering the profoundly negative, unexpected consequences that so many technologies yield.

Technology is subject to diminishing returns; that means that innovation will not end, only that it will become (on average) increasingly mundane, but it will continue to cost more and more. Moreover, technology cannot solve the underlying, systemic issues we face. Technology has its place, and it can be a wonderful thing — but it is not a panacea, and the exuberant faith of the Enlightenment in it is certainly misplaced.

Agriculture, information processing, sociopolitical control, economic activity and technological innovation are all subject to diminishing returns, because complexity itself is subject to diminishing returns. Tainter writes:

A society increasing in complexity does so as a system. That is to say, as some of its interlinked parts are forced in a direction of growth, others must adjust accordingly. For example, if complexity increases to regulate regional subsistence production, investments will be made in hierarchy, in bureaucracy, and in agricultural facilities (such as irrigation networks). The expanding hierarchy requires still further agricultural output for its own needs, as well as increased investment in energy and minerals extraction. An expanded military is needed to protect the assets thus created, requiring in turn its own sphere of agricultural and other resources. As more and more resources are drained from the support population to maintain this system, an increased share must be allocated to legitimization or coercion. This increased complexity requires specialized administrators, who consume further shares of subsistence resources and wealth. To maintain the productive capacity of the base population, further investment is made in agriculture, and so on.

The illustration could be expanded, tracing still further the interdependencies within such a growing system, but the point has been made: a society grows in complexity as a system. To be sure, there are instances where one sector of a society grows at the expense of others, but to be maintained as a cohesive whole, a social system can tolerate only certain limits to such conditions.

Thus, it is possible to speak of sociocultural evolution by the encompassing term 'complexity,' meaning by this the interlinked growth of the several subsystems that comprise a society.

Tainter then presents the idealized marginal returns curve below, and adds some discussion regarding key points along the way.

Tainter's graph of the diminishing marginal returns on complexity

At point $B1C1$, the marginal returns of complexity reach an inflection point as they near the point of diminishing returns ($B2C2$). Between $B1C1$ and $B1C3$, a complex society is at increasing risk of collapse. It is at $B1C3$ that collapse actually occurs. The costs of complexity relative to its benefits are simply too high, and substantial numbers across the society begin to see benefits to "dropping out" of the complexity of that society. In ancient Rome, we might see the baugaudae or the Allamanni as examples of this trend among the lower classes; various landlords who essentially "seceeded" from Rome as their wealthier analogues. In the contemporary United States, we might see the first stirrings of such signs among the Hippies; currently, we might see echoes of it among permaculture enthusiasts, voluntary simplicity advocates, and of course, primitvists. We might even see the open source movement itself as a reaction, trying to maintain the investments in technological complexity by creating greater simplicity in administration and information processing. We might find an upper-class echo of this behavior in the kind of elite resignment that Peggy Noonan discusses in her 27 October 2005 editorial for the *Wall Street Journal*, "A Seperate Peace."

It is at this point that collapse occurs, because the costs of complexity have become so high that the society is no longer willing to put forward any further investment in it. Tainter discusses the effect of energy subsidies — such as fossil fuels — which can extend the curve, heighten the curve, or even allow one curve to follow another. But these merely modify the situation; they do not change the basic fact that complexity is subject to diminishing marginal returns, and thus, any society that pursues greater complexity as the answer to every stress — that is, any civilization (*see* thesis #13) — must *eventually* collapse. The question is not *if*, but *when*.

Thesis #15: We have passed the point of diminishing returns.

In the previous thesis, we saw that complexity is subject to diminishing returns, because of each of its facets — subsistence, information processng, sociopolitical control, economics, and technology — are not only intertwined as a single system, but are themselves subject to diminishing returns. As such, any society which pursues complexity as an answer to every stress — which is to say, any civilization (*see* thesis #13) — must, eventually, collapse. This is only underlined by the basic fact that nothing can grow forever in a finite universe (*see* thesis #12). This leaves only the question of *when* collapse will occur, or, "is our current level of complexity before or beyond the point of diminishing returns?" To answer this question, let's again take a look at each of the elements we've previously broken out separately: subsistence, information processng, sociopolitical control, economics, and technology.

1. Agriculture and resource production.
2. Information processing.
3. Sociopolitical control and specialization.
4. Overall economic productivity.
5. Technological innovation.

Agriculture and resource production.

Industrialism allows the resource production of modern civilization to be reduced to a single figure: fossil fuels. Not only do fossil fuels provide energy for every segment of our economy, they even provide our food. In "The Oil We Eat," Richard Manning discusses the nature of our "petroculture":

« *The common assumption these days is that we muster our weapons to secure oil, not food. There's a little joke in this. Ever since we ran out of arable land, food is oil. Every single calorie we eat is backed by at least a calorie of oil, more like ten. In 1940 the average farm in the United States produced 2.3 calories of food energy for every calorie of fossil energy it used. By 1974 (the last year in which anyone looked closely at this issue), that ratio was 1:1. And this understates the problem, because at the same time that there is more oil in our food there is less oil in our oil. A couple of generations ago we spent a lot less energy drilling, pumping, and distributing than we do now. In the 1940s we got about 100 barrels of oil back for every barrel of oil we spent getting it. Today each barrel invested in the process returns only ten, a calculation that no doubt fails to include the fuel burned by the Hummers and Blackhawks we use to maintain access to the oil in Iraq. »*

The reason for the loss of caloric efficiency in agriculture, as Manning discusses in detail, is the loss of arable soil. Monoculture — planting whole fields with just one plant, as with agriculture — drains that soil very quickly. Different plants take different things from the soil, and put other things back, in much the same way as plants and animal harmonize with one another in the oxygen-carbon dioxide cycle. By planting only one type of plant in a field, those things that particular plant needs is drained, but not replenished. Meanwhile, its waste products saturate the soil.

Because of the increasing agricultural complexity of the Green Revolution, the marginal returns for agriculture have dropped to astonishingly negative values. Every calorie of agricultural product returned requires ten calories of input. This is sustainable even in the short term only because of our fossil fuel subsidies.

That subsidy may be running out soon, though. Hubbert's Peak, more popularly known as, "Peak Oil," is the midway point of global oil production. Energy Bulletin's *"Peak Oil Primer"* explains:

« For obvious reasons, people have extracted the easy-to-reach, cheap oil first. The oil pumped first was on land, near the surface, under pressure and light and 'sweet' and easy to refine into gasoline. The remaining oil, sometimes off shore, far from markets, in smaller fields, or of lesser quality, will take ever more money and energy to extract and refine. The rate of extraction will drop. Furthermore, all oil fields eventually reach a point where they become economically, and energetically no longer viable. If it takes the energy of a barrel of oil to extract a barrel of oil, then further extraction is pointless. »

In other words, the problem is not, strictly speaking, "running out of oil." Rather, it is a state where the oil that remains provides the same amount of energy as ever, but continues to entail greater costs for its extraction. In other words, the "Peak Oil" problem is a problem of the diminishing marginal returns for our fossil fuel subsidy.

Thus, the question of whether we have passed the point of diminishing returns for resource extraction is the same as the question, "Have we yet passed Hubbert's Peak?" There is increasing evidence that we may have done just that. Jeff Vail, an intelligence officer with the United States Air Force, wrote:

« I gave an intelligence briefing to the Assistant Secretary of the Interior, Tom Weimer, today. He's in charge of "water and science", which includes the US Geological Survey, the agency in charge of the official government calculations on oil reserves and depletion. Most Peak Oil nay-sayers rely on the USGS's 2000 report that shows an excessively optimistic projection for recoverable oil reserves, but what does USGS really think? All I can say for sure is that Weimer didn't have any objections to my assertion that Peak Oil may well be a Fall 2005 event, nor that the world is facing a serious energy supply crisis in the near future. Does the government have some master Peak Oil plan? I have no idea, but claims that they are ignorant about the problem are simply incorrect. »

OPEC, which provides most of the world's oil, may be peaking. Saudi Arabia, though very secretive about its reserves, is having difficulty selling its crude oil — it is heavy, sour crude, not light, sweet — suggesting that the Ghawar super-field has peaked. While previous estimates for the global Hubbert's Peak hovered around 2015–2025, revelations that Shell and Saudi Arabia may be lying about their reserves have revised those estimates closer to the present or recent past. The EIA released a report stating that demand would outstrip supply in 2005 Q4. And in fact, recent oil production has been consistent with the "plateau" one expects at the top of Hubbert's Peak.

While the case is as yet ambiguous, there is mounting evidence that Hubbert's Peak is now upon us, and thus, that we are currently passing the point of diminishing returns for resource production in an industrial context.

Information processing.

In the previous thesis, we cited Jeff Vail's analysis of what is perhaps the world's most efficient information processing hierarchy: the United States military. Vail highlighted that the *operational* span of control for each commander is 3, since the other 2 must be dedicated to information processing due to signal degradation problems through too many levels of hierarchy.

We have recently seen a drastic increase in information processing in global telecommunications, but this has been achieved by *sacrificing* hierarchy, and developing the technological infrastructure to allow for rhizome information processing. Open source methods have proven themselves far more efficient at information processing. "The Blogosphere" circulated news about the 2004 United States presidential election well ahead of the hierarchical mainstream media, while the Iraqi insurgency has successfully used the internet and "open source warfare" to counter the most powerful hierarchical military the world has ever seen. This investment in simplicity has yielded significant marginal returns, but it was made possible only by investments in greater technological and social complexity. And already, there are efforts to reassert hierarchical information processing methods over the internet, showing that such methods cannot long be tolerated by a civilized society.

Education also shows a point of diminishing returns has been reached. In *The Collapse of Complex Societies*, Tainter writes:

« *With increasing time spent in education and greater specialization, the learning that occurs yields decreased general benefits for greater costs. The greatest quantities of learning are accomplished in infancy; learning that occurs earlier in life tends to be more generalized. Later, specialized learning is dependent upon this earlier, generalized knowledge, so that the benefits of generalized learning include all derivative specialized knowledge. Axiomatically, therefore, generalized learning is of overall greater value than specialized.* »

Moreover, this early, generalized learning is accomplished at substantially lower cost. Malchup has compiled figures showing that, in 1957–8, education of pre-school children in the home cost the United States $4,432,000,000 (in income foregone by mothers), which yields $886,400,000 per year for ages 0 through 5. Elementary and secondary education cost $33,339,000,000, or $2,564,538,462 per year for ages 6 through 18. Higher education cost $12,757,000,000, or $2,514,000,000 per year for far fewer students, assuming an average of five years spent in higher education. In other words, the monetary cost to the nation of a year of education between pre-school, when the most generalized, highly useful education takes place, and college, when the most specialized learning is accomplished, increases by about 284 percent. And this increase would be even more dramatic if these figures took into account the fact that college enrollment is but a fraction of the available population.

Similarly ... the overall production of investment in higher education for the development of specialized expertise has declined substantially since 1900.

D. Price has demonstrated, in regard to the education of scientists, that educating more scientists causes those of average ability to increase in number faster than those who are most productive. Thus, increasing investments in specialized education yield declines in both marginal and average returns.

In 1924, S.G. Strumilin collected in the Soviet Union a set of educational data that reveal a corroborative pattern. He showed that the marginal return on investment in education declines with increasing education. The first two years of education, according to Strumilin, raise a Soviet worker's production skills an average of 14.5 percent per year. Yet the third year of education yields an increase of only an additional 8 percent, while the fourth through sixth years raise skills only a further 4.5 percent per year.

So, there is a definite diminishing marginal returns curve for each individual's education. This compounds to create a society's point of diminishing returns because, as Tainter points out, a society that can satisfy its needs based on general education will return far more on its investment than those that require more specialized education. In the modern United States, intensifying complexity has led to the rise of the four year college Bachelor degree as the expected minimum of education, rather than simply the high school diploma. This is driven by the need for workers with more specialized knowledge to handle the various components of a more complex society. As such, society's complexity is requiring heavier costs in education — passing a point of diminishing returns.

Sociopolitical control and specialization.

In the previous thesis, we mentioned the Bush administration's creation of the Department of Homeland Security in response to the terrorist attacks of 9/11. At one point in time, this move may have yielded significant returns. However, in 2002, all of the departments it was unifying already had significant hierarchies and complexities of their own. Creating another level of complexity to subsume them merely exacerbated this situation.

Tainter provides still more evidence:

« Between 1914 and 1967, the number of capital ships in the British Navy declined by 78.9 percent, the number of officers and enlisted men by 32.9 percent, and the number of dockyard workers by 33.7 percent. Yet during this period the number of dockyard officials and clerks increased by 247

percent, and the number of Admiralty officials by 769 percent. ... Between 1935 and 1954 the number of officials in the British Colonial Office increased by 447 percent. During this same period, of course, the empire administered by these officials shrank considerably. »

...

Bendix has compiled for private industry, in several nations, data similar to those Parkinson has uncovered in government. He was able to show that a pattern of increasing hierarchical specialization characterizes the private sector as strongly as Parkinson has demonstrated for the public. Clearly in the private sector, where economic succeess depends on efficiency, this pattern cannot be attributed to self-serving inefficiency. The reason why complex organizations must allocate ever larger portions of their personnel and other resources to administration is because increased complexity requires greater quantities of information processing and greater integration of disparate parts.

Even in 1977, Elgin and Bushnell concluded in "The Limits to Complexity: Are Bureaucracies Becoming Unmanageable?" that the United States government was a Stage III organization, marked by severe diseconomies of scale, and due to the "ratchet effect" (a specific case of the type of positive feedback loop discussed in thesis #12) must soon become stage IV, critical and prone to collapse.

Nor is this only a burden for the public sector. In recent years, enterprise search has become a necessary commodity for any large-scale enterprise. The information processing burden is simply too great. Even enterprise search products are now becoming insufficient for the complexity such organizations face, creating a niche that my employer, Vivísimo, has very successfully exploited, with the development of a sophisticated "clustering engine" to organize such an overwhelming amount of data. In a whitepaper distributed by Vivísimo, the annual savings for an organization with 100 employees over conventional search products is calculated to be $1,012,000. This suggests the amount of investment being made into information processing even in the "efficient" private sector for such complexity.

Overall economic productivity.

As the information processing burden increases, and as the marginal returns of sociopolitical complexity diminish, the overall economy cannot help but suffer the same curve. Tainter writes:

« Complex societies with large, well-developed economies have historically been able to sustain only rather inferior rates of economic growth. Latecomers to economic growth tend to have higher growth rates than early starters. ... [R]ates of economic growth are highest in middle income countries, followed by high income and low income nations. Kristensen infers from these data that, through time, rates of economic growth tend to slow down ... Such a trend suggests that societies with more developed economies face a situation in which the productivity of GNP for stimulating further growth tends to decline. »

...

Zolotas has argued that the productivity of industrialism for producing social welfare is declining. In partial support of this assertion he points out that while U.S. per capita product increased 75 percent from 1950 to 1977, weekly work hours declined by only 9.5 percent.

Technological innovation.

The very notion that we have passed the point of diminishing returns for technology would seem to be the only one even more absurd than the very idea that technology is subject to diminishing returns at all — at least, to the techno-salvationist. In fact, the evidence is quite clear. In "Getting better value from information management," published by *Information Economics Journal* in October 2003, Paul A. Strassmann notes:

« The prevailing view nowadays is that IT will remain stagnant for a while. ... An article by Nicholas Carr in the May 2003 issue of the Harvard Business Review resulted in a lively debate about its claim that IT spending will level off permanently because IT has become strategically irrelevant. »

...

Why were organisations unable to take advantage of IT capabilities? The explanation is simple. Each firm had to organise its IT department, train its managers, educate its executives, develop most of its software and integrate vendor offerings with disorderly legacy code. It was easier to junk and re-build instead of to accumulate and grow. Vendors and consultants thrived with revenues growing faster than IT budgets. Out of total 2002 worldwide IT spending of $2 trillion the vendors and consultants reaped about 30%.

Financial executives are now asking where they can find the gains from IT spending. They are not looking for a small amount of money. For US manufacturing firms IT investments accounted for over a third of all new capital expenditures. For the US financial and services sector the IT investments consumed most of the capital used for acquiring non-financial assets.

Strassman is clearly addressing concern for marginal returns — the cost of IT, versus its benefit — and finding that it does not live up to its promises. This is in information technology, the field that has seen the most strikingly successful technological development in the past 50 years. For other areas of technology, things have been even worse. Tainter writes:

« Despite Malchup's caution, a number of factors suggest that the productivity of research and development has indeed declined. ... [P]atents have been declining in respect to population and number of technical workers since about 1920, well before the R&D effort of World War II and thereafter. Even more significantly, patenting relative to numbers of scientists and engineers has declined continuously since 1900. Jacob Schmookler has compiled figures showing that, excluding government-financed projects, the number of industrial research personnel increased 5.6 times from 1930 to 1954, while the numbers of corporate patents rose between 1936–40 and 1956–60 by only 23 percent. »

...

There are, morevoer, other data suggesting declining productivity of inventing activity in the industrial world. Hornell Hart has demonstrated consistent patterns of increasing and then declining rates of patenting (logistic curves) in many fields that are partially or wholly unrelated to military R&D. These include airplanes, automobiles, cotton machinery, electric meters, radios, sewing machines, spinning machinery, sulky plows, telegraphy, telephony, typewriters, and weaving machinery. He also noticed that the same patterns are evident in the major inventions and discoveries of the Western world, and in patents sealed in Great Britain between 1751 and 1820, and between 1821 and 1938.

Thus, it seems that military R&D cannot account for more than a small part of the decline in patents. Furthermore, the decline is so widespread in so many fields, over such a long time, that declining propensity to patent can hardly account for it either. Recent research shows that there is in fact a strong positive relationship between R&D and patenting. Thus the patent statistics appear to be a reliable indicator of inventing accomplishment.

It would appear that there has indded been a genuine drop in the inventive productivity of research and development, and that as investments in R&D have increased (from 0.1 percent of gross national product in 1920 to 2.6 percent in 1960), the marginal product of these investments has declined. Although there are some demurrals, many economists recognize this trend.

That trend has continued. Jonathan Huebner charted the same trend from 1914 to 2005 in, "A Possible Declining Trend for Worldwide Innovation." A Japanese report from 2003 concluded that they, too, were suffering from having passed the point of diminishing returns in technology:

[W]e do not find strong evidence that Japanese innovative capacity has actually declined. However, that capacity has failed to grow at the rate of the 1980s. As a result, US and worldwide patent statistics suggest that Japanese firms in a number of sectors have fallen behind their US counterparts, even in areas where Japanese firms were formerly quite strong and rapidly converging on US levels of inventive output.

Medical technology, another field of significant investment in the past half century, has also shown signs of diminishing marginal returns. Penicillin, one of the most effective drugs ever devised, had a total production cost of approximately $20,000. According to a 2003 report by Bain & Co., the average cost of a new drug today is $1.7 billion. Writing about the study for Chemical & Engineering News, Rick Mullin writes:

« According to Bain, the cost of drug development — currently 55% higher than the average cost from 1995 to 2000 — is rising largely as a result of an increasing failure rate for prospective drugs in clinical trials. The rising cost of commercializing new drugs is another contributing factor — 12 months of sales and marketing costs are included in Bain's cost estimate but not in the Tufts figure. »

If this is true, then the cost of developing new drugs is increasing exponentially, and largely due to the fact that most prospective drugs fail in clinical trials. Medical technology is incuring greater costs for less benefit — in the case of medical technology, that would be more "misses," or work that never produce a viable drug.

* * *

Tainter provides another example of how we have surpassed the point of diminishing returns for complexity that does not fit easily under any of the above headings, as it applies to medical research and longevity:

« *Medical research and application provide a good example of a declining marginal return for increased investment in a scientific field. While it is less easy to measure the benefits of medicine than its costs, one sure indicator is life expectancy. Unfortunately, ever larger investments in health care do not yield proportionate increases in longevity. In 1930 the United States expended 3.3 percent of its gross national product (GNP) to produce an average life expectancy of 59.7 years. By 1982, 10.5 percent of GNP was producing a life expectancy of 74.5 years. ... [F]rom 1930 to 1982 the productivity of the U.S. national health care system (measured thus) declined by 57 percent. (In fact, it is likely that the decline in the productivity of medicine has been even greater, for the effects of improved nutrition and sanitation on increasing life expectancy have not been included.)* »

From this data, Tainter concluded in 1988 that collapse was neither an option, nor an immediate threat. The reason, he said, was that the United States existed in a peer polity system, and that no single polity can collapse in such a system without being immediately reabsorbed by the whole.

For such brilliant insight, Tainter shows a disappointing inability to grasp the implications of his own theory at the end. The difference he draws between the collapse of isolated civilizations (such as Rome) and peer polity systems (such as the Maya) is arbitrary. We are dealing with "global" systems, whether we are dealing with literal islands, "islands" isolated by distance, geography, or culture, or the entire globe itself. The global system of complexity must collapse as a system. No single part can collapse in isolation, this is true. This is a direct result of the fact that civilization must always pursue complexity (thesis #13), and must always grow (thesis #12). Thus, when New Orleans collapsed, the United States government eventually moved in to restore its former level of complexity. This is one, arbitrary level we could look at; or, we could look at the arbitrary level of nation-states, and cite the collapse of the USSR and its immediate reabsorption into a similar level of complexity.

However, it would be obviously untrue to conclude from this that collapse is impossible. The only caveat is that the entire system must collapse as a system, not as individual, constituent parts. Thus, the Roman Empire collapsed as a system; the Mayan city-states collapsed not as individual city-states, but as a single system. We do not face the collapse of the United States or any one nation-state; we face the collapse of industrialized society itself. The scale of the nation-state has become arbitrary as well. As globalization proceeds, multinational corporations have risen to an unprecedented level of power, bisecting nations and undercutting their influence (*see* Jeff Vail, "The New Map: Terrorism in a Post-Cartesian World"). If nation-states are vertical powers, then multinational corporations create horizontal powers across them. This trend raises the question of whether we still truly live in a peer polity system at all, or if we are seeing the rise of some new level of complexity in such organizations as the United Nations, International Monetary Fund and the World Bank — the inevitable conclusion to intensifying complexity, with the emergence of a single, global civilization? Ultimately, the distinction is still a semantic one, however; peer polity systems often behave as though they were a single civilization, because the political alliances and economic relationships between them fuse them into a single system of social complexity.

As we have seen, the crisis of the diminishing returns on complexity is not only present, it is global. The same problems can be seen in every country; we have highlighted the United States here only for its greater wealth of available data, and, as the "capital" of the globalized civilization/peer polity system, it provides perhaps the most striking example. We have passed the point of diminishing returns for agriculture, information processing, bureaucracy, technology and the economy itself. All of these are intertwined, as we saw in the previous thesis. Having passed the point of diminishing returns, the collapse of such a system is inevitable.

Thesis #16: Technology cannot stop collapse.

Invariably, the threat of our own civilization's collapse is readily answered with the hope of technological progress. Progressivists deny that we face any systemic problems, only technical problems, with technical solutions. As we have seen in the previous theses, this is most certainly not the case, but the question remains: could these systemic problems be solved through the proper application of technology? Technophiliacs and techno-utopians often wax poetic for the prospects of our technological future. Science fiction like *Star Trek* often portrays this vision, where technology has solved all of our problems. But ultimately, such hopes are statements of belief, not fact — and a belief that is not very well-grounded in reality, at that.

Primitivists often define themselves in regard to their dim view of technology, but they inherit from this a Romantic idea of "technology" as referring solely to the metal machines of the Industrial Revoluton. The genus *Homo* is separated from the Australopithecines by our use of tools. The creation of stone technology led to handedness, and was closely related to an expansion in cranium capacity, and the development of the areas of the brain used for language. Humans make technology, but to a significant extent, technology also made us. A *complete* rejection of *all* technology is a rejection of ourselves. Most of the great apes make and use tools. Even crows have technology. Obviously, there are sustainable levels of technology.

However, since the Enlightenment, most of our thinking about technology has been set by a different idea, the notion of unbounded progress, which is just as flawed. Foragers evidence little concern for the sweep of history. There is a certain sense of a timeless present in many such societies. Very often, there is only two real time periods — the present, and the mythic past. The Australian concept of the Dreamtime highlights how different forager conceptions of time can be — the Dreamtime is, simultaneously, the distant past, and coterminous with the present. Other societies, primarily agrarian, developed ideas of cyclical time. The best known of these systems is likely the Mayan and Aztec calendars, that charted out history in the same kind of cycles that governed the passage of days, seasons and years on a larger, historical level. Much more prevalent in past civilizations, however, has been a sense of degradation, of a lost "golden age," and the impression that the present is inferior to the past. This idea is found strongly in Greek and Hebrew beliefs. The idea of history as the story of human progress is largely a result of the Enlightenment, though it would be a mistake to claim it was entirely unrepresented before that. Robert Nisbet's *"The Idea of Progress"* highlights the pre-modern history of this notion. He concludes:

« As I have shown, the Western idea of progress was born of Greek imagery, religious in foundation; the imagery of growth. It attained its fullness within Christianity, starting with the Church Fathers, especially Augustine. Central to any genuinely Christian form of religion is the Pauline emphasis upon hope: hope to be given gratification in this world as well as the next. Basically, the Christian creed, its concept of Original Sin notwithstanding, is inseparable from a philosophy of history that is overwhelmingly optimistic about man's estate in this world and the next, provided only that due deference and commitment to God are given. »

This highlights the essentially religious nature of such belief in progress, no less religious than previous ideas about history as regress, or history as cyclical. While science itself may be wholly secular, the religious faith *in* science — and the salvific hope of future progress, *thanks* to science — is anything but. August Comte was more honest with himself than most of his contemporary fellows in his attempts to found the "Positivist *Church*."

In *Collapse*, Diamond refutes a number of "one-liner" objections, including "Technology will solve our problems," saying:

« This is an expression of faith about the future, and therefore based on a supposed track record of technology having solved more problems than it created in the recent past. Underlying this expression of faith is the implicit assumption that, from tomorrow onwards, technology will function primarily to solve existing problems and will cease to create new problems. Those with such faith also assume that the new technologies now under discussion will succeed, and that they will do so quickly enough to make a big difference soon. In extended conversations that I had with two of America's most successful and best-known businessmen and financiers, both of them eloquently described to me emerging technologies and financial instruments that differ fundamentally from those of the past and that, they confidently predicted, would solve our environmental problems. »

But actual experience is the opposite of this assumed track record. Some dreamed-of new technologies succeed, while others don't. Those that do succeed typically take a few decades to develop and phase in widely: think of gas heating, electric lighting, cars and airplanes, television, computers, and so on. New technologies, whether or not they succeed in solving the problem that they were designed to solve, regularly create unanticipated new problems. Technological solutions to environmental problems are routinely far more expensive than preventive measures to avoid creating the problem in the first place: for example, the billions of dollars of damages and clean-up costs associated with major oil spills, compared to the modest cost of safety measures effective at minimizing the risks of a major oil spill.

Most of all, advances in technology just increase our ability to do things, which may be either for the better or for the worse. All of our current problems are unintended negative consequences of our existing technology. The rapid advances in technology during the twentieth century have been creating difficult new problems faster than they have been solving old problems: that's why we're in the situation in which we now find ourselves. What makes you think that, as of January 1, 2006, for the first time in human history, technology will miraculously stop causing new unanticipated problems while it solves just the problems that it previously produced?

Diamond is touching on the first factor that makes technical solutions so ambiguous: unintended consequences. Diamond goes on to discuss the effects that CFC's have had on our atmosphere, but other examples abound — and not all of them negative. Benedictine monks invented the clock to help maintain their schedule of prayers, but, as Mumford put it, "Time-keeping passed into time-serving and time-accounting and time-rationing. As this took place, Eternity ceased gradually to serve as the measure and focus of human actions." Johannes Gutenberg was a devout Catholic, but, as Diamond discusses in *Guns, Germs & Steel*, the printing press helped create a shared linguistic world which, manipulated by politicians lke Ferdinand and Isabella of Spain, resulted in the myth of the "Nation." Bronze casting techniques invented for church bells revolutionized warfare by allowing the producton of bronze cannons. Science historian James Burke's 1978 television documentary series, *Connections*, presented the entire history of invention in terms of such unintended consequences, with the unintended consequences of one invention precipitating the next.

The problem with unintended consequences, however, is that since they are unintended, they can be good, bad, or indifferent. While we can certainly characterize any of the unintended consequences above as "good," there are others which are much less clear. The hygenic advances of the 1900s reduced diseases like cholera, cleaned up the cities, and had more to do with the extension of the industrialized life span than any of our investments in medical technology. However, the cities became *so* clean, it allowed a previously endemic disease to become epidemic. For the first two weeks after birth, a baby still has the mother's antibodies in its bloodstream. After two weeks, those are cycled out, and the baby relies on its own antibodies. Any pathogens the baby encounters in those two weeks will be counteracted by the mother's antibodies, and so, carries a low risk of actual illness. However, that exposure will allow the baby to begin creating her own antibodies to it. This is why *poliovirus* spent so many millennia endemic to humans. It is a relatively weak virus, but once the cities became sufficiently clean and babies were no longer encountering it in their first two weeks, an entire generaton grew up with no immunity to polio whatsoever. Though polio never achieved the truly terrifying numbers we normally associate with an epidemic, the personal toll the disease took on its victims created a pervasive aura of fear. The polio epidemics of the twentieth century were an unintended consequence of the hygenic advances of the decades prior.

This set the stage for what is perhaps the most clear-cut success story of Western biomedicine, alongside the eradication of smallpox: the polio vaccine. Yet the polio vaccine is not without its own unintended consequences. Though far from proven, it is possible that the research for a polio vaccine created AIDS. We know that the monkey tissue cultures used to develop the polio vaccine (for which Ender recieved the Nobel Prize in 1954, the same year Jonas Salk used the technique to develop the first working vaccine) introduced a number of simian virii (SV's) into the human population on a large scale for the first time. It is known now, for example, that SV40 went undetected in the first years of the polio vaccine, contributing to many patients developing cancer later in life. This, too, was an unintended consequence — SV40 went undetected because is was unknown at the time, and thus, impossible to test for. There is some indication that AIDS may have been caused similarly: by introducing a simian virus into a large human population, early polio vaccine trials in the Belgian Congo *may* have provided the perfect environment for such a simian virus to jump the species barrier and mutate into HIV as we know it today. To date, this theory has not yet been properly investigated, so conclusive evidence is lacking.

Bill Joy was one of the co-founders of Sun Microsystems in 1984, its chief scientist until 2003, and the programmer responsible for BSD. In short, he is one of the greatest innovators of new technology in computer engineering — itself the field of technology which still shows the greatest potential for future growth. Yet Joy's 2000 article for *Wired* magazine (according to

Wikipedia, the "Bible" of techno-utopians), *"Why the Future Doesn't Need Us,"* has become a significant work for ***primitivist*** thought. After a quotation from the Unabomber's manifesto, Joy writes:

« *I am no apologist for Kaczynski. His bombs killed three people during a 17-year terror campaign and wounded many others. One of his bombs gravely injured my friend David Gelernter, one of the most brilliant and visionary computer scientists of our time. Like many of my colleagues, I felt that I could easily have been the Unabomber's next target.*

Kaczynski's actions were murderous and, in my view, criminally insane [sic]. *He is clearly a Luddite, but simply saying this does not dismiss his argument; as difficult as it is for me to acknowledge, I saw some merit in the reasoning in this single passage. I felt compelled to confront it.*

Kaczynski's dystopian vision describes unintended consequences, a well-known problem with the design and use of technology, and one that is clearly related to Murphy's law — "Anything that can go wrong, will." (Actually, this is Finagle's law, which in itself shows that Finagle was right.) Our overuse of antibiotics has led to what may be the biggest such problem so far: the emergence of antibiotic-resistant and much more dangerous bacteria. Similar things happened when attempts to eliminate malarial mosquitoes using DDT caused them to acquire DDT resistance; malarial parasites likewise acquired multi-drug-resistant genes. »

Unintended consequences, however, are hit and miss. As unlikely as it is that no future technology will ever have unintended consequences when so many past inventions have, such consequences are sometimes beneficial. If this were the only limitations to technology's role, then we would merely have to be more careful with our innovation; it would not eliminate the possibility of a technical solution. However, unintended consequences is not the only, nor even the most pressing, limitation that technology faces.

William Stanley Jevons is a seminal figure in economics. He helped formulate the very theory of marginal returns which, as we saw in thesis #14, governs complexity in general, and technological innovation specifically. In his 1865 book, *The Coal Question*, Jevons noted that the consumption of coal in England soared after James Watt introduced his steam engine. Steam engines had been used as toys as far back as ancient Greece, and Thomas Newcomen's earlier design was suitable for industrial use. Watt's invention merely made more efficient use of coal, compared to Newcomen's. This made the engine more economical, and so, touched off the Industrial Revolution — and in so doing, created the very same modern, unprecedented attitudes towards technology and invention that are now presented as hope against collapse. In the book, Jevons formulated a principle now known as "Jevons Paradox." It is not a paradox in the logical sense, but it is certainly counterintuitive. Jevons Paradox states that any technology which allows for the more efficient use of a given resource will result in *greater* use of that resource, not less. By increasing the efficiency of a resource's use, the marginal utility of that resource is increased more than enough to compensate for the fall. This is why innovations in computer technology have made for *longer* working hours, as employers expect that an employee with a technology that cuts his work in half can do three times more work. This is why more fuel-efficient vehicles have resulted in longer commutes, and the suburban sprawl that creates an automotive-centric culture, with overall *higher* petroleum use.

Most of the technologies offered as solutions to collapse expect Jevons Paradox not to hold. They recognize the crisis we face with deplenishing resources, but hope to solve that problem by making the use of that technology more efficient. Jevons Paradox illustrates precisely what the unintended consequence of such a technology will be — in these cases, *precisely the opposite* of the intended effect. Any technology that aims to save our resources by making more efficient use of them can only result in depleting those resources even more quickly.

The best hope technology can offer for staving off collapse is to tap a new energy subsidy, just as the Industrial Revolution tapped our current fossil fuel subsidy. For instance, the energy we currently use in petroleum could be matched by covering 1% of the United States' land area in photovoltaic cells. However, the hope that human population will simply "level off" due to modernization is in vain (*see* thesis #4); human population is a function of food supply, and population will always rise to the energy level available. The shift to photovoltaics, like the shift to fossil fuels, is merely an invitation to continued growth — another "win" in the "Food Race." If our energy needs can be met by covering just 1% of the United States with photovoltaic cells, why not cover 2% and double our energy? Of course, then our population will double, and we'll need to expand again.

Such technological advances can postpone collapse, but they cannot stop it. However, there is also a cost associated with such postponements: each one makes collapse, when it eventually does happen, exponentially more destructive. Had the the timber crisis of the 1600s resulted in the collapse of Renaissance Western Europe, millions would have died, and Europe would have been ecologically ruined. New energy sources were found in New World colonies, and coal. Collapse was postponed, but the toll of collapse was increased by an order of magnitude. Now, we face a collapse that will kill billions rather than simply millions; rather than simply ravaging Europe, we have set off the single worst mass extinction in the history of the planet and set off massive global climate change, reversing a cooling trend that has guided the earth through geological time. A shift to photovoltaics would limit us only when we have covered so much of the earth's surface that there is no longer sufficient sunlight for green plants to grow — thus breaking the oxygen/carbon dioxide cycle, and damning humanity to extinction as we suffocate on our own breath.

Unless, of course, technology can deploy a solution to that, as well. That is the promise the techno-salvationist offers: to solve every problem just in the nick of time, thanks to the market forces that compel innovation, and eventually, to leave the earth behind and move from planet to planet, consuming the resources we need, and moving on. Most of them say we will "sow life throughout the universe" with such a plan, but they're neglecting a very basic fact: that our civilization is not devastating our planet because it is *evil*, but because these problems are *systemic*. Every resource has some rate at which it is replenished. Sometimes, that rate is "zero," but even fossil fuels are replenished over a sufficiently long time scale. Thus, the distinction between sustainable and unsustainable is the *rate* at which that resource is consumed — whether it is consumed faster, or slower, than it is replenished. Because complexity creates a self-reinforcing positive feedback loop (*see* thesis #12), complexity is a function of energy, and energy is obtained from resources, even a complex society that begins with sustainable practices must eventually become unsustainable as its complexity increases, and its need for more energy grows. Thus, civilization can never spread life through the universe. The brightest hope the techno-salvationist can offer is to become the alien villains of science fiction movies like *Independence Day*.

Fortunately, such a nightmare scenario, like "the Singularity," are merely fits of techno-salvationist hyperbole. The Singularity, sometimes called "the Rapture of the Nerds," predicts that the exponential curve of technological development will continue until we reach that point where the graph most resembles a straight, vertical line, and technological innovation comes at a pace too great for anyone to predict.

The problem with this scenario is that it only looks at a small part of the graph. If we see it in its whole, we see that technological invention is not following a graph of exponential growth at all — but a curve of diminishing marginal returns. We saw this in thesis #14, and in the previous thesis, we saw that we have *passed* the point of diminishing returns. Facile excitement about "the Singularity" is engendered by such ideas as "Moore's Law" ("computer chip performance doubles roughly every 18 months"), which remains "true" only because computer technology is younger than most other forms, and so is one of the very few areas of technological innovaton still seeing significant activity — because computer technology, unlike technology in general, has *not* yet reached the point of diminishing returns. However, even here, Moore's Law is beginning to fail. In "The Lives and Death of Moore's Law," Ilkka Tuomi writes:

« *Contrary to popular claims, it appears that the common versions of Moore's Law have not been valid during the last decades. As semiconductors are becoming important in economy and society, Moore's Law is now becoming an increasingly misleading predictor of future developments.* »

In a *Business Week* article, the difficulties of maintaining that pace — and the threat of diminishing returns being reached — is raised:

« *Now more than ever, though, upholding Moore's Law will require imagination. So far chip companies have relied mostly on one clever trick: They shrink the transistors on chips so that electrons have less distance to travel, thereby speeding up the processing of data. But that trick is getting harder to perform. In the 1990s, shrinking led reliably to faster speeds. It was "the cream-puff era," says Gary Smith, chief analyst at Gartner Dataquest (IT) in San Jose, Calif. Today, though, circuits are packed so closely that chips are heating up, and performance is starting to suffer. That's one reason giants such as Intel Corp., No. 52 on this year's Info Tech 100, and IBM, No. 44, have fallen behind schedule in launching new generations of microprocessors in recent years.* »

Even so, chipmakers think they can still pull off a few more generations of shrinking before they hit the wall. They're trying new materials and production tools, and most experts see an orderly progression deep into nanotechnology. Today's circuit lines measure about 90 nanometers in width — or 90 billionths of a meter. This year and next they'll go down to 65 nm, then 45 nm by 2010, 32 nm by 2013, and 22 nm by 2016, says

International Technology Roadmap for Semiconductors, an industry research group. After that, says Paolo A. Gargini, Intel's director for technology strategy, "it's unclear what will come next."

Computer technology is unique in that it has not yet reached the point of diminishing returns, but technology in and of itself most certainly has. Our greatest inventiveness is behind us, not in front of us. Technological innovations will continue to be made, but they will continue to be more rare, more modest, and more expensive. Eventually, even computer technology will suffer this fate, for it, too, is subject to diminishing returns. This means that the likelihood of a "techno-fix" is small, and growing smaller.

Ultimately, though, technology can never stop collapse because collapse is *caused* by greater complexity, and technology is one facet of complexity. The diminishing marginal returns of complexity make a society susceptible to all manner of various proximate causes for collapse, including invasion, ecological devastation, and others. Technological solutions address the proximate causes of collapse, but they do so only by exascerbating the ultimate cause of collapse, by introducing still greater complexity.

Technology is part of the problem we face, not because technology is, in itself, "bad," but because the accumulated unintended consequences of those technologies — especially Jevons Paradox — have continued to hound us. Technology can provide momentry relief or put off the inevitable, but only by compounding the problem still further. The crisis of too much complexity can never be solved by creating still more complexity, just as you can't save your burning house by spraying gasoline on it. Ultimately, what we face is a systemic problem. No technical solution is possible to systemic problems; they can only be solved by changing the system.

Thesis #17: Environmental problems may lead to collapse.

In *Collapse*, Jared Diamond argues that civilizations *choose* to collapse by neglecting their ecology. He spends most of his volume pointing to numerous examples of how civilizations collapsed because of ecological problems on Easter Island, Greenland, the southwest United States, and the Yucatan peninsula. He highlights the ecological role in conflicts in Rwanda, Haiti, Montana, China and Australia; he even provides a map which illustrates the nearly perfect overlap between the world's most ecologically distressed areas, and its most politically distressed areas. Perhaps to shield himself from the charges of geograhpical determinism that came of his previous volume, *Guns, Germs & Steel*, Diamond includes a few examples of societies that faced ecological problems and "chose" to survive: in the New Guinea highlands, Tikopia, and the Tokugawa shogunate. Yet, it is precisely in these "counter-examples" that we see where Diamond's model goes awry.

Though Tainter's work, already discussed at length, provides the cornerstone of most recent academic studies of collapse, Diamond spends only a single line in his dismissal. This is unfortunate, as Diamond's work provides an excellent case of Tainter's theory, were Diamond willing to accept that role. Instead, Diamond tries to argue that *all* collapses are due to ecology, and that is simply not the case. Diamond provides "counter-examples" to try to inject some element of "choice" into the matter, but all it accomplishes is to provide a theory which does not necessarily make any predictions, and thus, is unfalsifiable — making it unscientific, as well. Tainter's logic seems irrefutable, though. Managing ecological crises is one of the very reasons humans invest in complexity in the first place. Diamond's "success stories" illustrate that. The Tokugawa shogunate especially illustrates the use of greater complexity to handle an ecological crisis. So long as a society is still below the point of diminishing returns, this is an entirely sensible strategy. Diamond merely rephrases the question from, "Why do societies collapse?" to "Why do some societies collapse due to ecological pressure, and others don't?" That is the question Tainter so admirably answers. The diminishing returns of complexity are the ultimate cause of collapse, but there are other, proximate causes which ultimately deliver the *coup de grâce*. By analogy, no individual dies of AIDS; rather, AIDS creates a condition where otherwise harmless infections become fatal. Likewise, the diminishing returns of complexity is the ultimate cause of collapse by creating a condition where factors which otherwise might have easily been overcome, prove disastrous instead.

That said, Diamond's book provides an enormous catalogue of evidence for the position that the proximate cause of collapse is *very often* ecological. In the final section, Diamond warns of the possibility of our own society's collapse due to our environmental neglect. That neglect is born of a groundless mythology which is codified in our language, namely, the unique place humanity is accorded in the world. "The environment" is something outside ourselves — something we are distinctly not a part of. We separate the world into "artificial" and "natural" things; a dam made by a beaver is "natural," but a dam made by people is "artificial." We think of "nature" as all that which lies outside the sphere of human activity, thus allowing for such bizarre notions as "being close to nature." The duality of the English language may force upon us some idea of humans being separate from the rest of the world, but the poverty of our language to express our relationship does not alter it. Humans are animals, and subject to all the same basic, biological laws as any other animal. We require food, water and air. We depend on other animals, just as all animals do: we rely on plants to recycle the carbon dioxide we exhale into oxygen we can breathe, we rely on plants to convert sunlight into food we can eat and energy we can absorb, we rely on the bacterial ecology that naturally inhabits our bodies to digest food and fend off disease. We have as much to lose from catastrophic losses of biodiversity as any other animal.

Thus, the popular dichotomy that pits the economy and "the environment" is a false one. The ecology is the basis of all economies, and anything that harms that ecology threatens the economy more than any recession. The single greatest threat to any economy is the loss of the ecology on which that economy is utterly dependent for energy, raw materials, and the support base that allows both its consumers and producers to survive and continue consuming and producing.

Given that, the prominence of ecological problems in so many historical collapses is hardly unexpected. Societies, regardless of their level of complexity, are products of their ecology. This has led to great confuson between two senses of the term "collapse": social collapse, such as we have previously discussed in detail, and ecological collapse, which is an entirely different and unrelated phenomenon (save only in the case that ecological collapse is a proximate cause of social collapse).

Ecologies are inter-dependent, with many species relying on many others in complex webs of relationships. There is a great deal of resilience in this kind of formation, but it also makes for a somewhat chaotic system, where the loss of one member can initate cascades of change throughout the ecology, as some species die off, and others prosper from the emptied niches. Take, for example, the elimination of wolves from Yellowstone. Ill-studied at the time, the wolves were hunted as nuisances to livestock herds. In "Wolves' Leftovers Are Yellowstone's Gain, Study Says," John Pickerell writes:

« *Wolves were systematically hunted in Yellowstone and much of the Western United States from the 1800s onwards. Yellowstone's last pack was eliminated in 1926.* »

"In the early 1900s no one stopped to consider the ecological role of wolves," commented Robert Beschta, a forestry scientist at Oregon State University in Corvallis. "Wolves were considered a predator with no value and seen as a huge constraint on allowing a productive ecosystem to flourish," he said. Wolves, mountain lions (*Puma concolor*), and coyotes (*Canis latrans*) were all targeted as threats to livestock and game, he said.

When wolves were reintroduced to Yellowstone in 1995, changes cascaded through the ecology. In "Lessons from the Wolf," Jim Robbins writes:

« *The wolf-effect theory holds that wolves kept elk numbers at a level that prevented them from gobbling up every tree or willow that poked its head aboveground. When the wolves were extirpated in the park as a menace, elk numbers soared, and the hordes consumed the vegetation, denuding the Lamar Valley and driving out many other species. Without young trees on the range, beavers, for example, had little or no food, and indeed they had been absent since at least the 1950s. Without beaver dams and the ponds they create, fewer succulents could survive, and these plants are a critical food for grizzly bears when they emerge from hibernation.* »

After the wolves' reintroduction in 1995 and 1996, they began to increase their numbers fairly rapidly, and researchers began to see not only a drop in the population of elk but a change in elk behavior. The tall, elegant mahogany-colored animals spent less time in river bottoms and more time in places where they could keep an eye out for predatory wolves. If the wolf-effect hypothesis is correct, and wolves are greatly reducing elk numbers, the vegetation should be coming back for the first time in seven decades.

This is precisely what we have seen in the decade since the wolves' reintroduction. This specific case must stand to illustrate one of the most basic ideas of ecology: that ecologies are governed by complicated, intricate inter-relationships. Robbins sums this idea up at the end of his article, writing:

Wolves have brought other lessons with them. They dramatically illustrate the balance that top-of-the-food-chain predators maintain, underscoring what is missing in much of the country where predators have been eliminated. They are a parable for the unintended and unknown effects of how one action surges through an ecosystem. More important, the Yellowstone wolves are bringing into focus hazy ideas of how ecosystems work in a way that has never been so meticulously documented. Just as the actions of the wolf echo through Yellowstone, they will reverberate into the future as they help to increase the understanding of natural systems.

Thus, ecological problems cannot be considered in isolation. Every part of an ecology affects every other part. Nor can we recieve news of ecological problems with passivity: *nothing* is more vital to our survival as a species than the health of the ecology we are a part of. Though our cultural mythology has created a scientific "blind spot," by making the very question of what *our* inter-relationships might be, those inter-relationships still exist, and without a healthy, robust ecology, human survival itself — much less the fragile, complex societies we build on top of such ecologies — is imperilled. As E. O. Wilson described the position:

« *The first, exemptionalism, holds that since humankind is transcendant in intelligence and spirit, so must our species have been released from the iron laws of ecology that bind all other species. No matter how serious the problem, civilized human beings, by ingenuity, force of will and — who knows — divine dispensation, will find a solution. Population growth? Good for the economy, claim some of the exceptionalists, and in any case a basic human right, so let it run. Land shortages? Try fission energy to power the desalting of sea water, then reclaim the world's deserts. (The process might be assisted by towing icebergs to coastal pipelines.) Species going extinct? Not to worry. That is nature's way. Think of humankind as only the latest in a long line of exterminating agents in geological time. In any case, because our species has pulled free of old-style, mindless Nature, we have begun a different order of life. Evolution should now be allowed to proceed along this new trajectory. Finally, resources? The planet has more than enough resources to last indefinitely, if human genius is allowed to address each new problem in turn, without alarmist and unreasonable restrictions imposed on economic development. So hold the course, and touch the brakes lightly. »*

It is an unexamined bit of recieved wisdom, ridiculous once examined. Humans are animals like any other, and subject to the same laws and dictates.

Most of our current ecological problems can be organized under one of two general headings: the Holocene Extinction, and global warming. We will consider each in turn, before turning to the implications of these two looming crises.

The Holocene Extinction

In 1833, Charles Lyell introduced the name "Holocene," or "Recent Whole," for our current geological epoch, stretching back only 10 or 12 thousand years. This makes the Holocene an incredibly young geological epoch, the shortest by far. The International Geological Congress in Bologna adopted the term in 1885, and it has been the accepted terminology ever since. The preceding geologic epoch was the last ice age, the Pleistocene. It lasted for two million years, and while it was marked by significantly advanced glaciation, this was not the unremitting state of affairs. The Pleistocene had regular interglacial periods, during which the weather would turn warmer and the glaciers would temporarily recede. These interglacials typically lasted an average of 10 — 20 thousand years. In short, the "Holocene" is a perfectly typical interglacial. The Pleistocene — the "last ice age" — never ended. We're still in it; a warm spell, yes, but in it.

If anything, our current interglacial is most remarkable for its brevity. If it ended this week and the glaciers returned, it would be marked as the shorter side of normal. In fact, it would have ended some 5,000 years ago — an interglacial of just 5,000 years — were it not for the ecological devastation of the Agricultural Revolution (*see* Ruddiman, "The Anthropogenic Greenhouse Era Began Thousands of Years Ago," *Climatic Change* 61: 261 — 293, 2003). It was the threatened return of the glaciers, and the concommitant ecological changes, that pushed the first farmers in the Fertile Crescent to adopt their sedentary way of life. They were responsible for massive deforestation, and raising huge herds of livestock polluting the atmosphere with incredible amounts of methane — enough to hold the glaciers in check. For 5,000 years, our civilization has lived on borrowed time, extending our "Holocene" by balancing the earth's natural cooling trend against our reckless environmental abuse.

Yet, in that short time, the "Holocene" has joined the Cambrian-Ordovician, the Ordovician-Silurian, the Late Devonian, the Permian-Triassic, and the Cretaceous-Paleogene for the dubious distinction of contributing its name to a mass extinction event.

Until recently, the term "Holocene Extinction" referred to a rather minor spate of extinction which took place at the beginning of the Holocene, with the end of the megafauna — woolly mammoths, North American horses, sabertooth cats, and other large mammals. This occured at the beginning of the Holocene, as humans were first moving into many new environments, like the Americas and Australia. This has led to a long-standing debate between "overkill" and "overchill." Were the megafauna wiped out by climate change? Or by rapacious, brutal bands of overhunting human foragers? Both sides have their evidence, of course.

Nor is this merely an academic argument without reprecussion for the present. The "overkill" theory is routinely cited by some groups as if it were already a proven fact, and used as evidence that humans are an inherently destructive species. So we needn't worry ourselves with the ecological destruction we wreak. We can't help it. It's our nature.

As you might expect, the truth lies somewhere between overkill and overchill. Human populations were almost certainly too small to wreak such havoc all by themselves, and the same climate changes that opened the way for humans into Australia and the Americas also had to affect the other large mammals living across the globe. More importantly, however, alpha predators — like wolves, and like humans — play important, keystone roles in any ecology. The introduction of a new alpha predator can have dramatic effects, even causing cascades of extinction. This is not necessarily because the alpha predators overhunt or are even in the least bit maladaptive; this is simply the nature of alpha predators and how they relate in any given ecology. When humans came to Australia and the Americas, they were as harmless as wolves, lions, or any other big mammalian predator. Their presence caused cascades of changes throughout the ecosystem. Given that it was also a period of major climate change, a great number of species that were already under stress adapting to the new climate were tipped over the edge into extinction by the further ecological changes created by the adaptation of a new alpha predator. Our ancestors were hardly noble savages; but neither were they bloodthirsty killers bent on the destruction of all life on earth. They were animals, like any other.

While Australians and Americans established a new equilibrium in their given environments, the same climate changes that allowed them to cross the Bering Land Bridge and shortened the boat ride between the islands of Oceania and ultimately Australia, were having other effects, as well. In the Middle East, some foragers had come to rely increasingly on cereal grains. Their lives became more sedentary as they established static resources necessary for their food source, like granaries and mills. As the weather turned, they were forced to intensify their food production — and agriculture was born. The weather was already turning colder, causing the glaciers to expand, the sea levels to drop, and the ways to America and Australia to reveal themselves from the ocean floor. But the agriculturalists of the Fertile Crescent were seeing hard times with the colder, drier climate. They intensified their production, which gave them more food. More food increased their population, which naturally needed more food. The Food Race was off to a running start.

To refer to the "Fertile Crescent" today is a cruel joke, but this was not always the case. Once, this region was abundant. The arid desert we see today is the result of agriculture. The first farmers stripped it of all life, and then spread out to the east and west to consume the next region, like the alien invaders of some clichéd science fiction movie. Yet it was not malice or greed that drove them; they were locked into an endless cycle of exponential growth. Their way of life required constant expansion. Good or evil, nice or mean, they were compelled to conquer, whether they liked it or not (*see* thesis #12 and thesis #13).

Deforestation, desertification and the herding of methane-producing livestock increased the amount of greenhouse gases in the atmosphere — enough to halt the world's cooling trend. The two balanced each other, cancelling one another out, to unnaturally extend the "Holocene" interglacial. All the while, the massive ecological devastation wrought by the spread of agriculture perpetuated new cascades of extinctions — often, as a matter of policy.

Wolf species were systematically hunted down by farmers, until they became extinct, in both Japan and Europe. Such hunting has endangered wolf populations in North America, as well. Such hunts were conducted because wolves would prey on livestock. Agricultural societies often circulate tales demonizing wolves and other predators that prey on livestock, providing a cultural basis for such hunts. It is a unique strategy in the animal kingdom: no other species wastes its efforts trying to systematically eliminate its competition.

But more often, extinction has simply been the unforeseen side effect of our expanding agricultural way of life. These continuing extinctions have led to some confusion, and argument about an "on-going" Holocene extinction. In fact, there are two seperate phenomenon going on here, unfortunately obscured because both began with a common cause — the changing climate of 12,000 years ago. The first was simply the product of a readjustment in ecologies, to a changing climate and a new large mammalian predator migrating in. This was relatively benign. The second phenomenon is what makes the Holocene extinction such a pressing concern. It is far more devastating, and because it is a systemic consequence of agricultural society, it will never "iron itself out" as the first one did, except with the end of agricultural life — and civilization with it.

This, the *real* Holocene extinction, has been a significant problem for the entire history of civilization. Even all by itself, it would have eventually reached crisis proportions and *still* marked agriculture as "the worst mistake in the history of the human race."

Yet, this process has recently seen an incredible intensification, forcing us to face a crisis of unprecedented proportions *now*. This intensification began with the Industrial Revolution, which did not change the *nature* of agriculture nearly so much as it exponentially increased its *scale*. The intensification of cultivation had long before crossed a point of diminishing returns, where more calories of work were expended in cultivation than were returned in yields. This shortfall had previously been made up by animals, which could leverage energy sources that were otherwise unusable — for example, they could graze in fields too rocky for food crops. With first the Industrial Revolution, and then the Green Revolution, other energy sources — like petroleum — allowed us to push even further beyond the point of diminishing returns, to significantly increase yields simply by making the process unthinkably inefficient. Today, on average, every calorie of food we consume requires ten calories of work — primarily stored in fossil fuels — to cultivate, package and ship. Very little of the earth remains naturally arable; nearly all of it requires intense fertilization and irrigation. On the other end, the average piece of food an American eats has traveled 1,500 miles to the dinner plate.

The Green Revolution raised our carrying capacity to — essentially, wherever we want it to be. Human population jumped up in response, with growth slowing only now as we begin to approach a new asymptote somewhere near *9 billion*. There are, at the time of this writing, only 6.5 billion people on earth, yet just that many requires 40% of the earth's photosynthetic capacity. That is how much energy is required to support so many people, and the food that so many people require — and, as is often the case, the food that food requires. 40% of the total energy available to the entire planet is wrapped up in a single species; only 60% is currently portioned out among all the other millions of species on earth.

This is the essential reason for the Holocene extinction. Deforestation, desertification, climate change and other climatological and ecological disasters are often the immediate causes, but these are themselves symptoms of the ultimate cause — that we are, essentially, starving the world out. We are taking everything for ourselves, and laying siege to all life on earth.

The effects have been catastrophic. Extinctions are always happening, just like people are always dying. But like an explosively high death rate, an extinction rate far beyond the background rate is catastrophic. The normal background rate of extinctions is about two to five taxonomic families of marine invertebrates and vertebrates every million years. Normal background extinction would end one mammalian species every 200 years, on average. Some centuries might see two or three mammalian species lost; other times, several centuries may pass with no mammalian extinction whatsoever. Yet in the past 400 years, 89 mammalian species have gone extinct, and another 169 species are critically endangered — 45 times the normal rate of background extinction, just among mammals. The total current extinction rate is difficult to calculate, since we don't know precisely how many species there are on earth, but the most conservative estimates indicate that we are seeing *147 extinctions per day*. Most scientists estimate that we are now seeing extinction rates that are anywhere between *a thousand and ten thousand times* the normal, background rate.

This is unprecedented. None of the previous extinction events were this lethal, or this quick. We are doing more damage than when a comet carved out the Yucatan and blotted the sun out of the sky. In 2002, E.O. Wilson predicted that at current rates, one half of all species on earth will be gone in a century. Previously, the Permian-Triassic was the worst extinction event in our planet's history; it ended 95% of all species that then existed, but it took nearly a million years to unfold. We are seeing half of that in mere *centuries*.

No extinction occurs in a vacuum. All species exist in an ecosystem, and with each species lost, the ecosystem becomes weaker. If sharks go extinct, so too do remoras. Each extinction triggers a cascade of extinctions through its dependencies, running their course through the complex web of life on earth. The complex is too great to predict where those cascades will end, or what will be extinguished in its course. We are as dependent on our planet as every other species, and our willful blindness to this, our deluded, alienating fantasy of being higher and nobler than mere nature, does not change that basic fact.

The Holocene extinction, left unchecked, will ultimately claim *us* as well. All it will take is the wrong cascade, or simply weakening the earth's ecosystems to a tipping point that can no longer support our way of life. Cereal grains are fickle; a temperature change of a few degrees might kill them all off. With 90% or more of our diet coming from just a few, closely-related grasses, our entire, global population is essentially in the same precarious boat as the Irish of 1845.

Diversity is strength; diversity ensures survival. The human population is growing, while the number of species takes an unprecedented nose-dive. The amount of life is not changing, but biodiversity is plummeting. We are, pound by pound, replacing every single lifeform on this planet with a corresponding unit of human flesh. We are reducing the planet's biodiversity to a single species.

Taken to its extreme end-point, the insanity of this policy becomes evident. Humans will choke on their own breath and fall on each other in cannibalistic slaughter. We cannot survive all on our own. The general principle is more complex; long before we are alone in the world, this course will mean the end of our species. Therein lies the great irony of the Holocene extinction. It is the worst mass extinction in the history of the earth, and it is the only extinction ever driven forward by organisms themselves. But ultimately, those organisms — us, human beings — will be among the dead, if we do not soon wake up from our ten-thousand-year madness, and stop this before it's too late.

In the article cited above, E. O. Wilson considers the question, "Is humanity suicidal?" Like Wilson, I do not believe that it is. Humans are omnivores, making them incredibly adaptable to new environments. They are also alpha predators. They can be as harmless and well adapted as wolves, lions, or hawks. When humans found themselves in a new environment — such as the Americas or Australia — there were some changes that took place, but these were well within the normal bounds of ecological change. What we have seen since, however, is something entirely different. It is not humanity that is maladapted to life on earth; it is agriculture that is maladapted to humanity. We are still Pleistocene animals, no matter how many stories we spin about our vaunted "Holocene," and the agricultural life simply does not suit us. It forces us to grow exponentially, and wreak havoc on the earth.

Global Warming

As previously mentioned, ecological problems can never be considered in isolaton, and much of the cause of global warming can be found in the same causes of the Holocene Extinction. Humans have been causing the release of greenhouse gases and altering the earth's atmospheric composition and global climate for 10,000 years. However, while previously our excesses were checked by the earth's natural cooling trend as it tried to enter a new cycle of glaciation, the increases in scale since the Industrial Revolution have brought on a global climatological crisis.

Global warming is a subject of debate only because of the short-sighted nature of the modern corporation: a consequence of the nature of investment and the stock market. Because most of the proposed "solutions" to global warming are legal restrictons on economic activity, those companies which would suffer in the short-term (though they would propser in the long-term — as the benefits of their own survival and the survival of their customers) have invested a good deal of money in obfuscating the issue, in order to make global warming appear questonable, and thus avoiding the proposed political ramifications. It is worth noting that global warming is considered controversial only in the United States — the only other Western country than Australia that still considers evolution to be a controversial subject. With the United States as the single most significant consumer of petroleum and the worst producer of greenhouse gases, no international plan to reduce global warming can have any hope of succeeding without the support of the United States. The website Exxon Secrets maps the relationships through which ExxonMobil specifically funds nearly all of the "climate change skeptics" in the United States.

Yet global warming is an open question only in the arena of public policy. Among scientists and those who have honestly researched the topic, its reality is well known and widely accepted. Even the well-funded "climate change skeptics" can agree on the basics: that the greenhouse effect is real (and is even beneficial; with no greenhouse effect whatsoever, the earth would be too cold for mammalian life), and that the globe has been warming at a dangerous rate.

Political critics often allege that global warming is a non-issue, because mean global temperature has increased "only" a few degrees; specifically, as the IPCC WG I concluded, "0.6 ± 0.2°C." Even more importantly, that rate has increased over the past two decades to 1.0°C per century. The critics' use of the word "just" relies on our conventional concept of temperature, and dshonestly obfuscates the scale inside of which global climate operates. The difference between our current climate and an ice age is also "only a few degrees." Climate is a very different thing from weather, and while the temperature outside may change drastically, the *global average temperature* is a very static thing, and even minor changes can have catastrophic consequences.

Eleven of the warmest years on record have occurred since 1990, and the five warmest of all have occurred in the last decade (in descending order: 2002, 1998, 2003, 2001, 1997). The polar ice caps are shrinking. In 2005, that shrinking of polar ice meant that the Odden ice shelf did not fully form. Normally, the Odden ice shelf's melting in the spring releases a great deal of cold water into the Atlantic, providing one of the main forces pushing the Gulf Stream. The lack of much input from the Odden ice shelf made the Gulf Stream very weak through 2005. As a result, the hot water of the Gulf of Mexico remained in the Gulf, creating intense surface and deep sea temperatures — such that minor tropical storms that wandered over those hot waters became massive hurricanes. The record-breaking number of hurricanes in 2005 was entirely the result of normal mutli-decadal cycles, but the intensification of Katrina, Rita and Wilma into some of the most powerful hurricanes ever recorded in the north Atlantic was a direct result of global warming. At the same time, the lack of the Gulf Stream may continue to have devastating consequences, in the form of an especially bitter winter in northern Europe, which normally enjoys a climate much warmer than its latitude would normally allow, thanks to the Gulf Stream.

So we already see that the effects of global warming are chaotic, and are best described as, "increasingly erratic weather." Global warming drives weather into the extremes, rather than simply making everything hotter. This makes sense: the world is not uniform, why should we expect the effects of heating such a world to be uniform?

Of course, the world has been hotter in the past, but the question is not whether or not life on earth can survive; the question is not even whether or not humanity can survive. The salient question is whether a way of life that is utterly dependent on a small number of closely-related and fickle cereal grains that can barely survive the most minor perturbations of rainfall or temperature can endure in such a world. The U.S. Global Change Research Information Office outlines some of the threats our agricultural way of life might face:

It may be possible for global agricultural production to keep pace with increasing demand over the next 50–100 years if adequate adaptations are made, but there are likely to be difficulties in some regions. This conclusion takes into account the beneficial effects of carbon dioxide fertilization, i.e., given sufficient water and nutrients, plant growth will be enhanced by an increased concentration of carbon dioxide in the atmosphere. Changes in the spread and abundance of agricultural pests and the effects of climate variability were not reflected in this assessment. Regional changes in crop yields and productivity are expected to occur in response to climate change. There is likely to be an increased risk of famine, particularly in subtropical and tropical semi-arid and arid locations.

This is in addition to massive flooding, the spread of malaria with the spread of the tropics, and perhaps unpredictable crises we will face as our complex society faces the very same ecological problems that destroyed the Mayans and others.

In New Orleans, we may see a harbinger of things to come. Not only will the incidence of storms of Katrina's magnitude increase, but so will sea levels — setting up conditions where even milder storms can wreak such devastation.

Global warming is not new, but we have recently crossed a threshold in scale and set off a new environment in which previously tolerable acts have become intolerable. Our greenhouse gas emissions balanced the earth's natural cooling trend in the past, but our increases in scale have reversed that trend. Reductions in ice and snow cover make for darker land and water, which absorbs more heat from the sun. The Siberian permafrost is melting, releasing enormous amounts of methane. The frozen methane once locked beneath the arctic ice cap is also beginning to melt; that will drastically alter the atmosphere's composition, and make it hotter still. We are no longer emitting greenhouse gases into a world that's tending to become cooler: we're emitting greenhouse gases into a world that we've pushed into a positive feedback loop that will make it hotter and hotter.

That positive feedback loop will eventually end; they always do. Climate has states of equilibrium where ti comes to rest, and when pushed out of one, it moves quickly to the next. We have succeeded in moving the earth out of the Holocene's state of equilibrium, and the earth is now moving quickly — and catastrophically — towards a new, hotter state of equilibrium. It is by no means guaranteed that complex societies will be possible at this new state; in fact, it's very likely they will not be. Nor is a complex society already beyond the point of diminishing returns at all likely to be adaptable enough, quickly enough, to survive the catastrophic transition.

Diamond's Dozen

If the immediacy of our environmental crisis is still lost on anyone, Jared Diamond begins to draw down how crucial these concerns are at the end of *Collapse*:

« *Ask some ivory-tower academic ecologist, who knows a lot about the environment but never reads a newspaper and has no interest in politics, to name the overseas countries facing some of the worst problems of environmental stress, overpopulation, or both. The ecologist would likely answer: "That's a no-brainer, it's obvious. Your list of environmentally stressed or overpopulated countries should surely include Afghanistan, Bangladesh, Burundi, Haiti, Indonesia, Iraq, Rwanda, the Solomon Islands, and Somalia, plus others".* »

Then ask a first world politician, who knows nothing and cares less about the environment and population problems, to name the world's worst trouble spots: countries where state government has already been overwhelmed and has collapsed, or is now at risk of collapsing, or has been wracked by recent civil wars; and countries that, as a result of those problems, are also creating problems for us rich first world countries. Surprise, surprise: the two lists would be very similar.

Today, just as in the past, countries that are environmentally stressed, overpopulated, or both, become at risk of getting politically stressed, and of their governments collapsing. When people are desperate, undernourished, and without hope, they blame their governments, which they see as responsible for or unable to solve their problems. They try to emigrate at any cost. They fight each other over land. They kill each other. They start civil wars. They figure that they have nothing to lose, so they become terrorists, or they support or tolerate terrorism.

The results of these transparent connections are far-reaching and devastating. There are genocides, such as those that exploded in Bangladesh, Burundi, Indonesia, and Rwanda; civil wars or revolutions, as in most of the countries on the lists; calls for the dispatch of troops, as to Afghanistan, Haiti, Indonesia, Iraq, the Philippines, Rwanda, the Solomon Islands, and Somalia; the collapse of central government, as has already happened in Somalia and the Solomon Islands; and overwhelming poverty, as in all of the countries on these lists.

Hence the best predictors of modern "state failures" prove to be measures of environmental and population pressure, such as high infant mortality, rapid population growth, a high percentage of the population in their late teens and 20s, and hordes of young men without job prospects and ripe for recruitment into militias.

Those pressures create conflicts over shortages of land, water, forests, fish, oil, and minerals. They create not only chronic internal conflict, but also emigration of political and economic refugees, and wars between countries arising when authoritarian regimes attack neighbours in order to divert popular attention from internal stresses.

In short, it is not a question open for debate whether the collapses of past societies have modern parallels and offer any lessons to us. Instead, the real question is how many more countries will undergo them.

Diamond lists what he sees as the twelve most critical environmental problems we currently face:

1. Destruction of natural habitats (mainly through deforestation)
2. Reduction of wild foods
3. Loss of biodiversity
4. Erosion of soil

5. Depletion of natural resources
6. Pollution of freshwater
7. Approaching the "ceiling" for photosynthetic capacity
8. Environmental pollution
9. Introduction by humans of alien species
10. Artificially induced climate change
11. Overpopulation
12. Large and deep environmental footprints

Point #3 is the Holocene Extinction exactly, with points #1, #2, #7 and #9 as either its causes, or effects. Point #10 is global warming exactly. That leaves us with #4, #5, #6, #8, #11 and #12 as seemngly unaddressed.

But in fact it's in precisely these problems that we see the foregoing united under a single heading, and the illusion of Diamond's "choice" revealed. Because civilization must always grow (thesis #12 and thesis #13), resources must always be depleted more this year than last, population must always increase, and environmental footprints must always grow deeper. All of these environmental problems — including the Holocene Extinction and global warming themselves — are the natural consequence of the Food Race.

Erosion of soil.

Soils of farmlands used for growing crops are being carried away by water and wind erosion at rates between 10 and 40 times the rates of soil formation, and between 500 and 10,000 times soil erosion rates on forested land.

The rampant destruction of soil is a natural consequence of monoculture. In a balanced ecosystem, soil is shared by many different species of plant, creating mutually beneficial utrient cycles analogous to the oxygen-carbon dioxide cycle that benefits both plants and animals. The nutrient that one plant needs is the excretion of another, and vice versa. Planting a field entirely with a single crop is as suicidal as locking yourself in a garage with a running car, and for all the very same reasons.

This is what makes agriculture so disastrous for the land it's practiced on, and why agriculture leads to constant territorial expansion. This is why the Neolithic Revolution turned the Fertile Crescent into a blasted wasteland, why the situation in modern Australia is so dire, why agriculture leads to desertification and salination crises, and why merely farming in and of itself is sufficient to wreak environmental catastrophe on a very large scale.

Yet it is precisely monoculture that provides the large-scale yields of agriculture. Any plot of wild land has some percentage of human edible matter, but it is much less than 100%, because that same land also provides food for all manner of other species, as well. By clearing that land and planting a single variety of crop, the biodiversity and photosynthetic capacity of that land is converted purely into human food — and human mass. To back away from this would be stepping away from the Food Race — and like an arms race, that is a disastrous move unless everyone steps away from it at the exact same time.

Depletion of natural resources.

The prevalent view is that known and likely reserves of readily accessible oil and natural gas will last for a few more decades.

Here, Diamond addresses the end of our fossil fuel subsidies, a subject we'll broach in the full detail it deserves in the next thesis.

Pollution of freshwater.

« A good many prominent people have recently forecast, with a sort of gloomy relish, that wars will one day, probably soon, break out over water. These forecasts come not just from the environmental movement, which has long become accustomed to fits of Malthusian soothsaying, but from officials of so sober an institution as the World Bank. Ismail Serageldin, the bank's vice president for environmental affairs and chairman of the World Water Commission, stated bluntly a few years ago that the wars of the 21st century will be fought over water." Although he was roundly criticized for this opinion, he refused to disavow it and has frequently asserted that water is the most critical issue facing human development. The former UN secretary general Boutros Boutros Ghali said something similar about water wars. So did Jordan's late King Hussein, who had obvious cause to mean it. Egypt has more than once threatened to go to war over diversions of the Nile. »

The above quote comes not from Jared Diamond, but from Marc de Villiers' *"Water Wars of the Near Future."* That we are facing crisis conditions for lack of freshwater is not very widely recognized, but no less real. Water pollution forms one part of the threat; rising sea levels and the possible salination of existing freshwater reserves is another. Already, tensions over lack of freshwater have run high in the United States — one of the least affected regions in the world — west of the Mississippi. The term "water wars" presently refers to political maneuvering in the western United States, though the phrase is increasingly used to refer to looming armed conflicts in Africa and Asia. Erwin Klaas' *"Potential for Water Wars in the 21st Century"* provides an excellent introduction to the problem we face.

Environmental pollution.

Though the amounts detected in water from a Louisiana tap were small — just a few parts per trillion (ppt) — they can be biologically active, another study finds. At these concentrations, one of the hormones measured and another found in birth control pills alter the apparent gender of fish and, possibly, their fertility. In a suite of yet more studies, collaborating state, federal, and university scientists report finding male carp and walleyes in Minnesota that were producing "sky-high" quantities of vitellogenin, an egg-yolk protein normally made only by females. Such feminization might explain the suspected inability of some adult male fish to make sperm. The researchers had caught the walleyes in the effluent of a sewage-treatment plant — a type of facility that others have shown can release estrogenic pollutants.

That is also not from Diamond, but from Janet Raloff's June 2000 report, "Excreted Drugs: Something Looks Fishy." We are seeing increasing incidences of asthma and allergies — trends which are best explained by declining air quality. We all breathe, we all drink, and thus we all need clean air and water. We have neither. The toxins in our air and water are poisons that we take in daily, and are responsible for much of our deteriorating health.

Overpopulation.

The world's human population is growing. More people require more food, space, water, energy and other resources. ... What really counts is not the number of people alone, but their impact on the environment ... Our numbers pose problems insofar as we consume resources and generate wastes.

We'll consider points #11 and #12 together, since their separation was somewhat artificial to begin with. Overpopulation is the root cause of all other environmental problems. Even the most meager environment can sustain a few people — foragers have flourished in the Arctic, the Kalahari, and other regions because their populatons are low, and their footprint is light.

Overpopulation itself is the natural consequence of the Food Race — driven by the constant need to expand. That need is a systemic consequence of complex society. The alternative to overpopulation, then, is to reverse the trend of intensifying complexity and accept greater simplicity: in a word, collapse.

* * *

Complex societies are a luxury that a healthy ecology can afford. They grow out of a healthy ecology and are sustained by it. A complex society that is detrimental to its ecology assaults the very foundation on which it stands. It is bound for collapse.

Yet, that is precisely what complex societies *always* do. Diamond tries to paint collapse as a "choice," but the environmental problems we face are the direct result of the Food Race. Agricultural production creates more overpopulation, which is answered by more intensive agricultural production — resulting in still greater overpopulation, on and on for ten thousand years, however long it takes for the positive feedback loop to crash in on itself.

As Sam Vaknin worte in, "The Emerging Water Wars":

« *It takes 1000 tons of water to produce 1 ton of grain and agriculture consumes almost 70 percent of the world's water — though only less than 30 percent in OECD countries. It takes more than the entire throughput of the Nile to grow the grain imported annually by Middle Eastern and North African countries alone. Some precipitation-poor countries even grow cotton and rice, both insatiable crops. By 2020, says the World Water Council, we will be short 17 percent of the water that would be needed to feed the population.* »

The main driving force behind the Holocene Extinction is the twin forces of overpopulation and intensified agricultural production. As more land is converted into cultivated fields, we approach important tipping points in how much of the world's photosynthetic capacity is tied up in a single species. Deforestation is driven primarily by the need to feed an ever-growing populaton, but also for that population's other resource needs, such as lumbering and mining.

That deforestation has been responsible for anthropogenic atmospheric change for thousands of years, but as the positive feedback loop of the Food Race reached new levels, we were forced to either adopt fossil fuels, or collapse. Those fuels have intensified our atmospheric impact to obscene levels, yielding a new crisis in global warming.

We do not face a long laundry list of environmental problems: we face a single, multi-faceted crisis. That crisis is complex society itself. The problems we face are the direct consequence of the positive feedback loop of complex society, and the Food Race in particular.

Diamond points to several examples of societies that overcame their environmental problems, but all of those examples — and Diamond's own suggestions — rely on greater complexity. They solve one proximate cause of collapse by intensifying the ultimate cause of collapse: the diminishing marginal returns on complexity.

In the passage above, Diamond writes:

« *Today, just as in the past, countries that are environmentally stressed, overpopulated, or both, become at risk of getting politically stressed, and of their governments collapsing. When people are desperate, undernourished, and without hope, they blame their governments, which they see as responsible for or unable to solve their problems. They try to emigrate at any cost. They fight each other over land. They kill each other. They start civil wars. They figure that they have nothing to lose, so they become terrorists, or they support or tolerate terrorism.* »

Those people are right to blame their governments. One of the main excuses by which Leviathan justifies its existence is that it can "manage" the ecology. Yet it is the very existence of Leviathan that ultimately threatens the very ecology on which it depends. Tainter's logic is all too true: we cannot explain the collapse of complex societies in terms of their ecological resources, since managing those resources is precisely the promise complex societies offer. Why do such societies fail to deliver that promise?

The answer, of course, is the diminishing marginal return on complexity. The more a complex society manages its ecology, the harder it becomes to do so again. Diamond's examples of societies that cheated collapse all existed below the point of diminishing returns, when greater complexity — in the form of environmental laws and regulations — still had significant marginal returns. That is not our situation; we are far beyond that point. That is why governmental regulations can never be more than stop-gaps for us, and why our choices are not between the environment and the economy, but between complexity to its bitter end, and survival.

Ultimately, though, it is conceivable that some solution may appear to this crisis. None of the available solutions seem terribly likely to succeed, or even especially effective should they by some miracle be realized. The Kyoto Protocol is a wonderful example of this. Its passage by the United States would be a minor miracle, and without the signature of the world's single largest carbon consumer, it is completely ineffectual. Yet, even if it were somehow passed, it would be a mere stick in the river — the compromises already made to try to court the United States have made the treaty ineffective.

Ecological devastation is often the proximate cause of collapse — but not always. And, since complex societies specialize in managing their ecological resources, the possibility of some solution is possible, if miniscule and ever-shrinking. Ultimately, it is the diminishing returns on complexity that will end our civilization, but the final blow is difficult to predict. That said, it is extremely likely that the ecological devastation our complexity has wrought will be a proximate cause — and that our complexity will, in the end, be undone by its own consequences.

Thesis #18: Peak Oil may lead to collapse.

Energy, like matter, cannot be created — it can only be transformed. That is the Law of Conservation of Mass-Energy, which also entails that matter can be transformed into energy, making matter and energy differing states of the same thing. When you burn wood, part of the wood's matter is converted into energy — the light and heat of fire. Fossil fuels are created out of organic matter, by applying eons of pressure deep inside the earth to the remains of dead plants and animals. The result can be coal, petroleum, or natural gas. They all can be converted into energy with great efficiency, making them the most effective fuels ever discovered. In considering the quality of a fuel, the relevant measure is not simply how much energy the matter can yield, but how much energy it yields per energy put into it, or ERoEI, energy return on energy invested. On that score, fossil fuels were once unmatched. Petroleum once had an ERoEI near 100 — for the energy equivalent of 1 barrel of oil, you could extract 100 barrels of oil. But that, too, is subject to diminishing returns, and more recently, the ERoEI of fossil fuels has been dropping. "Peak Oil" is simply the law of diminishing returns applied to petroleum extraction.

A barrel of oil is a barrel of oil, and it will always have the same yield of energy as any other barrel of oil. The ERoEI changes based on how difficult and expensive that barrel of oil becomes to extract. The first oil reserves we extracted were the largest ones, those nearest the surface and/or those under pressure — often bubbling up all on its own. This oil was the lightest (meaning it had fewer impurities) and sweetest (less sulphur), which made it the easiest to refine. As these reserves were depleted, the pressure inside them dropped, and energy needed to be exerted on the reserve to move the oil up. This oil deeper in the earth tended to be heavier and more sour, which meant that not only did it take more energy to extract, it also took more energy to refine. Eventually, those reserves ceased to be economical, well before all the oil was exhausted. New reserves needed to be found, but these were obviously inferior. They were smaller, or they were deeper, or they weren't under any natural pressure, or any combination of those three. They started off less efficient and, like the original reserves, grew less economical as extraction proceeded.

The first to notice this phenomenon was M. King Hubbert, a geophysicist who worked for Shell from 1943 to 1964. As Energy Bulletin's "Peak Oil Primer" explains:

« In the 1950s a US geologist working for Shell, M. King Hubbert, noticed that oil discoveries graphed over time, tended to follow a bell shape curve. He posited that the rate of oil production would follow a similar curve, now known as the Hubbert Curve (see figure). In 1956 Hubbert predicted that production from the US lower 48 states would peak in 1970. Shell tried to pressure Hubbert into not making his projections public, but the notoriously stubborn Hubbert went ahead and released them. In anycase, most people inside and outside the industry quickly dismissed Hubbert's predictions. In 1970 US oil producers had never produced as much, and Hubbert's predictions were a fading memory. But Hubbert was right, US continental oil production did peak in 1970/71, although it was not widely recognized for several years, only with the benefit of hindsight. »

No oil producing region neatly fits bell shaped curve exactly because production is dependent on various geological, economic and political factors, but the Hubbert Curve remains a powerful predictive tool.

The peak of U.S. oil production in 1971 was the most significant event of the post-war era. Any economy can ultimately be understood purely in terms of energy transformations, and fossil fuels are the foundation of any industrial civilization. That transiton occurred because of a different "peak" problem — not fossil fuels, but timber. As Richard Cowen writes in the online, rough draft of *Exploiting the Earth* under contract with Johns Hopkins University Press, in chapter 11: "Coal":

« The situation was different in England and France. Much land had been cleared for agriculture in Roman and again in medieval times, and the population was much denser than in mountain Germany and Bohemia. Although metal mining was never on the enormous scale of the Central European strikes, many small mines exploited tin, lead, copper, and iron deposits. All these ores were smelted with charcoal, and with heavy demands on the forests for building timbers for castles, cathedrals, houses, and ships, for building mills and most machinery, for barrels for storing food and drink, and fuel for the lime-burning, glass and brewing industries and for domestic fires, the English and French found that they were approaching a major fuel crisis. »

A fuel "crisis" implies a lack of supply, and the other factors involved are supply and transport. Overland costs of transport were very high except for the highest-value goods, and it was simply not economic to carry bulky material like wood for very far on a cart. So thinly populated areas in forest land had no fuel crisis at all, whereas large cities soon felt a crisis as woodlands close by were cleared.

...

Nations were therefore faced with only two alternative solutions: to import timber from Scandinavia and Eastern Europe, and/or to substitute coal wherever possible. Transport costs imposed severe penalties on transporting timber long distances unless it was needed for special purposes such as building construction, pit props, or ship-building, and the coal-mining and coal-processing industries grew astonishingly, beginning in Elizabethan England and extending to European regions as the timber crisis overtook them.

Every economic indicator suggests that the timber crisis was most acute in England from about 1570 to 1630. It is at this time that we see an unwilling but dramatic change to coal as the nation's industrial fuel.

Wood was the preferred fuel for fires, as well as a primary construction material. As the population of northwestern Europe grew, so too did its appetite for wood. The forests of England were utterly destroyed. As Cowen points out, "You will search in vain today for Sherwood Forest. It exists only on road signs and movies that are filmed on sets somewhere else."

Coal was favored only by blacksmiths. For every other purpose, the black, dirty smoke was considered a major public nuisance. Laws were passed against the burning of coal, until it became a necessity. Obviously, Europe and France did not clear-cut the whole world, or we would have no trees today. Scandinavia and eastern Europe had very healthy forests — and lumber that was being exported to France and Britain. The question was how much did it cost to transport that wood to where it was needed. Shipments of wood from Scandinavia and eastern Europe added travel cost to the wood which were not previously necessary. So, while wood remained wood, the cost of that wood increased significantly, forcing northwestern Europeans to turn to an inferior, dirty fuel: coal. Cowen describes some of the social ramifications of this change:

A fundamental change in English domestic building followed, as more brick chimneys were built to accommodate the fumes from the smoky fuel. By 1618 London had 200 chimney sweeps, who would eventually give the world its first example of an environmentally produced cancer, from contact with soot. There were law suits against coal pollution, and there were courageous judges who would rule against the nuisance.

But with coal — and even moreso later with petroleum and to a lesser extent natural gas — Europeans had stumbled not only on a fuel with outrageously high EROEI, but a fuel that encouraged, rather than discouraged, technical innovation. As Joseph Tainter explains in his 1996 paper, "Complexity, Problem-Solving, and Sustainable Societies":

In one of the most interesting works of economic history, Richard Wilkinson (1973) showed that in late-and post-medieval England, population growth and deforestation stimulated economic development, and were at least partly responsible for the Industrial Revolution. Major increases in population, at around 1300, 1600, and in the late 18th century, led to intensification in agriculture and industry. As forests were cut to provide agricultural land and fuel for a growing population, England's heating, cooking, and manufacturing needs could no longer be met by burning wood. Coal came to be increasingly important, although it was adopted reluctantly. Coal was costlier to obtain and distribute than wood, and restricted in its occurrence. It required a new, costly distribution system. As coal gained importance in the economy the most accessible deposits were depleted. Mines had to be sunk ever deeper, until groundwater came to be a problem. Ultimately, the steam engine was developed and put to use pumping water from mines. With the development of a coal-based economy, a distribution system, and the steam engine, several of the most important technical elements of the Industrial Revolution were in place.

...

It generated its own problems of complexity and costliness. These included railways and canals to distribute coal and manufactured goods, the development of an economy increasingly based on money and wages, and the development of new technologies. While such elements of complexity are usually thought to facilitate economic growth, in fact they can do so only when subsidized by energy. Some of the new technologies, such as the steam engine, showed diminishing returns to innovation quite early in their development (Wilkinson 1973; Giarini and Louberge 1978; Giarini 1984). What set industrialism apart from all of the previous history of our species was its reliance on abundant, concentrated, high-quality energy (Hall et al. 1992). 5 With subsidies of inexpensive fossil fuels, for a long time many consequences of industrialism effectively did not matter. Industrial societies could afford them. When energy costs are met easily and painlessly, benefit/cost ratio to social investments can be substantially ignored (as it has been in contemporary industrial agriculture). Fossil fuels made industrialism, and all that flowed from it (such as science, transportation, medicine, employment, consumerism, high-technology war, and contemporary political organization), a system of problem solving that was sustainable for several generations.

Energy has always been the basis of cultural complexity and it always will be. If our efforts to understand and resolve such matters as global change involve increasing political, technological, economic, and scientific complexity, as it seems they will, then the availability of energy per capita will be a constraining factor. To increase complexity on the basis of static or declining energy supplies would require lowering the standard of living throughout the world. In the absence of a clear crisis very few people would support this.

Peak Oil poses a familiar crisis, then. Peak Oil is the moment at which we have extracted half of all the oil in the world — meaning another half remains. But the first half was light, sweet crude in large reserves near the surface and under pressure; the second half is heavy, sour crude in small reserves deep inside the earth where we must apply our own pressure. It is the half that costs more to obtain, but continues to deliver the same benefit as before. When it takes a barrel of oil to obtain a barrel of oil — when petroleum's ERoEI declines to 1 — then it doesn't matter how much oil is still left, it's no longer economically viable. The petroleum age is over.

The implications of that are profound and far-reaching. In "The Oil We Eat," Richard Manning elaborates the nature of agriculture in general, and the particular dependence of modern, industrialized agriculture on fossil fuels. He writes:

« *The common assumption these days is that we muster our weapons to secure oil, not food. There's a little joke in this. Ever since we ran out of arable land, food is oil. Every single calorie we eat is backed by at least a calorie of oil, more like ten. In 1940 the average farm in the United States produced 2.3 calories of food energy for every calorie of fossil energy it used. By 1974 (the last year in which anyone looked closely at this issue), that ratio was 1:1. And this understates the problem, because at the same time that there is more oil in our food there is less oil in our oil. A couple of generations ago we spent a lot less energy drilling, pumping, and distributing than we do now. In the 1940s we got about 100 barrels of oil back for every barrel of oil we spent getting it. Today each barrel invested in the process returns only ten, a calculation that no doubt fails to include the fuel burned by the Hummers and Blackhawks we use to maintain access to the oil in Iraq ».*

Industrial society itself is a product of petroleum — not because it produces energy (almost anything can do that), but because of its high ERoEI. As that continues to drop, we will find ourselves in the same position as the British and French did when they took up coal — in need of some other, inferior source of energy. The prospects for that are grim, to say the least. Most of the most promising "alternative fuels" suffer from some debilitating drawback. For instance, the energy that goes into producing a single photovoltaic cell drops its ERoEI to an estimated 1. Hydrogen cells are energy *carriers*, not energy sources. And Brazil's experiment with widespread biodiesel yielded very ambivalent results.

The image above comes from Stuart Staniford's 6 September 2005 entry at the Oil Drum explaining the thresholds between contraction and collapse, titled, "4%, 11%, Who the Hell Cares?" He writes:

I define the collapse threshold to be the depletion rate at which society collectively loses enough faith in the future that they are no longer willing to risk investments to preserve that future. This appears to be one of the fundamental characteristics in past societies that collapsed. The Easter Islanders gave up their intensive rock gardens, the Chaco Canyon people stopped building new Great Houses, the Mayans even stopped keeping track of their Long Calendar....

In our case, consider a potential investor in a company that is raising capital to open a lead mine to make batteries for anticipated future demand for plug-in hybrids. Let's say it takes five years to get the thing producing, and then the initial capital will take five more years to repay before it starts to really make money. So this investor has to believe society will hold together well enough over that time for his investment to really be worth it. Otherwise he's investing in gold instead (or vodka!).

Obviously, if our hypothetical investors do not feel enough confidence to make this investment, now society is in real trouble — the batteries needed to power the plugin hybrids are not going to be there when they are needed. And so on, across a thousand similar decisions across the economy.

Not only that, but the point at which wealthy investors are giving up hope about the future is also probably similar to the point at which the rest of society gives up hope too, and starts looking for alternative ways to survive. One of the leading effects of that is likely to be a loss of law-and-order. Things go downhill very rapidly from there as we have seen in the last week in New Orleans. We also know conflict was a major factor in the decline of Easter Island, Rome, and the Chaco Canyon Anasazi. Human beings can turn into bands of looters, and even cannibals (as at Chaco Canyon), with amazing speed once they lose faith in society.

Collapse occurs when the returns on complexity are no longer sufficient to warrant further investment — and that is precisely the problem that Peak Oil may very well pose.

There is much debate over when peak oil will occur. Many of the vested interests — including large American oil companies and Middle East monarchies — have a long record of deception with regard to their official numbers. Earlier estimates gave us another ten or more years to figure out what to do, but those estimates proved to be based on the over-reported reserves of Shell and Saudi Arabia. An increasing number of experts are suggesting that we may be at peak *right now*. This year's hurricane season may have caused a sufficient "bump" in production that we are now seeing the highest numbers we ever will. Saudi Arabia, the world's second largest supplier of oil (behind Russia), has been exporting crude oil that is increasingly heavy and more sour, to the point where they have experienced problems finding a buyer for it. Rumors persist that the Ghawar Superfield, the centerpiece of Saudi oil, has peaked. Princeton geology professor emeritus Ken Deffeyes even went so far as to predict a specific date for Hubbert's Peak: 24 November 2005, Thanksgiving in the U.S. According to Jeff Vail, Assistant Secretary of the Interior Tom Weimer, in charge of USGS, did not think that a fall 2005 date for Hubbert's Peak was an unreasonable estimate.

I said above that the North American Hubbert's Peak was the most significant event of the post-war period. The complexity of any culture is a function of energy, and it's energy that has always created the shape of history. Romans very explicitly fought for new farmland, for instance. The petroleum age has merely coalesced all of our needs into a single, needful resources. When our own supply of it began to run out in the 1970s, the famed "energy crisis" ensued, resulting in the widespread "hopelessness" and economic recession associated with that decade. The United States needed new sources of oil, and so developed the "twin pillar policy," to rely on Iran and Saudi Arabia. When Iran moved to nationalize its oil industry, the CIA assassinated the democratically-elected Mossadeq and backed the Shah — events that ultimately led to the Islamic Revolution in 1979, and a surging sentiment throughout the Mddle East that freedom from European powers and their meddling could be won through radical Islam. At the same time, the "twin pillar policy" collapsed, and the United States became dependent on Saudi Arabia.

That dependence has forced the United States to back many unsavory dictators and tyrants, or else allow economic recession. That U.S.-backed despotism led to many myriad resistance movements against our heinous allies, including the Ba'athists in Iraq and Syria, Mubarak in Egypt, Turkey, Algeria, and others. The goal of al-Qa'ida is to unite the local resistance movements into a pan-Arabic revolution with a short-term goal of destroying the countries that now dominate the region (being the legacies of arbitrary colonial divisions, and ruled by ruthless, Western-backed dictators), and a long-term goal of replacing them with a single caliphate. Al-Qa'ida focuses its ire on the United States because it is the common enemy of all of these local resistance movements, though in each case only a secondary one.

Al-Qa'ida's "rallying cry" to the Islamic world was sounded on 11 September 2001, and immediately appreciated as *carte blanche* by a far-sighted, visionary but ultimately ruthless group in American politics, the so-called "neoconservatives." Disciples of Leo Strauss, their political philosophy unites a Hobbesian worldview with avowedly Machiavellian pragmatism. With Saudi Arabia's reserves nearing their peak, these "neocons" saw an opportunity in 9/11 to sieze the resources the United States requires *before* we reach crisis levels, and prepared an invasion against our erstwhile ally, Saddam Hussein. The current war in Iraq, like every war in history, is about resources — in this case, the only resource that still matters: oil. The neoconservatives should be congratulated for their far-sighted preparations, if not for their ruthless lack of morality. Such is the cost of an industrialized civilization. As such, the invasion of Iraq may be seen as the first of the "oil wars" that so many have predicted to break out in the shadow of Hubbert's Peak.

Certainly we have seen a certain upsurge of violence to control petroleum reserves. In late September 2005, the Niger Delta People's Volunteer Force held Nigeria's oil production "hostage", taking over 10 oil flow stations and offering to return them only upon the release of their leader, Dokubo-Aasari.

Recently, Congress held sessions to "hold oil companies accountable" for record-high oil prices during the disasters of the 2005 Atlantic hurricane season. With record-high oil prices came record-high profits for oil companies, and the mainstream media worked to generate outrage for the oil companies who appeared to profit so much from the suffering of Katrina. Of course, the reality of the situation was the amoral grinding of capitalism's gears in the shadow of Hubbert's Peak. With peak production comes peak refinement demand — choking supply at the refining level. Oil companies sell to one another freely at every level; every oil company sells to every oil companies' refineries, including their own and their competitors'. The same occurs at the distributor and retail levels. A BP retailer is under no obligation to buy his oil from a BP distributor. The result is that oil prices are very much set by supply and demand, foiling any attempt an oil company might make to artificially raise or lower its prices. An industry insider and Oil Drum reader commented:

ExxonMobil, owning their own up and down stream divisions, could sell at a loss or reduced profit on the retail end, provided they compensated their convenience store owners for their lost gasoline revenues (these stores are franchises). But that would make whatever cut they did offer twice as financially painful — they would take the announced cut and associated reduction in profit, and then have to pay the store owners their traditional profit to keep them happy.

So you are not asking them to just fall on their own sword, but to get back up and hurl their bloodied body on it again...ouch!

So — if ExxonMobil did do this, it would be a huge gesture! But only those in the same business would understand the magnitude of what they had done. And whoever did it would shortly be replaced by the Board of Directors as the principal shareholders all called for his head on a pike! Remember, outside of the energy sector, the stock market is a total losing proposition.

While the world fights for the last few drops of good oil, though, the larger question seems to go unaddressed. Peak Oil is not such a unique problem. In fact, we have repeatedly faced the essential crisis with successive fuels throughout the history of civilization. In each previous iteration, we were saved by an alternative which, while initially considered inferior, proved to

156

have just as high an ERoEI — or, often, higher — as the fuel it replaced. Peak Oil has a strong possibility of bringing down civilization itself as a proximate cause of collapse, but it is by no means certain. This crisis has been averted in the past, and we might avert this one, as well. But with low research budgets and little interest in alternative fuels, that hope is becoming increasingly dim. In all previous iterations, there was, at this point, already a clear alternative in play. We have no such clear alternative. The closest we have to such an alternative is nuclear power, which will give us, at most, another 50 years. Nuclear power uses very little uranium, but there is very little uranium in the world.

Peak Oil does not ensure collapse, just as the timber crisis England and France faced did not ensure their collapse. That said, we should be deeply concerned, because where they had coal, we have nothing. In all previous cases, the alternative that prevailed was already known and widely available *before* the situation reached crisis levels. Not only do we not have that, but very little has been put into research and development efforts to develop such alternatives. Overwhelming resources will be needed, too. Not only is our need for an alternative no guarantee that it exists, but, as we have previously seen, we have already passed the point of diminishing returns for invention. So we see once again that the immediate problems posed (in this case, Peak Oil) are not so critical in and of themselves, but because of the larger context of complexity's diminishing returns, becomes unsolvable.

Cornucopians discount the threat Peak Oil represents by insisting that the market will adapt. Of course, they are correct, but they suffer a failure of imagination to consider what the market's adaptations might include. Genocidal warfare is a very efficient way to reduce demand, for example. As Tainter highlighted in *Collapse of Complex Societies*, collapse is an economizing process.

Many civilizations of the past have collapsed for precisely this diminishing return curve that Hubbert's Peak embodies. It was "peak wood" that ended Cahokia and the Hohokam, and brought on the Dark Ages that followed the Bronze Age. Obviously, Peak Oil has the potential to end our civilization, but it is by no means assured. Were it the only such crisis we faced, it might even be solvable. But with the peak likely already upon us, the time for coming up with a solution may already be passed. Solutions take time to implement, especially across an entire civilization, and the downside of the curve is always faster than going up. As Jared Diamond wrote in "The Ends of the World as We Know Them," "History warns us that when once-powerful societies collapse, they tend to do so quickly and unexpectedly. That shouldn't come as much of a surprise: peak power usually means peak population, peak needs, and hence peak vulnerability."

Thesis #19: Complexity ensures collapse.

Predicting the proximate cause of collapse is impossible, though, as we have seen, both environmental problems and peak oil present serious threats — precisely the kind of threat that has toppled civilizations in the past. On their own, however, such proximate causes are probabilistic. Peak oil may mean the end of civilization; or, perhaps we will be able to transition to some alternative. Environmental problems may destroy the most basic necessities of civilized life, or perhaps we will solve them, instead. What makes collapse a certainty, rather than a probability, is, ironically, the very thing that *defines* civilization in the first place: *complexity.*

Graph theory is ultimately the mathematics of relationships. Here, a graph means a set of nodes and the edges (lines) that connect those nodes to one another. Such a graph can represent nearly anything. A graph of air travel has nodes of airports, and edges of routes. A graph of the internet has nodes of webpages, and edges of hyperlinks. A graph of the electrical grid has nodes of power stations, and edges of power lines. A graph of social power has nodes of people, and edges of power relationships. Graphs can be directed, where edges are all one-way, or bidirectional.

Take, as an example, our power grid. It is, as mentioned above, a graph. We can define the nodes as the power stations, and the recipients who need power. The edges, then, are power lines. There are obviously a great many nodes here, and a great many edges. But buildng a new edge is expensive, and redundancy is only useful when something goes wrong. By taking the resources that might be used to create more redundancy and instead creating new edges, any power company can increase the number of nodes connected by its edges for the same cost. The problem, though, is that the resulting graph is complex, and *fragile.* Removing a single edge can disconnect a huge sub-graph from the rest of the graph — and in the case of a power grid, that can mean an enormous blackout.

That's what happened on 14 August 2003, when insuffecent tree trimming in a Columbus, OH caused a single power line's capacity to wear. That caused a power surge throughout the power grid, and the largest electrical blackout in North American history. One-seventh of the United States' population, and one-third of Canada's, went without power. The economic toll was estimated at $6 billion. All for an untrimmed tree in Ohio.

Increasing complexity without increasing redundancy means an escalating probability of disaster for the whole network. We can look at the power grid as such a graph, or we can broaden our scope and see all of civilization as such a graph. We now see a global economy, with currencies pegged to the American dollar or the Euro, and interdependent stock markets. Hospitals and security rely on power grids that themselves rely on a complex network of commodities and components some of which, while crucial, yet have no redundancy. Were any natural or political disaster to befall Taiwan, for example, the "Information Age" would come grinding to a halt, with 80%of the world's mainboards and graphics chips, 70% of the notebooks, and 65% of the microchips suddenly disappearing from the table.

The solution to such vulnerabilities, of course, is simple: create redundancy. That is the only solution to such a conundrum, but it is a solution civilization is incapable of implementing.

As we have already seen, civilization must always grow (thesis #12 and thesis #13). That kind of competition creates an environment where building redundancy is impossible. An entity that spends its resources building in redundancy to guard against possible future vulnerabilities is not using those resources to grow. A competitor that chooses to grow is more vulnerable, but has significant short-term advantages that will allow it to out-compete its more forward-thinking competitor, and makes all her planning for the future a moot point. Running two power stations, or twice as many power lines, makes a power grid more robust, but it also makes it more expensive to maintain. Another grid with less redundancy costs much less to maintain, and so will out-compete the other — at least, until something goes wrong. On a long enough timeline, something *always* goes wrong.

While some part of the globe remains unincorporated into that graph, there is room to grow. However, once that room is consumed, room for growth can only be bought at another entity's expense — meaning that the overall graph is incapable of any further growth. In the case of civilization, that means that the process of collapse begins. As Jeff Vail writes in "Rhizome, Communication, and Our 'One-Time Shot'":

« *In the past, such peer-polity resource races led to periodic regional collapse. Today such a collapse is not possible — with the 'Closing of the Map' it is no longer possible for one region of the world to collapse while progress, technology, and "civilization" are maintained in another location, much like epidemic diseases. Instead, our global civilization simply swallows up non-performers or attempts at regional collapse and immediately reintegrates them into the global system. ... In today's world, without the ability for regional collapse and reconstitution, the entire world functions as an integrated system. We have had a remarkable run of development, fueled by the twin processes of improving energy subsidy (coal, nuclear, oil, petroleum based fertilizer, etc.) and globalization (always newer and cheaper labor pools, newer and cheaper resource sources). But this will soon come to an end. The fundamental reality of the finite nature of resources upon which we depend (fossil fuels, uranium, metals), combined with the accelerating depletion of renewable resources which without regional collapse can no longer recover (forests, topsoil, clean water) is leading down the road to an inevitable global collapse. »*

Thus, we find ourselves hemmed in by the very complexity that has so often solved our problems in the past. The diminishing returns of complexity make it increasingly difficult to use complexity to solve our future problems, even as our complex society finishes its 10,000 year march to complete domination of the earth, and we find that the result is more fragile than anything we could have foreseen, and disastrous because it has finally succeeded in eliminating all those alternatives it had once relied on when it had previously failed. The result is a fine, gossamer web of a culture that is doomed to fall apart in the slightest breeze — wherever that breeze may come from.

Thesis #20: Collapse is an economizing process.

Many will no doubt find the long foregoing discussion of collapse depressing or pessimistic. In "How Civilizations Fall: A Theory of Catabolic Collapse" John Michael Greer hints at why this is, writing, "Even within the social sciences, the process by which complex societies give way to smaller and simpler ones has often been presented in language drawn from literary tragedy, as though the loss of sociocultural complexity necessarily warranted a negative value judgment. This is understandable, since the collapse of civilizations often involves catastrophic human mortality and the loss of priceless cultural treasures, but like any value judgment it can obscure important features of the matter at hand." Greer goes on to characterize collapse in terms of ecological succession. In *The Collapse of Complex Societies*, Joseph Tainter makes a distinct point that collapse "is an economizing process."

The notion that collapse is a catastrophe is rampant, not only among the public, but also throughout the scholarly professions that study it. Archaeology is as clearly implicated in this as is any other field. As a profession we have tended disproportionately to investigate urban and administrative centers, where the richest archaeological remains are commonly found. When with collapse these centers are abandoned or reduced in scale, their loss is catastrophic for our data base, our museum collections, even for our ability to secure financial backing. (Dark ages are rarely as attractive to philanthropists or funding institutions.) Archaeologists, though, are not solely at fault. Classicists and historians who rely on literary sources are also biased against the dark ages, for in such times their data bases largely disappear.

...

Complex societies, it must be emphasized again, are recent in human history. Collapse then is not a fall to some primordial chaos, but a return to the normal human condition of lower complexity. The notion that collapse is uniformly a catastrophe is contradicted, moreover, by the present theory. To the extent that collapse is due to declining marginal returns on investment in complexity, it is an *economizing* process. It occurs when it becomes necessary to restore the marginal return on organizational investment to a more favorable level. To a population that is receiving little return on the cost of supporting complexity, the loss of that complexity brings economic, and perhaps administrative, gains.

In other words, collapse happens precisely because it improves our lives — and it happens when the alternative is no longer tolerable. The process of catabolic collapse becomes self-reinforcing, as individuals decide that further complexity is not a worthwhile investment and refuse to make further investments, which makes the prospect even less attractive to other individuals. In the same manner as a "run" on a given company's stock, the process of catabolic collapse snowballs quickly, until support for a complex society drops so low that that society can no longer be maintained. A "freefall" of lowering complexity follows, until it reaches a level where the marginal returns for it have become favorable again, and people are willing to invest in it again. In "The Old Cause," Joseph Stromberg illustrates this process with the example of the Roman Empire:

« Collapse loomed, but collapse had definite advantages, as shown by its aftermath. The Germanic kings who replaced the empire in the west were better at defending their (smaller) territories against invaders and could do so more cheaply than the overextended empire. In North Africa, the Vandals (victims of a bad press) lowered taxes and economic well-being grew, until Justinian brought back Roman rule and, with it, imperial taxes. "Investment" in this lower level of political "complexity" paid for itself, so to speak, by being less costly. Collapse is not all bad: a disaster for the state apparatus may not be one for people as a whole. Devolution of power to smaller geographical units is "a rational, economizing process that may well benefit much of the population." »

In another light, the essential crisis of civilization is a problem of scale. There are inherent problems to creating any society of humans of the size and scope that civilization requires. When a cell in your body becomes too large, it becomes more difficult for nutrients to reach the nucleus from the outer wall. Civilizations that grow too large face similar problems of scale; they become too large to administer, and face increasing problems with a diminished ability to answer those problems. In the face of such pressures, they fission into smaller entities that are easier to maintain.

Humans are adapted to a band-level society (*see* thesis #7), and have a very difficult time operating in any unit of society with much more than 150 persons. To accomodate such a maladapted scenario, drastic measures must be taken. These measures make an ill fit to the human animal, and it is precisely this adaptation that leads to all those social ills which we find endemic to civilization, but startlingly absent, or at the very least in a much diminished form, among band-level, foraging societies, such as war, poverty, corruption, chronic stress and even hunger and disease. These are the penalties a large-scale society pays for force-fitting humans into a society larger than they are adapted to. These penalties may be outweighed for a time by the high marginal returns of complexity, but when those marginal returns diminish, civilizations collapse.

In such a collapse, the complexity that allows for such large-scale societies crumbles first, meaning that for a time, there is still a large-scale society and all the problems of scale that accompany it, but without the benefits that complexity offers. During these periods, all those social ills mentioned above — war, poverty, disease, hunger, etc. — spike remarkably. Those ills also serve to reduce that large population by catastrophic means. Though it is a terrible, brutal process, it is so far the only one that has reliably allowed humans to escape the positive feedback loop of ever-increasing complexity, and reap the benefits humans gain from living in the kind of small-scale, band-level societies to which they are best adapted.

Because our civilization has now succeeded in spanning the whole earth with a fragile network of interdependence, no one element can collapse independently, even though much of the world has "collapsed" in the past century. Rwanda, Haiti, the former republics of the Soviet Union and much of the Third World shows what happens when part of a complex system needs to collapse, but remains artificially propped to a higher level of complexity by neighboring concentrations. This trend of localized collapses has even begun to intrude into these concentrations themselves. The destruction of New Orleans by Hurricane Katrina in 2005 was an example of a localized collapse inside the United States itself.

Collapse has already begun, and progressed quite far without our notice. Rumblings of awareness have become increasingly ambient in the popular imaginaton in recent years, though full acceptance of the situation remains rare. The current level of complexity cannot be maintained, and individual regions cannot collapse on their own — they must collapse *as a system*. Whether the final blow is dealt by environmental problems, health issues, or the inability of diminishing resources to fuel our continued growth, the fragile interconnectedness of our globalized, industrial civilization will eventually propogate a catastrophic, catabolic collapse that will cascade through the entire system, feeding on itself until we have reached the next lowest level of sustainable complexity: the Stone Age.

There were great fluctuations of complexity throughout the Stone Age. Throughout most of human existence, social complexity was at its most basic. The Upper Paleolithic Revolution introduced art, music, philosophy, religion, science, medicine, mathematics and all those other things that we value as defining our humanity. These are all at least four times older than civilization, and universal to the entire human race, whether civilized or not. Human societies found a new dynamic equilibrium about a new, higher level of complexity that was sustainable and allowed humans to prosper for 30,000 years.

It was only 10,000 years ago that another jump in complexity was made with the Neolithic Revolution, and the twin innovations of agriculture and hierarchy (*see* thesis #10). This one proved distinctly unsustainable, and touched off a positive feedback loop of ever more complexity (*see* thesis #13), leading inevitably to collapse (*see* thesis #14). Thus, the global collapse of such a system is its inevitable destiny. That destiny has been averted at various times in the past, but each aversion has merely postponed that collapse — and, in postponing it, intensified it, by allowing for even more complexity that must be collapsed, a smaller surviving resource base to fall back on, and a larger population dependent on that complexity.

At the same time, while the *sustainable* complexity of the Upper Paleolithic Revolution gave us many of those things we value most about our species, the only innovations unique to the *unsustainable* complexity of the Neolithic Revolution have been the unnecessary evil of hierarchy (*see* thesis #11), the difficult, dangerous and unhealthy life of the agriculturalist (*see* thesis #9), and the dehumanizing denial of the open, egalitarian tribal life to which humans are adapted (*see* thesis #7).

Collapse ends those things that define complex society — hierarchical oppression, war, disease, toil and others. It restores society to the lower level of complexity to which humans are best adapted, a level which still enjoys art, medicine, science, mathematics, and technology. It is no idyllic utopia, but it is a life to which humans are naturally adapted. We are not descended from "noble savages"; what nobility there is in savagery is simply the product of humans living in a manner to which they are adapted, rather than a dehumanizing system that denies and hems in human nature. It is, in the words of Marshall Sahlins, "the original affluent society."

The transition, however, will be the greatest ordeal that any species has ever endured. Industrial society currently supports a population of some 6.5

billion humans. The Stone Age can only support a human population measured in millions. The loss of the complexity on which so many people depend for survival can only mean catastrophic die-off. Genocide, war, disease, starvation and widespread suffering will be involved. Essentially, complexity has allowed us to overshoot our sustainable carrying capacity, and that will have to be addressed — catastrophically, if need be.

Unfortunately, it will almost certainly need to be. The alternative to catastrophic increases in mortality would be an unprecedented memetic feat. As we have already seen, the escalating complexity of civilization is a game of prisoner's dilemna, and thus, a tragedy of the commons. Appeals to conscience, or to any kind of reformed, ecological "vision" are ultimately self-defeating in such a context. Incredible shifts of a population's ideology have occured in the past — but always in the context of catastrophe. When the Hohokam and Anasazi collapsed, those that survived did so by adopting a new vision of the world and living in a manner that was independent of complexity. They became the Pueblo Indians, one of many Native American groups so often mythologized for ther sustainable, ecologically wise way of life. To the extent that such a characterization is true, it is the product of collapse, and it arose because the alternative was their own destruction.

The collapse of our globalized, industrial civilization will be most similar to the collapse of the ancient Pueblo peoples. Like them, we have left little behind us to rebuild a civilization out of, precluding the possibility of a new civilization in its place, or simply a lower level of agrarian life. Also like them, an alternative already exists: namely, to adopt a new vision of the world now, to divorce ourselves from complexity, to form band societies in the midst of civilization, and to end our dependence on it so that when it collapses, we do not need it.

Collapse will mean the death of billions, and in aggregate, there is nothing that can save the mass of humanity. But, to quote one of the twentieth century's most cold-blooded murderers: "One death is a tragedy. A million deaths is a statistic." As we have previously discussed, the human brain is incapable of understanding more than 150 full persons. We aspire to a philanthropic love of the whole human race, but ultimately such concerns become little more than posturing. Worse, our pretenses have often motivated our worst atrocities. While the Chinese remained in haughty dismissal, Christians enslaved whole continents to bring heathens the « redemption » of Jesus Christ — and shatter their sustainable, affluent societies in the process. In Nazi ideology, the extermination of "inferior races" was a project undertaken for the good of all mankind. "Tribalism," though, in its usual, pejorative sense — looking solely to you and yours — preserved human tribes for millennia sustainably, in a "peace" that was, if not absolute, at least sufficient to leave no archaeological hint of *mass* violence before the Neolithic. It is difficult to consider our own morals in such an analytical light, but philanthropy has caused great suffering, and "tribalism" was a vital component of the only true balance our species has ever known. Finally, as guilty as it seems, we must all confess that the fate of an abstract "humanity" does not truly interest us in the least. We are concerned with our own fate, and the fate of our family, our friends, and those close to us – *our own tribe*. We may not be able to do anything for the abstract, anonymous hordes of "humanity," but the fate of those we *truly* care about is entirely in our own hands.

Though collapse will be the most terrible ordeal ever endured and billions will die in its course, any given individual can still decide his fate. There is a choice in it, even for those who do not understand that choice. Nearly all of humanity will choose to stay true to their culture to the very end, just as they have in all previous collapses. Some, though, will choose to create a new society, to embrace a new vision of who they are, what humanity is, what the world is, and how they all relate. Like the ancestors of the Pueblo Indians, some will choose to live sustainably.

Such a future may be less complex, but it will have *more* diversity. Michael Green's *Afterculture* is an inspiring collection of art that explores some of the limitless syncretic possibilities that are far more plausible than the dystopian "Mad Max" scenarios of post-apocalyptic fiction. Green waxes poetic about his project:

« *The truth is that for the first time we are bereft of a positive vision of where we are going. This is particularly evident among kids. Their future is either* Road Warrior *post-apocalypse, or* Blade Runner *mid-apocalypse. All the futuristic computer games are elaborations of these scenarios, heavy metal worlds where civilization has crumbling into something weird and violent (but more exciting than now)* ».

The *Afterculture* is an attempt to transmute this folklore of the future into something deep and rich and convincingly real. If we are to pull a compelling future out of environmental theory and recycling paradigms, we are going to have to clothe the sacred in the romantic. The *Afterculture* is part of an ongoing work to shape a new mythology by sources as diverse as Thoreau and Conan and *Dances with Wolves* and Iron John. The *Afterculture* is not "against" the problems of our times, and its not about "band-aid solutions" to the grim jam we find ourselves in. It's about opening up a whole new category of solutions, about finding another way of being: evolved, simpler, deeper, even more elegant. Even more cool. Even very cool.

Our way of life is unsustainable, and it will not go on much longer. Willingly or otherwise, it will soon end; the only question is whether or not we will be ready and able to survive without it. The greatest crisis in the history of the human race looms before us, but that also means that the greatest opportunity in the history of the human race will also soon be opened. In sum, I must agree wholeheartedly with Steven Lagavulin, who concluded "The Future is a Free-For-All" with this:

« But the one thing we should not be doing is just sitting on our hands. Because if the future is a free-for-all, then that means there is great opportunity to be seized as all the old rules, the ingrained habits, the institutionalized systems and the hard-fought hierarchies get shaken up and "redistributed" a little bit, and the playing field is levelled. I'm not saying this will happen completely or that it will happen overnight, but when our system collapses there will be as much creative energy released as there is destructive. It will be a time for gaining new things even as we're being stripped of the old, a time for us to experience expansive new freedom as well as a desperate clinging for control. It will be a time of soul-searching and of blame-casting, of unanswered questions and unquestioned answers. But when all is said and done, we will no doubt look back on the events that are still to come with a bittersweet fondness, the way we do all our growing pains. Thankful that they're over, but even more thankful that we had them. »

Thesis #21: Civilization makes us sick.

The Paleolithic was not an era of perfect health. The Neanderthals, for instance, show signs of trauma consistent with those of rodeo cowboys — suggesting a certain rough and tumble life with big game. They were certainly a few diseases in circulation, and of course things happened. However, the claim so often made by progressivists that civilization has made us healthier could not be more incorrect. Civilization has most definitely made us much *less* healthy, and in innumerable ways.

The first has been the introduction of the epidemic disease. Epidemiologists typically divide diseases into one of two broad categories: endemic and epidemic. Endemic diseases are always circulating in a population. Most members of the population have some immunity to it. Endemic diseases can be serious, but for the most part, they are accepted as a simple fact of life, as the population grows used to them. Chicken pox is endemic to most First World populations, for example. Formally, an endemic is an infection that can be maintained in a population without external inputs. Mathematically, an endemic is a steady state, $R0 \ x \ S = 1$, where every single individual who is infected passes the infection on to exactly one other person. If the rate of contagion is less than that, the infection will simply die out. If it is more, it will become an epidemic.

Epidemics are another thing altogether. Epidemics are new to a population, and so burn through it without meeting any immune response whatsoever. Epidemics burn themselves out quickly, but leave much mortality and suffering in their wake. Eventually, some will begin to develop an immune response, and eventually the epidemic will kill or infect everyone it can — leaving only the immune alive (with the exception of some minority protected by the "herd effect," who cannot be infected because they're surrounded by people who are immune). The Plague which ravaged Europe several times over was an epidemic; each iteration was slightly less devastating than the last, as each left a larger segment of the population with immunity. When an epidemic infects the worldwide population of a species, it is a *pandemic*.

The epidemic disease is something new, a gift of civilization. Most epidemics are zoonotic — they come from animals. That is how we become exposed to so many unfamiliar pathogens, because once a pathogen mutates sufficiently to jump the species barrier, what was endemic to our domesticates is epidemic to us. Chicken pox, easles, smallpox, influenza, diphtheria, HIV, Marburg virus, anthrax, bubonic plague, rabies, the common cold, and tuberculosis all came from animal domestication. If epidemic diseases did arise in the Paleolithic, they were short-lived: hunter-gatherer bands were too small, and had contact with one another too infrequently to allow an epidemic to spread. It may have wiped out the whole band, but it would die out there. Domestication brought humans into sufficiently close contact with other animal species to allow their germs to adapt to our bodies, created concentrated populations where diseases could incubate, and even provided long-range trade to export those germs, once fully developed, to other concentrated populations. In *Guns, Germs & Steel*, Jared Diamond points to these titular germs as one of the main reasons that civilization was able to destroy all other societies. By the time the conquistadors had set into the New World, smallpox had already wiped out 99% of the native population.

Civilization did not only introduce us to disease as we know it, though. It also introduced a novel way of life that was completely at odds with the evolutionary expectations of the human body. Humans remain Pleistocene animals; the short 10,000 years since the end of the last ice age has been meager time to adapt ourselves to such a radically different way of life. One factor that aided the spread of such disease was the rampant malnutrition that accompanied the Neolithic. Where foragers rely on a vast diversity of life that is nearly impossible to eliminate, and thus almost never starve, agriculture introduced the concept of "famine" to humanity be relying completely and utterly on a small number of closely related species. Starvation in the Neolithic was rather the norm. In "The Worst Mistake in the History of the Human Race," Jared Diamond wrote:

« *One straight forward example of what paleopathologists have learned from skeletons concerns historical changes in height. Skeletons from Greece and Turkey show that the average height of hunger-gatherers toward the end of the ice ages was a generous 5'9" for men, 5'5" for women. With the adoption of agriculture, height crashed, and by 3000 B. C. had reached a low of only 5'3" for men, 5' for women. By classical times heights were very slowly on the rise again, but modern Greeks and Turks have still not regained the average height of their distant ancestors.* »

Another example of paleopathology at work is the study of Indian skeletons from burial mounds in the Illinois and Ohio river valleys. At Dickson Mounds, located near the confluence of the Spoon and Illinois rivers, archaeologists have excavated some 800 skeletons that paint a picture of the health changes that occurred when a hunter-gatherer culture gave way to intensive maize farming around A. D. 1150. Studies by George Armelagos and his colleagues then at the University of Massachusetts show these early farmers paid a price for their new-found livelihood. Compared to the hunter-gatherers who preceded them, the farmers had a nearly 50 per cent increase in enamel defects indicative of malnutrition, a fourfold increase in iron-deficiency anemia (evidenced by a bone condition called porotic hyperostosis), a theefold rise in bone lesions reflecting infectious disease in general, and an increase in degenerative conditions of the spine, probably reflecting a lot of hard physical labor. "Life expectancy at birth in the pre-agricultural community was bout twenty-six years," says Armelagos, "but in the post-agricultural community it was nineteen years. So these episodes of nutritional stress and infectious disease were seriously affecting their ability to survive."

Over the course of millennia, we have gradually recovered from the enormous mortality of the Neolithic, to the point where most First Worlders now enjoy a quality of life just shy of our Mesolithic ancestors. That doesn't mean our current diet is healthy, only that it is plentiful enough to keep us alive. Boyd Eaton called it "affluent malnutrition" — we eat a great deal of food, but what we eat is horribly maladapted to the human body. Affluent malnutrition is so lacking in basic micronutrients that many of us require vitamin supplements. Other criteria of affluent malnutrition include:

- Highly processed foods that are deficient in important vitamins and minerals
- Synthetic food compounds
- High in refined sugars
- High in saturated fat
- Deficient in fibre
- Mega-size portions
- High in calories

The human body evolved to expect a diet primarily of animals. Fat provided most of the body's energy, and protein provided the necessary materials for the large human brain. Wild edibles provided vitamins and minerals in abundance. A single cup of crushed dandelion leaves contains more vitamin C than 2 glasses of orange juice.

Instead, some 99% of the world's current diet is supplied by either wheat, rice or corn. Ben Balzer's "*Introduction to the Paleo Diet*" outlines the main problems with these cereal grains and their adaptation to the human body:

« *Consider our friend, the apple. When an animal eats an apple, it profits by getting a meal. It swallows the seeds and then deposits them in a pile of dung. With some luck a new apple tree might grow, and so the apple tree has also profited from the arrangement. In nature as in finance, it is good business when both parties make profit happily. Consider what would happen if the animal were greedy and decided to eat the few extra calories contained within the apple seeds — then there would be no new apple tree to continue on the good work. So, to stop this from happening, the apple seeds contain toxins that have multiple effects:*

1. *Firstly, they taste bad — discouraging the animal from chewing them*
2. *Secondly some toxins are enzyme blockers that bind up predators digestive enzymes — these also act as "preservatives" freezing the apple seed enzymes until sprouting — upon sprouting of the seed, many of these enzyme blockers disappear.*
3. *Thirdly, they contain lectins — these are toxic proteins which have numerous effects. They act as natural pesticides and are also toxic to a range of other species including bacteria, insects, worms, rodents and other predators including humans.*

Of course, the apple has other defenses — to start with it is high above the ground well out of reach of casual predators, and it also has the skin and flesh of the apple to be penetrated first. Above all though is the need to stop the seed from being eaten, so that new apple trees may grow.

Now, please consider the humble grain. Once again as a seed its duty is mission critical- it must perpetuate the life cycle of the plant. It is however much closer to the ground, on the tip of a grass stalk. It is within easy reach of any predator strolling by. It contains a good source of energy, like a booster rocket for the new plant as it grows. The grain is full of energy and in a vulnerable position. It was "expensive" for the plant to produce. It is an attractive meal. Its shell offers little protection. Therefore, it has been loaded with toxic proteins to discourage predators- grains are full of enzyme blockers and lectins. You may be surprised to learn that uncooked flour is very toxic... »

Once again, it is a simple matter of adaptation. In fact, some varities of anthropoid *have* adapted to eating grain in the past, such as *Paranthropus bosei*; however, that is a variety that is unrelated to us. We are descended from the *Australopithecus* branch, which focused on scavenging while *Paranthropus* focused on grain, and died out. Humans lack the necessary enzymes to digest these cereal grains properly, the way birds do. Instead, they lead to a host of health problems — including, possibly, cancer.

Lectins — found in cereals, potatoes, and beans — have effects throughout the body as widespread and significant as our own hormones, but originating from outside our bodies, they react with our physiology in ways that are often quite harmful. They can strip off protective mucous tissues, damage the small intestine, form blood clots, make cells react as if stimulated by a random hormone, stimulate cells to *secrete* random hormones, make cells divide at improper times, cause lymphatic tissues to grow or shrink, enlarge the pancreas, or even induce apoptosis. In an editorial for the *British Medical Journal* titled "Do dietary lectins cause disease?" David L. J. Freed answers the question affirmatively, writing:

« *Until recently their main use was as histology and blood transfusion reagents, but in the past two decades we have realised that many lectins are (a) toxic, inflammatory, or both; (b) resistant to cooking and digestive enzymes; and (c) present in much of our food. It is thus no surprise that they sometimes cause "food poisoning." But the really disturbing finding came with the discovery in 1989 that some food lectins get past the gut wall and deposit themselves in distant organs.* »

The question of whether or not the lectins in grain causes cancer is still open, but there is certanly a good deal to suggest it. Lectins are well-known to cause cancer-like reactions in colon cells in a test tube. Franceschi, et.al; "Intake of macronutrients and risk of breast cancer" (Lancet 1996;347(9012):1351–6) showed that while risk of breast cancer went down with total fat intake, it rose with carbohydrate intake, but the original study on a correlative "cause" of cancer remains the most compelling: Stanislaw Tanchou's 1843 study that found a nearly perfect correlation between cancer in major European cities, and grain consumption. Tanchou predcted that no forager would ever be found with cancer, initiating a frenzied search to find the counterproof. Though no such forager was ever found, cancer often became commonplace among those same populations once they were settled into an agricultural lifestyle. Between the effects of grain and more recent environmental factors, it seems evident that the natural occurence of cancer among our foraging ancestors must have been negligible. In the modern United States, some 50% of men and 33% of women will suffer from some kind of cancer. Among foragers, we have significant difficulty producing even a single example.

There is also significant and widespread intolerance to grain. Writing of intolerance to the gluten in grain in "Why So Many Intolerant To Gluten?" Luigi Greco writes:

« *Having had over 25 years of variegated experience with gluten intolerance I find hard to imagine that the single most common food intolerance to the single most diffuse staple food in our environment might provoke such a complexity of severe adverse immune-mediated reactions in any part of the human body and function. The list is endless, but malignancies, adverse pregnancy outcome and impaired brain function are indeed complications above the tolerable threshold of this food intolerance.* »

Dairy is also a new and disastrous introduction to the human menu. All mammals lose their ability to produce lactase — the enzyme that breaks down the lactose in milk — when they reach maturity. At about 4000 BCE, a mutation occured in Sweden and the Middle East, allowing those populations to continue producing lactase into maturity. This was a useful adaptation in their societies, with their adoption of herds of domesticated cattle, and so the mutation spread. However, "lactose intolerance" remains the norm across most human populations. The prevalence of this bizarre mutation amongst the socio-politically powerful northern Europeans has led to a strange stuation where the normal state of affairs is referred to as if it were a malady. While humans with this mutation *can* digest milk, it remains something that the human body is ill-equipped for. Cow milk is tailor-suited for calves, just as human milk is suited for human babies — but the requirements of cows differ markedly from humans. Consumption of cow milk has been linked to iron deficiency anemia, allergies, diarrhea, heart disease, colic, cramps, gastrointestinal bleeding, sinusitis, skin rashes, acne, increased frequency of colds and flus, arthritis, diabetes, ear infections, osteoporosis, asthma, autoimmune diseases, and more, possibly even lung cancer, multiple sclerosis and non-Hodgkin's lymphoma.

The "Paleolithic Diet" is often referred to as a "low-carb diet," which it is, and while it retains the weight-reducing properties of the more popular Atkins diet (since your body does not know how to turn protein or fat into body fat, but only carbohydrates), it is far more sustainable and conducive to long-term health than Atkins. Individuals on a Paleolithic Diet report not only dramatic weight loss, but less hunger, more energy, and even greater mental acuity. Even in civilization, taking up only the *diet* of a forager leads to dramatic improvements in health.

The "diseases of civilization" are so well known as to hardly bear repeating. While we work far longer hours than even the most overworked forager, our work is quite different. Affluent First Worlders are too busy working extraordinarily long hours sitting behind desks to exercise, while agrarian societies emphasize back-breaking labor for the torso, back and arms. A cursory examination of the human body's construction shows that it is adapted best to one activity: walking. Whether hunting or gathering, most of a forager's short work day consists simply of walking for hours at a time. The sedentism of First World life has led to a host of maladies.

At the same time, we suffer from the psychosomatic and mental disorders that are the result of such stressful lives. We are primates adapted to small, egalitarian bands, but we find ourselves locked into large-scale, hierarchical societies. Even primates that are adapted to hierarchy show signs of stress when they occupy the lower ranks — and theirs are hierarchies that are not nearly as pyramidal, as if to increase the number of stressed-out unfortunates as much as possible. Our personality and our ability to cope can allow us to survive such a maladaptive situation, but we feel it all the same, particularly with the constant, ever-escalating competitiveness of a civilization that must always grow or die. High stress is endemic to the civilized population. It has become the leading cause of death in the United States. At the same time, while one quarter of U.S. citizens suffer from some form of mental illness, one would be hard-pressed to find any examples of mental illness among foragers.

Indeed, even those maladies which we consider to be merely the onset of old age, such as frailty and senility, are difficult to find among foragers, suggesting that even these may be the result of a maladapted, civilized diet.

Pleistocene humans were not always in perfect health, but the natural state of health for most animals in the wild is far, far superior to that which we find ourselves in. Humans did not evolve to be unique in the animal kingdom for our sickly, malnourished, and weak forms. We evolved to enjoy the same level of health as every other animal, but for 10,000 years, we have lived contrary to human nature, creating a great deal of stress and mental anguish.

We eat foods that are not entirely edible for us as staples, and in ever-increasing quantities to counterbalance their anti-nutritional effects.

Thesis #22: Civilization has no monopoly on medicine.

In the previous thesis, we saw some of the many ways that civilization has been catastrophic for human health: the introduction of epidemic disease, the promotion of a diet utterly divorced from the expectations — or even abilities — of human digestion, and the adoption of a generally unhealthy, maladaptive lifestyle turned civilization into a Pandora's Box of horrors unleashed on the human race. If that is the case, though, then, like Pandora's Box, civilization also offers hope to deal with all of those terrible afflictions, in the form of medicine. Interestingly, the Cherokee tell a similar story, wherein the plants take pity on humans and give them medicine. That in itself gives the lie to the terrible trick played on us; though we have more than paid for it in diseases and generally terrible health, the hope we have thus bought is universal among all human cultures. Every culture has its own ethnomedicine — and though our afflictions are greater, our medicine is not proportionally more powerful.

This is not to say that Western biomedicine is ineffective in the least. The very fact that it is powerful enough to sufficiently balance the disastrous health effects of civilization and not only keep us alive, but even allow us to live nearly as long as the natural human lifespan is a great testimony to it. That said, we have also often over-valued its contribution. In thesis #16, we discussed the great hygenic efforts of the early twentieth century to clean up the cities, and how that medical victory led to the rise of polio. Then, another medical victory was won with the polio vaccine, but there is some evidence to suggest that *that* victory may have created AIDS. No medicine is 100% effective — not even ours. Any doctor can tell you a series of terrible stories of patients they could do nothing for. Our pharmaceuticals, as powerful as they are, still owe most of their effectiveness to the placebo effect. For all the diseases our medicine has cured, they are more often cured by our own bodies — or they simply run their course. For all the strides we have made, Western biomedicine has — and will always have — its limitations.

Some of those limitations are systemic. There is a growing awareness, even among the professional practitioners of Western biomedicine, that the Cartesian duality of mind and body is very misplaced. The brain is an organ like any other, and its operation is as integrally tied to the condition of the body as the operation of the heart or liver. Though many quarters have been resistant to the notion, the natural implication of this contention is that psychological is basically a *biological* phenomenon, like heart rate or the immune response. Given the deep, indivisible interrelationships between all the regions of the brain, and the brain with the body as a whole, it should not be at all surprising that the brain can also have an effect on the condition of the body, just as the body forms the conditon of the brain. That is to say, because Descartes' duality of body and mind is no longer defensible, we should not be surprised that our psychology impacts our physical health — as the objection to such notions has always been a reiteration of such disproven Cartesian duality.

Evolution has not left us without a certain ability to see to our own health, and as any medical student knows, the human body is replete with any number of systems to fight infection and disease, ease symptoms, or simply kill the pain. When the brain expects to be cured, that becomes something of a self-fulfilling prophecy, as the brain activates those systems. This is what we call the placebo effect, and it is probably the single most powerful force in any medicine. The reverse is also true; believing ourselves ill can have observable, negative, physical effects, too. This is called a nocebo effect, but the division is largely arbitrary, based on our perceptions of "good" and "bad"; in both cases, the body's own, internal systems work to match one's health to the expectations in one's mind.

This has led to the distinction adopted by many medical organizations, including WHO, of "illness" and "disease." Marshall Marinker's distinction is still the most generally accepted form:

Disease ... is a pathological process, most often physical as in throat infection, or cancer of the bronchus, sometimes undetermined in origin, as in schizophrenia. The quality which identifies disease is some deviation from a biological norm. There is an objectivity about disease which doctors are able to see, touch, measure, smell. Diseases are valued as the central facts in the medical view...

Illness ... is a feeling, an experience of unhealth which is entirely personal, interior to the person of the patient. Often it accompanies disease, but the disease may be undeclared, as in the early stages of cancer or tuberculosis or diabetes. Sometimes illness exists where no disease can be found. Traditional medical education has made the deafening silence of illness-in-the-absence-of-disease unbearable to the clinician. The patient can offer the doctor nothing to satisfy his senses...

Sickness ... is the external and public mode of unhealth. Sickness is a social role, a status, a negotiated position in the world, a bargain struck between the person henceforward called 'sick', and a society which is prepared to recognise and sustain him. The security of this role depends on a number of factors, not least the possession of that much treasured gift, the disease. Sickness based on illness alone is a most uncertain status. But even the possession of disease does not guarantee equity in sickness. Those with a chronic disease are much less secure than those with an acute one; those with a psychiatric disease than those with a surgical one ... . Best is an acute physical disease in a young man quickly determined by recovery or death — either will do, both are equally regarded.

Western biomedicine, with its historical basis in the naturalism of Hippocrates, and later Cartesian dualism, has excelled in the treatment of *disease*, but has been utterly abysmal in its treatment of either *illness* or *sickness*. This emphasis has led to a maligning of the single most powerful healing effect we have ever found, the placebo effect. We speak of something as "*just* a placebo," and when someone recovers by placebo, they believe there was never any physically wrong with them in the first place if, after all, it was "all in my head." This laser-like focus on only one dimension of health has made Western biomedicine myopic, and constitutes its single greatest institutional limitation.

Western biomedicine is an ethnomedicine, comparable to other ethnomedicines. The fact that it is *our* ethnomedicine means we believe it *a priori* to be more effective than all other ethnomedicines, which are only superstitous mumbo-jumbo. Of course, other cultures say the same of us. This is merely an expression of ethnocentrism — an evolutionarily adaptive attitude to hold, but not necessarily related to reality in any way.

Where Western biomedicine tries to eliminate the placebo effect, most traditional ethnomedicines are built around *enhancing* the effect. They spend more time treating illness and sickness, and thus are usually less effective at treating disease. Overall, though, the effectiveness of other ethnomedicines remains roughly comparable to our own, more specialized variety. For example, Michael Winkelmann makes a strong case in *Shamanism: Tne Neural Ecology of Ecstasy and Healing* that shamanism helps to activate and enhance the body's natural healing systems. He revisits many of those same arguments in his 2002 paper for *American Behavioral Scientist*, "Shamanism as Neurotheology and Evolutionary Psychology," where he writes:

« *Shamanic ASCs* [altered states of consciousness] *and their slow-wave synchronization patterns activate functions of the paleomammalian brain involving self, attachments, and emotions. Shamanic cognitive capacities based in presentational symbolism, metaphor, analogy, and mimesis express the dynamics of the lower brain systems and provide a medium for ritual and symbolic manipulation of these systems. These physiological aspects of ASCs facilitate healing and psychological and physiological well-being through physiological relaxation; facilitating self-regulation of physiological processes; reducing tension, anxiety, and phobic reactions; manipulating psychosomatic effects; accessing unconscious information in visual symbolism and analogical representations; inducing interhemispheric fusion and synchronization; and facilitating cognitive-emotional integration and social bonding and affiliation. The neuroendocrine mechanisms of meditation indicate that stress reduction also occurs through enhancement of serotonin functioning and stimulation of theta brain wave production.* »

While shamanic healing differs from Western biomedicine in its emphasis on — rather than its shunning of — the placebo effect, neither is this the entirety of ethnomedicine. While these methods are extremely effective at treating illness and sickness, and are far more effective even at treating disease than we normally give them credit for, most traditional ethnomedicines also have more directly physical means of treating disease.

Perhaps the most impressive example would be the archaeological evidence that foragers in the Mesolithic successfully performed brain surgery. The procedure, called trepanation, involves boring a hole in the skull, and is often effective to treat head trauma or pressure. A news brief in *Archaeology* magazine described one such discovery:

« *New accelerator radiocarbon dating of the Dnieper Rapids cemeteries near Kiev in Ukraine by the Oxford Radiocarbon Laboratory has produced evidence that trepanation, the surgical removal of bone from the cranial vault, was performed during the Mesolithic period. During a study of 14 individuals at the Vasilyevka II cemetery, Malcolm C. Lillie, a geoarchaeologist and palaeoenvironmentalist at the University of Hull, found one skeleton (no. 6285–9) to have evidence of trepanation. The cemetery, excavated in 1953 by A.D. Stolyar, has been dated to 7300–6220 B.C., making the trepanned cranium the oldest known example of a healed trepanation yet discovered. The skull, which was originally reported in Russian by I.I. Gokhman in 1966, has a depression on its left side with a raised border of bone and "stepping" in the center showing stages of healing during life. The complete closure indicates the survival of the patient, a man who was more than 50 years old at his death. The dates for the individual are 1,000–2,000 years earlier than those of the skull at Ensisheim in France, recently reported by Kurt Alt to be the earliest evidence for trepanation ».*

Today, trepanation is still done around the world and with great success by many primitive peoples, including the Gusii and the Tende from the hills east of Lake Victoria.

There is also an interesting point that, having past its point of diminishing returns (*see* thesis #15), medical research is increasingly relying on ethnobotanical knowledge of medicinal plants for drug development, by isolating the active compounds in traditional remedies used by shamans for millennia. Perhaps the single most effective drug ever developed by Western biomedicine is aspirin — originally isolated from willow bark, a remedy for headaches used by Native Americans as much as by Hippocrates in the fifth century BCE. One pharmaceutical company built on this premise, "Shaman Pharmaceuticals," explains its rationale thus:

« *Tropical forest plant species have served as a source of medicines for people of the tropics for millennia. Many medical practitioners with training in pharmacology and/or pharmacognosy are well aware of the number of modern therapeutic agents that have been derived from tropical forest species. In fact, over 120 pharmaceutical products currently in use are plant-derived, and some 75% of these were discovered by examining the use of these plants in traditional medicine. ... Yet while many modern medicines are plant-derived, the origins of these pharmaceutical agents and their relationship to the knowledge of the indigenous people in the tropical forests is usually omitted.* »

In both of these cases, traditional medical knowledge is often rejected on the basis of the religio-philosophical frame it is placed in. When shamans speak of good or evil spirits, Western researchers usually stop listening. This neglects the fact that shamanic knowledge usually operates on multiple, simultaneous levels, and they are usually fully aware of the physical level. For instance, one example of shamanic "fraud" often cited is the practice of some shamans to spit out rolled up plants and tell the patient that they are the evil spirits sucked out of his body. In fact, the shaman placed those plants in his mouth prior to the ritual and hid them there. This is often cited as an

181

example of shamans as charlatans, but it actually fits in well with the shamanic worldview. The plants hold the same spirit that is being sucked out of the patient — the shaman holds them in his mouth to "catch" the spirit so he does not become infected himself. When they are spat out, the shaman indicates that they are the evil spirits — and to him, they are: the evil spirits were trapped inside of them. This display prompts a stronger placebo effect, and is not in the least bit deceitful from the shamanic worldview.

Under this same notion of disease coming from invasive evil spirits, we have a means for shamans to memorize ethnobotanical information. By placing plants and diseases into a mythic context, the shaman can keep a full medical library in his memory using the same mnemonic tricks that help astronomers keep track of the stars by reference to a full mythology of constellations. It is also interesting to ponder the strange similarities between "evil spirits" and germs: neither can be seen, both invade our body, both have "good" analogues that actually help us; both make us sick by the way they seek to use our bodies; both can be driven out by ourselves, or by introducing new elements to fight them. The distinction between germ theory and the superstitions of "evil spirits," in that regard, seems to become little more than insistence that another culture express one's same ideas in the same, mechanistic terms.

Every culture believes its own ethnomedicine to be the only valid one. Every ethnomedicine is based in a given view of the world, a given understanding of human nature and the world. Each culture's ethnomedicine is based in that. The inustrialized West sees the world as a physical clockwork mechanism, and though we can easily recognize the fallacious cornerstones of other cultures' worldviews, we are blind to our own, such as the bankruptcy of Cartesian dualism. Our ethnomedicine — Western biomedicine — is based in our worldview. We see other ethnomedicines as superstitious poppycock, because they are not based in our mechanistic worldview. They are based in the worldview of the culture they come from — in the case of foragers, that is usually an animistic worldview. Yet, we cannot deny their effectiveness, even as they cannot deny ours — even when we can't explain that effectiveness (and when they can't explain ours).

In the final analysis, the effectiveness of Western biomedicine has been greatly exaggerated and its limitations conveniently forgotten, while traditional ethnomedicines have been denigrated. A correction for these problems reveals that our ethnomedicine, while unique in many ways, by no means has a monopoly on medical knowledge or effectiveness. In fact, though an overall comparison is difficult, most ethnomedicines fall within a fairly narrow general range of effectiveness. Even our own does not significantly outclass the others, while there is a minimum effectiveness required to keep a society competitive.

Thus, the protest that civilization improves our health is utterly without merit. The overall effect of civilization on human health has been disastrous, introducing innumerable diseases and maladies unknown before. A more nuanced argument cites a "Pandora's Box": civilization has unleashed these terrible diseases on the world, and we cannot rewind time to undo the damage. We need civilization now to produce the medicines necessary to combat the diseases civilization unleashed. But, as we have seen here, that is not the case, either. Most of those diseases are the effects of the civilized lifestyle, and would be cured as a consequence of rewilding. Of those that remain, their ability to sweep across the world as an epidemic would be greatly reduced in a world of small, nomadic bands. And finally, as we have seen above, every culture — civilized or not — has medicine. Other forms of medicne tend to be less specialized in treating disease only, and instead also treat illness and sickness, but none of them are much more effective than any other, including our own. Our ability to treat disease would not be diminished without civilization, only the means by which we do so. It would mean a shift in emphasis from the dehumanizing, clinical introduction of foreign substances to combat invasive pathogens by an aloof, unquestionable authority to a method that emphasized communal bonds and deep emotions in a process that helps the patient take control of his own illness and, ultimately, empowers him to heal himself.

Thesis #23: Civilization has no monopoly on knowledge.

Where all else fails, science is held up as a distinctly civilized pursuit, and something that can justify whatever other problems it may entail. This supposition works well against our general impression of primitive society as "stupid, ignorant, or superstition-dominated." The animistic beliefs of so many foragers convince us that they inhabit a terrifying world of evil spirits, where they are driven by their superstitious fears. The progressivist myth articulated explicitly in the Enlightenment posits a narrative of human history where civilization frees us from such a life of fear and ignorance by the ennoblement of reason. The very term, "the Enlightenment," points to the salvific role it bestowed upon reason, logic, and the scientific process. Yet, as E.O. Wilson discusses at length in *Consilience*, as powerful as the reductionary mode of thought may be, we also need an integrative form to turn our collected facts into a full body of knowledge. Though science may be unique to modern civilization, impressive bodies of knowledge are not. Our belief that science is the only valid way to gain knowledge is an ethnocentric farce that denies enormous swaths of human potential, as illustrated by the impressive means of gathering knowledge exhibited by primitive peoples, and the incredible bodies of knowledge they have formed with them.

First, we must address the fundamental issue of the "superstitious" primitive mindset which has been so often remarked. Psychologists and anthropologists alike have written whole volumes on this subject, but even from such an ethnocentric frame, the systematic curiosity inherent to human nature everywhere is all too often self-evident. Evans-Pritchard once wrote of the Azande:

« Their blindness is not due to stupidity, for they display great ingenuity in explaining away the failures and inequalities of the poison oracle and experimental keenness in testing it. It is due rather to the fact that their intellectual ingenuity and experimental keenness are conditioned by patterns of ritual behavior and mystical belief. Within the limits set by these patterns they show great intelligence, but it cannot operate beyond these limits. Or, to put it another way: they reason excellently in the idiom of their beliefs, but they cannot reason outside, or against their beliefs because they have no other idiom in which to express their thoughts. »

This passage says more of Evans-Pritchard's biases, than it does of the Azande's knowledge. All of us are bound by our cultural norms; as Daniel

184

Quinn suggested, the advance of knowledge is not limited by knowledge itself (which is usually easy to attain), but curiosity to seek that knowledge in the first place. For example, the notion that the Azande may have intellects equal to his own is something that Evans-Pritchard cannot conceive of in the above quotation. He displays "great ingenuity in explaining away the failures and inequalities" of his own theories, but he is ultimately "conditioned by patterns of ... belief. Within the limits set by these patterns, he shows great intelligence, but it cannot operate beyond these limits."

In fact, primitive thought more often operates on multiple, simultaneous levels, such that a statement may be a straightforward, physical formula, an allusion to mythology, and a statement of metaphysics all at once. This is a common occurence in oral societies, where knowledge is often encoded in stories, myths, and other mnemonic devices to aid necessary memorization. A statement that seems, on its surface, to be pure superstition to us, is often very clearly a statement of physical practicality to its tribal speaker. As Paul Radin explained in *Primitive Man as Philosopher*:

« *Primitive peoples will, for instance, indulge in magical rites for the attainment of purely practical ends — the killing of deer, for instance — under circumstances in which they could by no conceivable means fail to do so. Yet they will seek the most tenuous of religious sanctions for a hazardous undertaking such as a warpath. They may tell you, if directly interrogated, that a poisoned arrow discharged for a short distance into a deer trail will cause the death of a deer that is to be hunted on the following day. What inference can we very well expect a person to draw from such a statement but that a magical nonrational rite has achieved a practical and all-important result? Must we not insist, then, that the mentality of people who accept such a belief is different in degree and possibly in kind from our own? There seems indeed to be no escape.* »

The first error that we commit is that of expecting the answer to a direct question put to a native to be either complete or revealing. It is similarly an error even to expect that such a question touches the core of the real problem involved. Let us take the last example given. We are not to imagine that after discharging the arrow into the deer trail our native returns to his family and informs them that he has potentially killed a deer, nor are we to imagine that he tells them he has performed the preliminary part of his work. What he has done is one indissoluble whole — he discharges the arrow in the proper way, waits for the morrow, and then follows the trail until he has killed the deer. Any question whereby it is assumed, consciously or unconsciously, that one part of this series of activities is more important than the other or that a causal relation exists between them, is misleading and entails a misleading answer. So much for our initial error. But we have likewise no justification for assuming that some general principle underlies the native's activities in this particular instance. He did not select any trail at any time of the year, but a particular trail at a particular time of the year. We must assume that he knows from unlimited practical experiences that he is selecting the proper conditions for his task. I once asked a Winnebago Indian whether the rite of shooting an arrow into a trail of which he had no knowledge would be effective and received a prompt and amused denial. Similarly it was discovered that although in certain tribes a vision from a deity was regarded as adequate sanction for embarking on a war party, in actual practice certain very practical conditions had to be fulfilled before an individual was permitted to depart.

So we see here that the juxtaposition of science and religion we experience in our own society is by no means universal, and in fact in many oral, tribal societies, religion is the language in which one expresses natural knowledge. We have concluded that these societies are superstitious based on their invocations of "spirits" — a conclusion that says more of our own lack of understanding of oral societies, than of their natural knowledge.

Some circles have been trying to advance the study of "aboriginal science," but this is misleading. Though it is intended to legitimize native modes of thought and knowledge, it in fact does harm to that cause, first by eroding our notion of science from one particular, useful means of gathering knowledge, to a generalized — and thus meaningless — synonym for "knowledge" itself. Secondly, it further supports the notion that science is the only respectable means of gathering knowledge, an ethnocentric fetish for our own, particular mode of thought. Science is a very particular way of thinking. It is a rigorous, minimalist process that relies on reductionism and analyticism. If our goal is to create a minimalist database of truly reliable information, there is probably no better approach. Yet, this cannot — and should not — be our *only* epistemological goal. Such a database is invaluable as a base to begin with, but as E.O. Wilson argues, such a database is of value primarily as the foundation of an integrative consilience. As Kerim Friedman wrote for *Savage Minds* in "Aboriginal Science":

« *The problem is that to accept all belief systems about the natural world as science makes nonsense of the term science. Whether it is intelligent design or aboriginal knowledge, these forms of knowledge are important to those*

*who embrace them, but why do we need to label them as being "scientific"
as well? It is true that many things aborigines know through their traditional
forms of knowledge have, in fact, been proven to coincide with scientific
knowledge as well. But some have not. This alone shows that traditional
forms of knowledge can never be coterminous with science....*

*But the solution to the relative status of traditional knowledge compared to
science is not to simply label knowledge as "science." It is to find ways
create space within which it can find legitimate expression in our society
and be accorded a status other than "superstition." It is also to better
educate people about scientific knowledge and its limits, so that all citizens
can better distinguish between good and bad science. Seeking to give
traditional forms of knowledge the same status of science accomplishes
neither of these goals. Even worse, it makes it harder for us to understand
why we should care about traditional knowledge. After all, if it is simply
science with another name, why bother? »*

Many of us believe that science is the only worthwhile way of knowing, and
everything else is superstition. This is a false dichotomy created by the
peculiar nature of our particular epistemological history. The Enlightenment
was a reactionary movement that ultimately owes itself to the Protestant
Reformation, being in many ways a more extreme reaction to "the Age of
Faith." These are not the only two possible poles, nor are these necessarily
opposites. Religion can spring out of reason and support it. Pantheism has
often been espoused by scientists as a type of religion that melds easily with
scientific thought — being, at its base, nothing more than a sense of awe for
the unvierse we inhabit. Shamanism and animism can be close natural allies
of pantheism. Shamanism is ever adaptive, willing to change its most basic
conceptions to fit new visions or evidence — just as science does, allowing
it to grow and change with our changing ideas and theories. Shamanism can
also prompt scientific discovery and the curiosity that leads to greater
knowledge, because of its insistence on experiencing the numinous for
oneself and learning from the spirits themselves. It would be a contradiction
in terms to propose a shamanic fundamentalism.

The basic curiosity that underlies all science is evident in all cultures. As the
Evans-Pritchard passage above indicates, the Azande showed "experimental
keenness" in their methodical, systematic testing. In their 1970 study,
Nicholas Blurton Jones & Melvin J. Konner of the Harvard Kalahari
Research Group supposed that such methodical hypothesis testing might be

a basic function of the human brain that was necessary for tracking. They wrote:

« Such an intellective process is familiar to us from detective stories and indeed also from science itself. Evidently it is a basic feature of human mental life. It would be surprising indeed if repeated activation of hypotheses, trying them out against new data, integrating them with previously known facts, and rejecting ones which do not stand up, were habits of mind peculiar to western scientists and detectives. !Kung behavior indicates that, on the contrary, the very way of life for which the human brain evolved required them. That they are brought to impressive fruition by the technology of scientists and the liesure of novelists should not be allowed to persuade us that we invented them. Man is the only hunting mammal with so rudimentary a sense of smell, that he could only have come to successful hunting through intellectual evolution. »

The knowledge thus achieved by primitive peoples is truly staggering when we consider it. The proliferation of invention and technology we currently characterize as "civilized" is a very recent development, stemming from the peculiar nature of the Industrial Revolution. Before then, even civilized invention was generally frowned upon, though the Agricultural Revolution did usher a surge of invention to cope with such a radically different, maladaptive lifestyle. Nonetheless, the most impressive intellectual feats that our species has achieved have been made not by civilized men working within the paradigms thus set down, but by the primitives who discovered those paradigms in the first place.

For instance, the most pure science of mathematics. In "Two Precursors of Writing: Plain and Complex Tokens," Denise Schmandt-Besserat writes:

« The invention of zero and place notation has been heralded as a major accomplishment of the civilized world, but the literature does not treat the advent of abstract numerals because of the common but erroneous assumption that abstract numbers are intuitive to humans. The token system is one piece of artifactural evidence proving that counting, like anything else, is not spontaneous. Instead, counting is cultural and has to be learned ».

We have evidence for counting, and thus the basics of mathematics, even among *Homo neanderthalensis* and *Homo erectus*, up to 70,000 years ago, in the form of counting sticks: bit of bone with sets of strikes cut into them in specific patterns. Some of these are quite complex, mathematically, and have even been described as "calculators" to aid in basic arithmetic in much the same fashion as an abacus. Many of these counting sticks appear also to be lunar calendars, indicating the beginnings of astronomy, as well. The Pleiades are known as "the Seven Sisters" among natives to North America, Siberia and Australia — suggesting that they must have been named before those groups went their separate ways, at least 40,000 years ago. While Stonehenge in England, and Woodhenge at Cahokia, were monolithic structures built by agricultural societies, the finely tuned astronomical knowledge they exhibit comes from the primitive societies they came from.

Perhaps the most powerful example of primitive mathematics comes from the quipu lines of the Andes. The Inka Empire was on par with any of the Old World civilizations for its bureaucracy, attention to detail, and supreme power. However, they did so without writing. Instead, they had quipu lines. One string would have a number of other strings tied to it; each, with some number of knots tied in it. In *Ethnomathematics*, Marcia Ascher describes the quipu lines as a data structure:

« *The Incas can be characterized as methodical, highly organized, concerned with detail, and intensive data users. The Inca bureaucracy continuously monitored the areas under its control. They received many messages and sent many instructions daily. The messages included details of resources such as items that were needed or available in sotrehouses, taxes owed or collecte,d encsus information, the output of mines, or the composition of work forces. The messages were transmitted rapaidly using the extensive road system via a simple, but effective, system of runners... The message had to be clear, compact, and partable. Quipu-makers were responsible for encoding and decoding the information.*

A quipu is an assemblage of colored knotted cotton cords... The colors of the cords, the way the cords are connected together, the relative placement of the cords, the spaces between the cords, the types of knots on the individual cords, and the relative placement of the knots are all part of the logical-numerical recording. »

Gary Urton's *Signs of the Inka Quipu* shows that we can also see the quipu lines as encoding information in binary — a primitive sort of computer. Had the Spanish not conquered the Inka, might we have had computers centuries earlier? It is impossible to speculate, but the ingenious elegance of the quipu lines certainly show that the potential exists in primitive societies. Though the quipu lines were used to hold together the bureacracy-intensive Inka Empire, it was not an Inka invention. Rather, quipu lines predated the Inka, and are found first among the primitives the Inka conquered, "to bring civilization to them," as Inca Garcilaso de la Vega — a half-Spaniard, half-Inkan historian soon after the Spanish conquest — might have put it. The quipu lines — and binary counting — may well have been primitive inventions the Inka took by conquest.

Native knowledge abounds — even systematic, experimental thought is found in abundance. Working from a definition of "civilization" dependent on advanced knowledge (a definition we **rejected** in thesis #13), Richard Rudgley's *Lost Civilizations of the Stone Age* concludes that *all* societies are civilizations (making the term somewhat worthless). Along the way, Rudgley fills three hundred pages with examples of the impressive knowledge gathered by primitive peoples. That said, that knowledge is not science. It is often gathered systematically, and with "experimental keenness." It is often retested and falsified, but there is no set scientific method that tribal peoples use. Their mode of investigation is very often inegrative, rather than reductionist. Native forms of knowledge are precisely the integrative forms of consilience that E.O. Wilson discusses as our next great epistemological need. We have followed the Enlightenment as far as it is likely to carry us; it is time to understand that it was a reactionary movement, and thus suffered from the same failings as all other reactionary movements. Science, as invaluable as it is, is not the only way of knowing, nor necessarily the best. Indigenous knowledge is also invaluable. Though science is unique to civilization, knowledge and reason are not. As Nicholas Blurton Jones & Melvin J. Konner of the Harvard Kalahari Research Group in their 1970 report:

« *The accuracy of observation, the patience, and the experiences of wildlife they have had and appreciate are enviable. The sheer, elegant logic of deductions from tracks would satiate the most avid crossword fan or reader of detective stories. The objectivity is also enviable to scientists who believe that they can identify it and that the progress of science is totally dependent upon it. Even the poor theorisation of our !Kung left one uneasy; their 'errors,' the errors of 'Stone Age savages,' are exactly those made today by many highly educated western scientists ... Just as primitive life no longer can be characterised as nasty, brutish and short, no longer can it be characterised as stupid, ignorant, or superstition-dominated.* »

Thesis #24: Civilization has no monopoly on art.

When the case is laid out against the material benefits of civilization, and the progressivist is forced to admit that hierarchy is an unnecessary evil (thesis #11), that it is a difficult, dangerous and unhealthy way of life (thesis #9), that it makes us sick (thesis #21), and that it cannot provide medicine (thesis #22) or knowledge (thesis #23) beyond that which is universal to all cultures, civilized or not. The typical last resort is the ephemeral. Civilization, the progressivist then claims, is still of value for the art, music, and poetry it creates. Primitive cultures have no Beethoven, no Rembrandt, and no Shakespeare. Again, the progressivist case is predicated on an abysmal ignorance of what primitive cultures can boast. In fact, art is universal to all human cultures, not just including primitive ones, but *especially* primitive ones. Art is essential to human nature — and thus, it is always at odds with civilization's basic, dehumanizing trends — and it is found wherever one finds humans.

The nature of tribal art is somewhat different, though, in that it emphasizes a communal vision, rather than the work of a single "genius" — hence the oft-repeated refrain that tribal cultures lack a Beethoven, a Rembrandt, or a Shakespeare. Each storyteller tells a story, and in so doing taps a story that has been told and retold through the generations. At the same time, this particular telling is new, and different from every retelling before it; it is a perfect, sublime moment that never has been, and never will be again. This is a common theme through primitive art, a means by which the tribal ideal is reinforced: the simultaneous apotheosis of both the individual, and the collective, with neither one more important than the other. We see this reflected again and again in primitive art, music, dance, storytelling, and all their other forms of art.

Music is universal across all cultures. In "The memetic origin of language," Vaneechoutte and Skoyles argue that humans are naturally and biologically musical, and furthermore, that it was song that laid the foundation for language. They suggest that music is very much central to our nature, and that it may also explain human sexual behavior.

We typically judge the artistic quality of music based on its complexity, but even by such a metric as "complex music," civilization can claim no monopoly: the polyphonic complexity of Pygmy songs, though unwritten, was not matched by Europeans until the 14th century. That said, in *Nature and Madness*, Paul Shepard offers this insight:

« In conventional history/progress thinking, the complexity and quality of music have steadily grown in the course of cultural evolution from something repetitive and simple like the Kalahari bushman's plucking his bowstring to the symphonies of the nineteenth century. But a very different view is possible. Suzanne Langer observes that "the great office of music is to ... give us insight into ... the subjective unity of experience" by using the principle of physical biology: rhythm. Its physiological effect is to reduce inner tensions by first making them symbolically manifest, then resolving and unifying them... One interpretation is that the more complex the music, the more fundamental the problem; or, one might say, the more elaborate the music, the more fragmented the vision of the world. Composer and musician Paul Winter has said that we are now habituated to an overstructured format, especially in so-called classical music, from which we need to escape into a more informal extemporaneous performance and audition. But if, indeed, music is a kind of final refuge serving to hold things together, this might be impossible in modern life. »

Every culture now on earth has music. Archaeologically, our first evidence of musical instruments date back to the Upper Paleolithic, including bone whistles and pipes. Many anthropologists and ethnomusicologists have long conjectured that one of the first instruments may simply have been a hunter strumming his bowstring.

The first art in Europe appears in the Upper Paleolithic, long before the beginning of civilization. The cave art painted by Upper Paleolithic foragers is a wonder even today. Usually paintings of animals, they used the rock itself. One bull at Lascaux, for instance, uses a bulge of rock to form its haunches. These Paleolithic foragers did not simply paint on a flat, two-dimensional canvas; their paintings seem almost to walk out of the very walls, even today. An emerging trend of modern artists have tried to replicate the feats of Paleolithic artists, but have found them to be difficult masterpieces to imitate.

Art is made by foragers all around the world. From the famous totem poles of the sedentary Kwakiutl and other forager chiefdoms of the Pacific coast, to the sacred art of the !Kung in the Kalahari, art is universal. Being subjective, we may be free to interpret our art as "superior," but on what objective grounds could we possibly draw such a conclusion?

The usual matter of art's quality is the abstract thought it reflects. In that, too, we find a richness in primitive societies on par with anything civilization has produced. The complex theology of Austrlian aborignes features songlines, and a Dreamtime that is both present, and in the mythic past, simultaneously. Paul Radin's *Primitive Man as Philosopher* explores the depth of some forager philosophical systems, especially the Ho-Chunk, and finds they are easily comparable to the philosophical depth found in civilization. The question of how well primitive art reflects that complex, intellectual world is answered by David Lewis-Williams' *The Mind in the Cave*, where he compares the cave paintings of the Paleolithic to the rock art of the !Kung and the Native Americans, and finds many of the same images and motifs. Ethnographically, as Lewis-Williams shows, these images are shamanistic elements, bound up ultimately in the structure of the human brain itself.

Lewis-Williams suggests that art began as a means by which shamans could share their visions with others. Among the !Kung, stone is seen as a porous membrane separating our world from the spirit world. In both the beliefs of modern foragers, and in archaeological theories of Paleolithic art, the role of art is to connect people with a common vision of the world, and to communicate with the spirit world, drawing us back to Tolstoy's observation, "art is a means of union among men, joining them together in the same feeling."

The reality of such profound, primitive art is something that John Zerzan does not engage in his influential essay, "The Case Against Art." Zerzan's argument has informed many primitivists' views against art and language, that it was the innovation of symbolic thought, rather than the innovation of civilization, that led to hierarchy. Lewis-Williams and Zerzan agree on many ideas. They agree that art began with shamanism, for example, and they agree that shamanism and art are bound up inextricably in the formation of hierarchy. Where Zerzan sees this as something that must be undone, Lewis-Williams sees it as a great advance for humanity.

Where Lewis-Williams' argument falters is in his application of Max Raphael's Marxist interpretations of the meaning of art as a mediator of class struggle. Lewis-Williams makes the argument that the "classes" in conflict here were "behaviorally modern humans" versus the Neanderthals, wherein "behaviorally modern humans" used art to flaunt their cognitive superiority to Neanderthals. In this, his argument becomes very tenuous, because there is a significant body of evidence which suggests that Neanderthals may in fact have had some types of art. While misinterpretation of some may be likely, Lewis-Williams seems to be on increasingly shaky ground as he argues that they are *all* misinterpretations of the archaeological evidence. Neanderthal cranial capacity was larger than our own, and while some of that may well have been to ennervate their shorter, stouter bodies, the undeniable contention remains that as far as the archaeological evidence can show, Neanderthals' cognitive capacity was at least equal to our own. Besides the evidence of art that Lewis-Williams tries to dismiss, the Neanderthals also show the only evidence of adaptation evidenced in the Paleolithic, with the Chatelperronian toolset — a synthesis of the Neanderthals' own Mousterian toolset, with the blade technology of the Aurignacian, associated with our own ancestors. It was not our ancestors who adapted the best parts of Mousterian technology, but the Neanderthals who showed that they could learn and adapt to new ideas. Given this, Lewis-Williams' premise that Neanderthals lacked the capacity for symbolic thought that our ancestors expressed in cave and rock paintngs is sketchy, at best, and if the Neanderthals were able to understand symbolic thought just as well as our ancestors could, then the use of art for conflict and hierarchy cannot follow.

Where Lewis-Williams sees humanity's abstract thought as the crown of creation, Zerzan sees it as our expulsion from Eden. Zerzan connects art and hierarchy simply by stating, "The shamanistic origin of visual art and music has been often remarked, the point here being that the artist-shaman was the first specialist." This is a common view, but nonetheless a distinct abuse of the term "specialist." Shamans usually have the same responsibilities as everyone else; they must hunt and gather like anyone else. Their station does not afford them any kind of command or undue influence. While in some societies, shamans guarded their "secret knowledge" jealously as a source of power, in many other societies, shamanism was open to anyone who wished to try, making shamanic specialization a matter of emphasis, rather than exclusivity.

Zerzan goes on to explain how, in the mediated life of symbolism, the symbol comes to replace the thing itself, thus separating humans from actual reality and providing a critical layer of symbols that can be manipulated by specialists like shamans, priests, artsts and ultimately rulers, to control us. He follows the progression of art through changing ideas and religions, showing how the increasing alienation of symbolism leads to increasing hierarchy and control. Consistently, Zerzan has also written against language ("Language: Origin and Meaning"), numbers ("Number: Its Origin and Evolution") and time ("Time and Its Discontents"), creating a significant force in modern primitivism that is hostile to any symbolism that mediates sensory reality. In this view, it is symbolism that creates civilization and its problems, rather than any kind of material motivations. Zerzan's view of history is driven by ideas, with a culture that changes its material reality to fit changing ideas — and thus, it is at odds at its most basic level with memetics and cultural materialism, where ideas are shaped by material reality.

Such an extreme view is as much contrary to human nature as civilization's own. As we have seen, art is universal to all human cultures, and almost certainly intrinsic to our very nature. The truth of the matter is, the shaman's exploration of his own psychology and the murky depths of the Dreamtime are far more real than the world we seem to experience. No satisfying answer has ever been proposed to allay our nagging suspicions of Descartes' "little demon" — an inescapable doubt that returns to haunt us again and again in various forms, be it "a brain in a jar," or more recently, *The Matrix*. The fact that we cannot escape is that we have never directly experienced the world around us. It is always mediated by symbols. We see a narrow band of electromagnetic energy as "light"; how would our view of reality shift if, instead of color, we saw infrared, or ultraviolet? We do not taste foods; buds on our tongue and in our mouth react to given chemicals in food, producing electrochemical responses in our brain. What we experience first-hand are the impulses conducted to our brain via our senses; what we experience first-hand are, ultimately, nothing more than another kind of symbol. The taste of an apple is a symbol in our mind for what that taste might really be, but we do not experience the taste itself; we experience only the neurological symbol conducted through our taste buds, to our nerves, and finally to our brains.

The external symbol merely extends that inescapable layer of neurological abstraction to create another layer through which we can deal with and experience reality. That layer is ambiguous. It can create, or it can destroy. It can open, or it can close. Many Native American shamanic traditions were very secretive, and created in the shaman a focus of power and authority, and thus, incipient hierarchy. Among the !Kung, shamanism was open and egalitarian, a matter of reconciling the dreams and visions of many into a great vision of the world — a vision they painted on rock to show their dreams to one another, and to all their children to come. That abstract layer of thought, symbol and art can be used to conceal things, as Zerzan argues;

it can be used to coerce and control. But it can just as easily be used to reveal, open and share.

Zerzan's condemnation of abstract symbols in and of themselves is as radical as it is short-sighted. The ultimate proof lies in the fact that civilization's propaganda is wrong. Every culture has art, a rich symbolic world, abstract thought and deep philosophy. Yet, only some of those cultures possess hierarchy, evidence coercion, or maintain a population showing the signs of being cut off from experiential reality, as Zerzan decries. It is part of human nature; it connects us to one another; it is universal. In condemning art, Zerzan condemns us all, just as civilization does.

Art has always been the refuge for those sensitive souls who cannot face civilization's horrors. Even in civilization, it is a lifeline to human nature, and thus to some extent, stands in defiance of civilization. Every power has tried to co-opt it towards its own ends, but ultimately, art serves only the human spirit. It is irrepressible, and it cannot be claimed solely by any one culture — not even ours.

Thesis #25: Civilization reduces quality of life.

Nothing in human existence has had a more profoundly negative impact on our quality of life than civilization. As we have already seen, it introduced the unnecessary evil of hierarchy (*see* thesis #11); it introduced the difficult, dangerous, and unhealthy agricultural lifestyle (*see* thesis #9); it makes us sick (*see* thesis #21), but provides no better medicine to counterbalance that effect (*see* thesis #22). It introduced endemic levels of stress, a diet and lifestyle maladapted and deleterious to our health, war as we know it, and ecological disaster, but it has given us nothing to counterbalance those effects; it has no monopoly on medicine, or knowledge in general (*see* thesis #23), or even art (*see* thesis #24), making the overall impact of civilization on quality of life disastrous.

Measuring quality of life is always a tricky thing, but the United Nations' "Human Development Index" looks at three criteria: longevity, knowledge, and standard of living. In the case of the HDI, all three are measured in ways biased towards civilization. For example, longevity is measured by life expectancy at birth — a measure which presumes the common civilized assumption that life begins at birth. It does not weight the average with abortions, for example, even though there is disagreement even within our own culture of when life begins. Given such disagreement, we should not be terribly surprised to learn that other cultures have different measures of when life begins. Foraging cultures, for example, often believe that life begins at *age two*, and thus classify infanticide and abortion in the same category. Children are often not named or considered persons until that time. A !Kung woman goes into labor, and walks into the bush — maybe she comes back with a baby, and maybe she doesn't. Whether stillborn or killed at birth, it's not considered any business of anyone else's. This kind of attitude has given foragers a very high infant mortality rate, leading many naive commentators to assume that their way of life must be terribly afflicted with disease to claim so many infants, and ultimately taking the skewed statistics that arise from such a practice to make statements on forager quality of life. In fact, all such commentary provides is a glimpse of the power of ethnocentrism to skew even what we might consider unbiased statistics.

A less biased measurement might take expected age of death at a given age. Richard Lee noted that up to 60% of the !Kung he encountered were over 60 (in Western countries, that number is 10–15%). The table provided by Hillard Kaplan, et. al, in "A Theory of Human Life History Evolution: Diet, Intelligence, and Longevity" (*Evolutionary Anthropology*, 2000, p. 156–

185) is quite instructive. Comparing the Ache, Hazda, Hiwi and !Kung shows an average probability of survival to age 15 of 60% (reflecting the enormous impact of normative infanticide), but the expected age of death at age 15 shoots up to 54.1. In Burton-Jones, et. al, "Antiquity of Postreproductive Life: Are There Modern Impacts on Hunter-Gatherer Postreproductive Life Spans?" (*American Journal of Human Biology*, 2002, p. 184 — 205) another table is presented on p. 185, showing that at age 45, women of the !Kung could expect to live another 20.0 years for a total of 65 years, women of the Hadza could expect to live another 21.3 years for a total of 66.3 years, and women of the Ache could expect to live another 22.1 years for a total of 67.1 years. We should also bear in mind that all of the forager cultures examined to derive these statistics live in the Kalahari Desert — an extremely marginal and difficult ecosystem, even for foragers. Could we expect significantly higher numbers from foragers, if they were allowed to roam the sub-Saharian savannas to which humans are adapted, or verdant forests? We can only speculate, though the inuitive assumption would be affirmative.

An expected age of death even at 54.1, or even 67.1, may seem dismal to us in the United States, but even here in 1901, life expectancy was 49. It has only been very recently that civilized life expectancy has caught up to even the most marginal foragers. Moreover, in thesis #8, we explored the relationship between the First World and the Third World. Focusing on First World statistics produces the same skewed result as focusing only on medieval royalty, to the exclusion of the peasants they relied upon for their abundance. The worldwide average life expectancy, then, is the far more relevant measure than the United States'. That number is currently 67 years — exactly the number Burton-Jones found for !Kung women eking out a living in the Kalahari. Given the marginality of the ecosystems these foragers exist in, it seems that we could easily conclude from these data that the incredible advances made in our life expectancy — advances which are now slowing, due to the diminishing marginal returns of medical research (a point addressed explicitly in thesis #15) — we have managed to raise our life expectancy to that of the most meager and marginalized foragers.

Archeological evidence, however, does not entirely bear this out. Life expectancies in the Mesolithic were quite low. How do we reconcile these conflicting data? Caspari & Lee suggest an answer in "Older age becomes common late in human evolution," (*Proceedings of the National Academy of Sciences, USA*, 2004, p. 10847–10848), where they note a trend of increasing longevity that goes back not to the origins of civilization, but to the Upper Paleolithic Revolution. If we work under this assumption — that modern, abstract behavior had led to increasing longevity — then the data makes much more sense. We see forager longevity extending through the Upper Paleolithic, Mesolithic, and into historical times prior to being wiped out by the advance of civilization. In those meager areas where they have not been wiped out yet, forager longevity continues to grow longer, even though the marginal nature of their ecosystem makes for a fairly harsh life.

What we also see, archaeologically, is a massive crash in life expectancy associated with the innovation of agriculture. Dickson's Mounds, already discussed in thesis #6, shows a catastrophic drop-off in life expectancy. We see the same pattern repeated wherever agriculture enters. Until recently, average agricultural life expectancy tended to vary between 20 and 35 years, while even the Kalahari foragers likely enjoyed the same 54.1 years they do today. Today, life expectancy in the First World is in the low 70's; in the Third World, however, it is still often in the 30's.

The second criteria the U.N.'s index measures is knowledge, but here they use literacy as a stand-in. We have already discussed the high level of knowledge in primitive cultures in thesis #23, but such systems of knowledge are rarely written. Though impressive, they are of a different kind than literate knowledge. The U.N.'s measure systematically ignores this body of knowledge, however, by judging only by literacy. As Walter Ong takes such pains to express in *Orality and Literacy*, orality, though it differs greatly from literacy, is by no means inferior to it.

It is by the third criterion, "standard of living," that the disaster of civilization is laid bare, though it is once again obscured in the U.N. index by a systematically biased metric, in this case, gross domestic product (GDP) per capita at purchasing power parity (PPP) in U.S. dollars. This is an intrinsically consumeristic metric that systematically sidelines the world's "original affluent societies" by measuring a wealth they have no need for, and neglecting the wealth they possess in such abundance. Where foragers only equal civilization on the first two criteria, it is the third in which they excel.

On the very first day of any introductory economics class, a student will learn the concept of scarcity, presented as an unassailable truth which forms the rock-solid cornerstone of all economic theory. Scarcity simply means that there is not enough of a given resource to satisfy the desires of everyone;

therefore, some system must be established to control access to the scarce resource. As Marshall Sahlins points out in his famous essay, "The Original Affluent Society":

« Modern capitalist societies, however richly endowed, dedicate themselves to the proposition of scarcity. Inadequacy of economic means is the first principle of the world's wealthiest peoples.

The market-industrial system institutes scarcity, in a manner completely without parallel. Where production and distribution are arranged through the behaviour of prices, and all livelihoods depend on getting and spending, insufficiency of material means becomes the explicit, calculable starting point of all economic activity....

Yet scarcity is not an intrinsic property of technical means. It is a relation between means and ends. We should entertain the empirical possibility that hunters are in business for their health, a finite objective, and that bow and arrow are adequate to that end. »

Sahlins goes on to explain the wealth that foragers enjoy. They do not place much value in possessions, since these are a double-edged sword to the nomad. Since the items they need are so easily manufactured from freely available, abundant raw materials, foragers typically display a "scandalous" nonchalance with them. As Martin Gusinde remarked regarding his time with the Yahgan in *The Yamana*:

« The European observer has the impression that these Indians place no value whatever on their utensils and that they have completely forgotten the effort it took to make them. Actually, no one clings to his few goods and chattels which, as it is, are often and easily lost, but just as easily replaced... The Indian does not even exercise care when he could conveniently do so. A European is likely to shake his head at the boundless indifference of these people who drag brand-new objects, precious clothing, fresh provisions and valuable items through thick mud, or abandon them to their swift destruction by children and dogs.... Expensive things that are given them are treasured for a few hours, out of curiosity; after that they thoughtlessly let everything deteriorate in the mud and wet. The less they own, the more comfortable they can travel, and what is ruined they occasionally replace. Hence, they are completely indifferent to any material possessions. »

Sahlins also notes that foragers enjoy a terrifically varied diet, and one that is virtually assured against famine. Le Jeune despaired of the Montagnais' laid-back attitude, writing:

« In the famine through which we passed, if my host took two, three, or four Beavers, immediately, whether it was day or night, they had a feast for all neighbouring Savages. And if those People had captured something, they had one also at the same time; so that, on emerging from one feast, you went to another, and sometimes even to a third and a fourth. I told them that they did not manage well, and that it would be better to reserve these feasts for future days, and in doing this they would not be so pressed with hunger. They laughed at me. 'Tomorrow' (they said) 'we shall make another feast with what we shall capture.' Yes, but more often they capture only cold and wind. »

The European Le Jeune was anxious about how they would survive, but the foragers were so completely confident in their ability to feed themselves that they refused to store food, and ate recklessly. Among most foragers, the concept of starvation is unthinkable. If this represents any kind of primordial "Eden," then it is typified by the injunction of the gospels, "Look at the birds of the air; they do not sow or reap or store away in barns, and yet your heavenly Father feeds them." (Matthew 6:26) Of course, foragers have lean times like any other, and Sahlins supposes that there may be more to their lack of food storage than simple ideology. Food storage would encumber their movement, which would push them towards sedentism — and thus push them towards over-exploiting a given area, noting, "Thus immobilised by their accumulated stocks, the people may suffer by comparison with a little hunting and gathering elsewhere, where nature has, so to speak, done considerable storage of her own — of foods possibly more desirable in diversity as well as amount than men can put by."

To gather such a bounty, foragers work much less than we do today. Richard Lee's initial assessment of the !Kung work week is neatly summarized by Sahlins:

« Despite a low annual rainfall (6 to 10 inches), Lee found in the Dobe area a "surprising abundance of vegetation". Food resources were "both varied and abundant", particularly the energy rich mangetti nut- "so abundant that millions of the nuts rotted on the ground each year for want of picking." The Bushman figures imply that one man's labour in hunting and gathering will support four or five people. Taken at face value, Bushman food collecting is

more efficient than French farming in the period up to World War II, when more than 20 per cent of the population were engaged in feeding the rest. Confessedly, the comparison is misleading, but not as misleading as it is astonishing. In the total population of free-ranging Bushmen contacted by Lee, 61.3 per cent (152 of 248) were effective food producers; the remainder were too young or too old to contribute importantly In the particular camp under scrutiny, 65 per cent were "effectives". Thus the ratio of food producers to the general population is actually 3 :5 or 2:3. But, these 65 per cent of the people "worked 36 per cent of the time, and 35 per cent of the people did not work at all"!

For each adult worker, this comes to about two and one — half days labour per week. (In other words, each productive individual supported herself or himself and dependents and still had 3 to 5 days available for other activities.) A "day's work" was about six hours; hence the Dobe work week is approximately 15 hours, or an average of 2 hours 9 minutes per day. »

This is the oft-quoted "two hours a day" statistic, but it has come under fire from critics who point out that Lee did not add in other necessary activities, such as creating tools, and food preparation. So, Lee returned to do further study with these revised definitions of "work," and came up with a figure of 40–45 hours per week. This might seem to prove that hunter-gatherers enjoy no more leisure than industrial workers, but the same criticisms laid against Lee's figures also apply against our "40 hour work week." Not only is that increasingly a relic of a short era sandwiched between union victories and the end of the petroleum age as the work week stretches into 50 or even 60 hours a week, but it, too, does not include shopping, basic daily chores, or food preparation, which would likewise swell our own tally. Finally, the distinction between "work" and "play" is nowhere nearly as clear-cut in forager societies as it is in our own. Foragers mix the two liberally, breaking up their work haphazardly, and often playing while they work (or working while they play). The definition of work which inflates the total to 40–45 hours per week includes every activity that might be considered, regardless of its nature. Even the most unambiguous "work" of foragers is often the stuff of our own vacations: hunting, fishing, or a hike through the wilds.

We often contemplate how the greater leisure afforded by agriculture allowed people the time to develop civilization. On the contrary; agriculture drastically cut our leisure time, and much of our quality of life. Civilization, then, is a contrivance to try as much as we can to make such a difficult and maladaptive way of life the least bit bearable. The typical means of measuring quality of life are all distinctly biased, and for good reason: the abundance and affluence the forager enjoys is of a kind that we are now blind to, and can no longer even concieve of. They have their health, unlike us; they have a reliable, diverse diet, unlike us; they have liesure time, unlike us. The past 10,000 years have constituted an umitigated disaster in every dimension possible. Civilization is unprecedented in all our knowledge both as such an absolute failure, and for such a swift failure — lasting only 10,000 years before coming to this point of collapse. For us, its victims, it has caused a catastrophic loss of quality of life, regardless of however one might choose to define it.

Thesis #26: Collapse is inevitable.

Agricultural societies have the unique ability to arbitrarily raise their food supply, simply by intensifying their cultivation. By bringing more land under cultivation, or by cultivating what land they have more intensively, or by the occasional technological innovation, agriculturalists can increase their output. By raising the food supply, agriculturalists can arbitrarily raise their population (*see* thesis #4). Thus increasing the energy throughput of their society, agriculturalists can arbitrarily raise their level of complexity. This draws all individuals in that society, and all neighboring societies, into a catastrophic game of prisoner's dilemna (*see* thesis #12). Because complexity is subject to diminishing returns (*see* thesis #14), the effort required to further increase complexity rises, while the value of such an investment drops. Competition, however, keeps driving the assemblage forward, even after further investment in complexity has long ceased to be an economical decision. If any party *does* decide to make that investment — however large it may be — then they will enjoy an edge — however slight — over everyone else, forcing all parties to move to the next level of complexity to remain competitive. Thus, competition drives civilization headlong towards collapse.

The diminishing returns of complexity represent an escalating probability of disaster. As that probability approaches one, disasters continue at their normal pace. Sometimes, as we can see in our own world, our own complexity may accelerate that pace, as with our environmental problems (*see* thesis #17), or it may even create those problems, as with Peak Oil (*see* thesis #18). Even were these not the case, there is a regular, background pace of problems any society faces. Answering all of them with increased complexity — whether by pursuing technical solutions to systemic problems, inventing new technologies, or creating governmental bureaucracies in response — only aggrevates the greater, underlying crisis of complexity's diminishing returns. Following this strategy, a routine crisis will eventually arise, but the response of greater complexity will be impossible due to its prohibitive cost.

Thus, a society faces catabolic collapse.

In dealing with some of the problematic details of Tainter's model, John Michael Greer offered a refinement with, "How Civilizations Fall: A Theory of Catabolic Collapse." Greer noted that, contrary to Tainter's definition, many of the collapses he considered took place over significant periods of time — centuries or more — while others collapsed catastrophically. This led Greer to develop a model that distinguishes between a "maintenance crisis" and a catabolic collapse.

A society that uses resources beyond replenishment rate ... when production of new capital falls short of maintenance needs, risks a depletion crisis in which key features of a maintenance crisis are amplified by the impact of depletion on production. As $M(p)$ exceeds $C(p)$ and capital can no longer be maintained, it is converted to waste and unavailable for use. Since depletion requires progressively greater investments of capital in production, the loss of capital affects production more seriously than in an equivalent maintenance crisis. Meanwhile further production, even at a diminished rate, requires further use of depleted resources, exacerbating the impact of depletion and the need for increased capital to maintain production. With demand for capital rising as the supply of capital falls, $C(p)$ tends to decrease faster than $M(p)$ and perpetuate the crisis. The result is a catabolic cycle, a self-reinforcing process in which $C(p)$ stays below $M(p)$ while both decline. Catabolic cycles may occur in maintenance crises if the gap between $C(p)$ and $M(p)$ is large enough, but tend to be self-limiting in such cases. In depletion crises, by contrast, catabolic cycles can proceed to catabolic collapse, in which $C(p)$ approaches zero and most of a society's capital is converted to waste. ...

Any society that displays broad increases in most measures of capital production coupled with signs of serious depletion of key resources, in particular, may be considered a potential candidate for catabolic collapse.

Once begun, the process of catabolic collapse creates a self-reinforcing feedback loop: the same kind of unbreakable, self-reinforcing process that propels civilization's anabolic growth, as we discussed in thesis #12. That process only ends when that society reaches the next lower sustainable level of complexity.

The question, then, is not whether or not these processes wll hold for our own civilization, but the timeframe to expect of them. As we have seen, we have already passed the point of diminishing returns (*see* thesis #15), leaving us open to the possibility of collapse. Peak Oil (*see* thesis #18) and environmental problems (*see* thesis #17) are already poised as potentially unsolvable problems that could lead to collapse in the near future, but ultimately, predicting the proximate cause of collapse is much more difficult than predicting its timeline. The best answer to that question is almost certainly, "soon."

The U.N. expects human population growth to "level off" at 9 billion in the next century, but humans already take up 40% of the earth's photosynthetic capacity to feed the 6.5 billion we already have. That is the ultimate cause behind the Holocene Extinction — already the worst mass extinction ever seen on the planet, and driven entirely by human agriculture. Global warming is radically altering the fragile interglacial climate that agriculture requires, and the fossil fuel subsidy that is so fundamental to our civilization's current mode of existence is running out. As Tainter wrote in his 1996 paper, "Complexity, Problem Solving and Sustainable Societies":

With subsidies of inexpensive fossil fuels, for a long time many consequences of industrialism effectively did not matter. Industrial societies could afford them. When energy costs are met easily and painlessly, benefit/cost ratio to social investments can be substantially ignored (as it has been in contemporary industrial agriculture). Fossil fuels made industrialism, and all that flowed from it (such as science, transportation, medicine, employment, consumerism, high-technology war, and contemporary political organization), a system of problem solving that was sustainable for several generations.

Of course, any course of action is "sustainable" over a sufficiently short time frame. Burning your house down for heat is sustainable for several minutes. The use of fossil fuels was sustainable for almost two centuries, but now we are facing the end of that subsidy — meaning that all those costs that we ignored in the past must now be paid.

Nothing can grow forever in a finite world. That basic truism is the ultimate doom for civilization. Its very nature will not permit it to exist in a steady state; it must grow. If it is not growing, it is dying. If the economy is not growing, and most investments will have negative returns, who is willing to invest? Without investment, how can we build the infrastructure to continue the civilized life — the roads, telephony, satellites or buildings we need now, much less the investments in future technology and complexity we will need to continue such a pace? That makes investment in complexity even less compelling, since there is no one else investing in it, either, and its total cost must be divided among fewer investors. Being the last one "holding the door," so to speak, is the worst possible strategy. The snowball may take some time to build up, but ultimately, if investment in complexity were a traded stock, collapse works in much the same way as a "run."

Thus, the "point of no return" in the collapse of any society is when an increasing percentage of the population begins to believe that further complexity is no longer worth it. That fringe always exists, in small numbers; collapse comes when that fringe begins to grow. As such, we can see the first signs of collapse in the growth of primitivism itself. The spread of ideas like slow food, voluntary simplicity, Ethan Watters' *Urban Tribes*, or "The Hunter-Gatherers of the Knowledge Economy" — even less obvious attacks on complexty, like open source and blogging — show a general discontent with the current level of complexity, and a growing antipathy for further investment in it.

Much of the world has already collapsed, but are propped up now only by the peer polity system they are enmeshed in. The following map shows those countries in red, showing how far along in the process of collapse we already are.

Currently collapsed regions in red.

In collapse, all the rules reverse themselves. Sustainabilty becomes not only feasible, but advantageous. Small, egalitarian groups out-compete large, hierarchical ones. Human nature becomes adaptive, rather than something we must suppress. That process is the inevitable end of any civilization, because nothing can grow forever and without limit in a finite universe. Moreover, that process will begin sooner, rather than later. It has already begun, and in all likelihood, most of us alive today will live to see its completion.

Thesis #27: Collapse increases quality of life.

We have seen what disastrous effect civilization has had on our quality of life (*see* thesis #25), but the alternative — collapse — seems little better. However superior the Paleolithic way of life might have been, it is long gone, and there does not seem to be any way back. For the past ten millennia, that sentiment has been true. But, as we have seen, we are now nearing the limits to our growth, and we are past the point of diminishing returns for our investments in further complexity (*see* thesis #15). Collapse is now inevitable (*see* thesis #26) — it is already underway. Collapse is an economizing process (*see* thesis #20) that begins when the alternative — continuing civilization — is no longer tolerable. We stand on the brink of collapse. That is a statement that would terrify most people, but it shouldn't: collapse increases our quality of life.

Our views of collapse are filtered through the lens of literary tragedy. The fall of Rome is our archetype, and it is viewed through the eyes of the aristocracy who lamented the loss of their power, and those who yearned to join the aristocracy in that power. After the sack of Rome, St. Jerome famously opined, "In the one city, the whole world dies." Or take for another example the famous Old English poem, "The Ruin":

The city buildings fell apart, the works

Of giants crumble.

Tumbled are the towers

Ruined the roofs, and broken the barred gate,

Frost in the plaster, all the ceilings gape,

Torn and collapsed and eaten up by age. And grit holds in its grip, the hard embrace

Of earth, the dead-departed master-builders,

Until a hundred generations now,

Of people have passed by.

Why would an Anglo-Saxon, a barbarian, pine so for the ruins of the Roman occupation — an occupation that the Britons themselves routinely rose up against? The motivations of the barbarians who overran the Roman Empire was not hatred of Rome — far from it. The barbarians wanted to become Roman themselves. The allure of *Romanitas* spread around the world. The "barbarian invasions" were primarily matters of *foederati* — mercenaries — hired by Rome. The Senate then saw fit not to pay them — after all, they were only barbarians. Alaric led one of the ensuing rebellions when he sacked Rome in 410 CE, leading St. Jerome to make his famed lament. For the powerful, the loss of empire was the loss of power and privelage. For those far removed from its reality, *Romanitas* lingered as the aura of gods who could achieve such wonders, and the Empire was a mythological "golden age."

But what of those masses who had to endure the actual empire itself? In "The Old Cause," Joseph Stromberg neatly summarizes Tainter's analysis of the Roman Empire.

Of the collapses which he describes, Tainter's discussion of the Western Roman Empire is the most interesting, perhaps because it is the best-documented. The Roman Empire was initially successful because stolen goods from each conquest financed the next one. The broad logistical limits of the process were reached by the time of Augustus. Thereafter, territorial changes were minimal. Without further loot (a sort of primitive accumulation of statist capital), Roman rulers had to defend vast territories out of current revenues drawn from a contracting economy. In general, the Roman state crippled and ruined the developed east (Greece, Egypt) so as to hold onto the less productive west. Making citizens of all free men in the Empire (212 AD), in order to tax them, acknowledged the decline.

Faced with rising costs and declining revenues, emperors debased the coinage while trying desperately to extract taxes out of a demoralized people. But by the third century, taxes were eating up citizens' capital and savings. In the following two centuries, further imperial inroads brought about "a drop in actual output." Later emperors, from Diocletian onwards, undermined society's capacity to pay at all. Some of these things, too, will sound familiar.

Collapse loomed, but collapse had definite advantages, as shown by its aftermath. The Germanic kings who replaced the empire in the west were better at defending their (smaller) territories against invaders and could do so more cheaply than the overextended empire. In North Africa, the Vandals (victims of a bad press) lowered taxes and economic well-being grew, until Justinian brought back Roman rule and, with it, imperial taxes. "Investment" in this lower level of political "complexity" paid for itself, so to speak, by being less costly (pp. 88–89). Collapse is not all bad: a disaster for the state apparatus may not be one for people as a whole. Devolution of power to smaller geographical units is "a rational, economizing process that may well benefit much of the population."

Our fear of collapse is an irrational one; one that is projected onto us by our leaders, who truly do have something to fear. This is the same class of elites that are the drivers and architects of all the problems we have so far discussed (*see* thesis #10). Now that we can see that civilization did not give us medicine (*see* thesis #22), or knowledge (*see* thesis #23), or art (*see* thesis #24) — but it *does* give us illness (*see* thesis #21), makes our lives difficult, dangerous and unhealthy (*see* thesis #9), destroys the way of life to which we are most adapted (*see* thesis #7), and submits us to the unnecessary evil of hierarchy (*see* thesis #11) — the true nature of civilization should now be plain to see: it is the means by which elites maintain their power and privelage, at the cost of everyone else.

Collapse undoes civilization. As Tainter highlights, such incredibly high levels of complexity as we have today are a bizarre abberation in the history of our species. Collapse returns us to the normal state of affairs — a state of affairs humans are well-adapted to. The benefits of living a well-adapted life are things we, in our maladaptive civlization, usually dismiss as utopian daydreaming. Lower stress, less work, better food, more liesure, more art and music, less violence, more security, less disease, more health — such is the human birthright intended for Esau the Hunter, and stolen by our forebear, Jacob the Farmer. Our plight is not normal; it is what happens when an animal lives contrary to its nature. It is an intractably stressful position, and adaptations must be made to allow such an unnatural state to continue. Coercion and control by authorities must be accepted, to take the place of a natural adaptation to the situation which we lack. More work must be exerted to tasks we have no natural ability for. Much of our energy must be expended simply keeping us alive on a diet we can scarcely digest (and is still mostly toxic to us), while never exercising the faculties that two million years of evolution has led our bodies to expect just over the course of another liesurely day. Today, in the United States — the most complex society our species has ever developed — the number one killer, by far, is stress.

The result of collapse is a reversal of all the quality of life issues that civilization raises. Rather than being the exclusive domain of Western countries, people everywhere will enjoy the normal human lifespan. The epidemic diseases released by civilization are now released for good. Eventually, they will burn themselves out, but not for some time. Yet even this does not justify our efforts to sustain civilization; since we have passed our point of diminishing returns, the likelihood of developing a cure without the kind of massive paradigm shift a collapse entails becomes increasingly small. Moreover, collapse would also end the far-ranging travel and dense population centers such epidemics thrive on.

Living and working as humans are adapted to all have distinct advantages, as well. Though there is no doubt a great deal of exaggeration in Zerzan's *Future Primitive,* (for instance, the example of the Dogon has been fairly effectively debunked), the preponderance of evidence is too great to dismiss entirely.

The Andaman Islanders, west of Thailand, have no leaders, no idea of symbolic representation, and no domesticated animals. There is also an absence of aggression, violence, and disease; wounds heal surprisingly quickly, and their sight and hearing are particularly acute. They are said to have declined since European intrusion in the mid-19th century, but exhibit other such remarkable physical traits as a natural immunity to malaria, skin with sufficient elasticity to rule out post-childbirth stretch marks and the wrinkling we associate with ageing, and an 'unbelievable' strength of teeth: Cipriani reported seeing children of 10 to 15 years crush nails with them. He also testified to the Andamese practice of collecting honey with no protective clothing at all; "yet they are never stung, and watching them one felt in the presence of some age-old mystery, lost by the civilized world."

DeVries has cited a wide range of contrasts by which the superior health of gatherer-hunters can be established, including an absence of degenerative diseases and mental disabilities, and childbirth without difficulty or pain. He also points out that this begins to erode from the moment of contact with civilization.

Relatedly, there is a great deal of evidence not only for physical and emotional vigor among primitives but also concerning their heightened sensory abilities. Darwin described people at the southernmost tip of South America who went about almost naked in frigid conditions, while Peasley observed Aborigines who were renowned for their ability to live through bitterly cold desert nights "without any form of clothing." Levi-Strauss was astounded to learn of a particular [South American] tribe which was able to "see the planet Venus in full daylight," a feat comparable to that of the North African Dogon who consider Sirius B the most important star; somehow aware, without instruments, of a star that can only be found with the most powerful of telescopes. In this vein, Boyden recounted the Bushman ability to see four of the moons of Jupiter with the naked eye.

"In the kingdom of the blind, the one-eyed man is king," the proverb says. If these all seem like miraculous super-powers, they should not. We often marvel that all animals are faster and stronger than we; have we truly been so neglected by evolution? Is it not more reasonable to conclude that our faculties are equal to those of any other animal — if only we were to use them in such a manner as evolution has fitted them for us? The "amazing" abilities of foragers should not amaze us; rather, we should marvel at how much we have lost to live such a maladaptive life, and in trade for so little.

Most importantly, civilization reduces human life to a cog in an enormous machine, a large-scale, complex, industrial society far beyond the human brain's capacity to understand on a human level. Instead, it can only be understood by analogy to a machine — and the human himself becomes mechanical. In a small scale, simple society, where individuals can know each other, they can be appreciated as individuals. We can form close groups that still respect our autonomy. Egalitarianism and rule by concensus becomes possible. In our present state, we are, ourselves, domesticated — and as with all the other animals we have afflicted with that fate, we domesticates are but a shadow of our proud, wild ancestors. Yet, beneath it all, we remain wild; and wild we shall be again. As Richard Heinberg said in "The Primitivist Critique of Civilization":

« *Many primal peoples tend to view us as pitiful creatures, too — though powerful and dangerous because of our technology and sheer numbers. They regard civilization as a sort of social disease. We civilized people appear to act as though we were addicted to a powerful drug — a drug that comes in the forms of money, factory-made goods, oil, and electricity. We are helpless without this drug, so we have come to see any threat to its supply as a threat to our very existence. Therefore we are easily manipulated — by desire (for more) or fear (that what we have will be taken away) — and powerful commercial and political interests have learned to orchestrate our desires and fears in order to achieve their own purposes of profit and control. If told that the production of our drug involves slavery, stealing, and murder, or*

212

the ecological equivalents, we try to ignore the news so as not to have to face an intolerable double bind. »

The collapse will mean a sharp cut-off of that supply, and as we shall see in the next thesis, it will not come easily. The process of collapse itself will be the most terrible thing any animal has ever endured, as ten thousand years of damage are all paid back at once. But for those of us who are able to end our dependence on that "drug" gradually, rather than catastrophically, a whole new world awaits.

Thesis #28: Humanity will almost certainly survive.

As beneficial as collapse may ultimately prove to be for the state of humanity (*see* thesis #27), the process itself will likely be horrific. Ultimately, the only sustainable level of complexity is the stone age (though this allows a great deal more complexity still than the popular imagination permits, as we discussed in theses #22–24). But complexity is a function of energy; complexity allows more energy to pass through a society. Most of that energy takes the form first of food, and then, of people (*see* thesis #4). In short, we face a severe problem of overshoot — and the drop in our carrying capacity to its sustainable level will mean the die-off of some 90% or more of the current population.

We can certainly excuse those authors who have worried for the extinction of our entire species facing such a grim scenario, as with Christchurch's comments in 2004, "...if we continue our present growth path, we are facing extinction. Not in millions of years, or even millennia, but by the end of this century." Or, Sun Microsystems' co-founder Bill Joy's "Why the Future Doesn't Need Us," first published in *Wired* magazine, long acknowledged as the "Bible" of techno-utopians, where he writes about how our technology may succeed in driving us into extinction.

We must remember two crucial facts, both of which are contrary to everything we've been raised to believe. First, civilization is fragile, and second, humans are not.

John M. Shanahan once called civilization, "a thin veneer over barbarianism." That quote was repeated often during the weeks that followed Hurricane Katrina's 2005 landfall on the Gulf Coast. The exaggerated media reports of looting and violence showed us what we have come to expect of uncivilized humanity, "anarchy," in all its pejorative meaning. However, in the months that followed, we learned that portrayal was grossly exaggerated. What was underreported, however, was the formation of small, egalitarian "tribes" among New Orleans' survivors. Allen Breed wrote "French Quarter Holdouts Create 'Tribes'" for the Associated Press, published 4 September 2005, which began with:

« *In the absence of information and outside assistance, groups of rich and poor banded together in the French Quarter, forming "tribes" and dividing up the labor. As some went down to the river to do the wash, others remained*

214

behind to protect property. In a bar, a bartender put near-perfect stitches into the torn ear of a robbery victim. »

While mold and contagion grew in the muck that engulfed most of the city, something else sprouted in this most decadent of American neighborhoods — humanity.

"Some people became animals," Vasilioas Tryphonas said Sunday morning as he sipped a hot beer in Johnny White's Sports Bar on Bourbon Street. "We became more civilized."

By such a definition, civilized behavior is the antithesis of civilization. New Orleans collapsed in the face of Katrina. The rebuilding efforts that have followed are precisely what we see whenever one region collapses in a peer polity sytem. This makes New Orleans a microcosmic preview of what awaits us with collapse.

As we saw in New Orleans, it does not take much to disrupt civilization's control. More importantly, civilization's very foundations are extremely weak. Civilization is utterly dependent on cereal grains for the bulk of its diet — a small handful of closely-related grasses. They are extremely tempermental plants, susceptible to even minor fluctuations in temperature, sunlight, and rainfall. A proverb of unknown attribution asserts that every civilization is three meals away from revolution; it is a basic application of Maslow's hierarchy of needs. Whatever need we may have to remain members of a large-scale, hierarchcial, exploitative society is not the equal to our basic, physical needs. If those cannot be met by a civilization, that civilization will dissolve. With a changing climate, the end of the era of fossil fuels, and the increasing fragility of complexity and its escalating probability of a cascading disaster in an era of diminishing marginal returns, how much longer can civilization provide for our basic needs?

That said, humans are omnivores. Wild foragers enjoy a far more varied diet than we do. To starve an agriculturalist requires nothing more than a dry spell, or a hot year; to starve a forager would require the extinction of nearly the entire of the plant and animal kingdoms (and even then, the forager might have a chance of surviving off of fungi). Before the advent of civilization, humans had adapted to nearly every environment on the planet. Culture allows us a means of adapting more quickly, and omnivorism makes us virtually impervious to starvation. That has made the human being comparable to the cockroach as one of the most adaptive organisms on the planet.

We must understand, then, that collapse is the end of civilization — and not necessarily the end of humanity. Those who depend on civilization for their survival will perish along with it; those who are able to make themselves independent of civilization will enjoy the foragers' bounty, and as much an assurance of survival as this world ever provides.

If survival is so easy, why are we facing such a catastrophic die-off? That sad fact is a testimony to the power of acculturation. The ultimate cause of death will be lack of food. Violence or disease may constitute proximate causes, but these will be ultimately the result of the contracting flow of energy through society. Lack of food will give rise to food riots; riots will give way to mobs and gangs and ultimately, the grisly cannibalism that seems to mark the final moments of every collapsing civilization. Before that, nation-states will wage war for the resources they need, invading oil-rich countries and maneuvering against each other for those fields. Of course, lack of nutrition inhibits the immune response, and the "Four Horsemen of the Apocalypse," historically, have always ridden together: war disrupts the growing and harvest seasons, leading to famine, which in turn leads to pestilence, and all of them to death. So why is it that people starve to death? Most commonly, people starve to death surrounded by edible matter — just no food. There is the essential issue, because "food" is not just edible matter, it's the *culturally constructed subset* of edible matter. That mismatch has garnered a small fortune for the producers of "Fear Factor." Bull's penis is entirely edible — it's even a high-priced delicacy consumed by China's elites to bestow sexual potency — but it isn't "food." At least not in *our* culture.

One of the examples of this mismatch are simply astounding. The single most famous example of cannibalism in American history is that of the Donner party — a group of 31 settlers bound for California who became trapped in the Sierra Nevadas in the winter of 1947. Though fed with pine nuts by Paiute Indians earlier in their travels, they still resorted to cannibalism and ultimately starved to death — in the middle of a large pine grove. They used the pine trees for fuel and even cut many of them down, but they never used them for food. It simply never occured to them: pine nuts and pine bark simply were not "food." Pine had long been a "starvation food" for Native Americans in these areas; when all else failed, you could always eat the pine. It was rarely the first choice, but in desperate

216

circumstances, it would suffice. The Donner party was desperate, and ate every "food" they could think of — even rawhide, bones and leather. But they didn't eat things that weren't "food" — and pine simply wasn't "food," even though they had been fed a meal of pine nuts a short time before.

Or, consider the plight of the Viking colonists of Greenland, as related by Jared Diamond in *Collapse*. Fish had long been a staple of Norse life, and like other staples (bread in European cultures, or rice in Japan), that entailed two, seemingly discordant attitudes. First, every meal required some portion of it: it is the prescence of some amount of the staple, more than portion size, that separates a "meal" from a "snack." Secondly, eating *just* the staple is a sign of poverty, as in "bread and water." Yet, in Greenland, we find no sign of fish associated with the Viking settlements. Couldn't it simply be a matter of the fish not being preserved very well, or otherwise hidden from us? Diamond runs through a number of the theories proposed on this account, most of which are patently ridiculous, and comes to a very good point with this:

The trouble with all those excuses for the lack of fish bones at Greenland Norse sites is that they would apply equally well to Greenland Inuit and Icelandic and Norwegian Norse sites, where fish bones prove instead to be abundant.

Yes, fish bones decompose faster, so we need to look at contemporary Norse sites for comparison, to see how much of their fish bones survived. Short answer: a lot. Even more at the Inuit sites, because Greenland isn't just a fisherman's paradise — it's also an archaeologist's dream. The soil composition and the cold means that nearly everything in Greenland is incredibly well preserved. We have preserved sheep lice and fecal pellets from the Norse colonies — both of which decay far more quickly than fish bones. As Diamond put it:

« *Every archaeologist who comes to excavate in Greenland refuses initially to believe the incredible claim that the Greenland Norse didn't eat fish, and starts out with his or her own idea about where all those missing fish bones might be hiding ... I prefer instead to take the facts at face value; even though Greenland's Norse originated from a fish-eating society, they may have developed a taboo against eating fish.* »

In the end, the Viking colonies of Greenland starved to death — next to a sea teaming with fish. To the end, they never touched them. Their Norse cousins lived on fish; they knew this. They lived in full view of the Inuit, who lived happily as they starved to death. They called them *skraelings* — "wretches" — because they were naught but ignoble savages. Savages who survived — and quite happily — while the civilized Europeans died a long, agonizing death. They ate their herds of cows, even the young, all the way down to the hooves — a clear sign that they had given up on the future. They ate their dogs. And again, in the end, they ate each other. But to the very end, they never ate fish.

The Arneborg study does show that the Greenland Norse were incredibly adaptive, learning to change their diet to match changing circumstances. It's not a lack of desperation that's at fault here; it's a lack of imagination. It's the cultural construction of food. We like to point to such stories with modern pride and think how *we* could never be so foolish, but unlike them, we *don't* know that we can eat pine bark, or dandelions, or plantain, or burdock root, or any of the other thousands of plant and animal species that surround us — even in the middle of the city. These things are easily learned, but as Daniel Quinn once suggested, the greatest impediment to learning is not the difficulty of acquiring knowledge — that is done easily — but the curiosity to seek that knowledge in the first place. We have defined "food" to be solely our domesticates. They are clearly packaged and labelled. We need not concern ourselves with those things in the wild that we can eat; they are not food.

We feel the cultural construction of food very deeply, because it is the primary means of our species' adaptation. Culture can learn far more quickly than biology, and what we are willing to eat or not is very literally a matter of life and death. Acculturation sets our notion of food at a level as powerful as any genetic instinct, and for the most part, this is highly adaptive. It allows us to use culture to learn what is edible and what is poisonous in a new environment quickly, and its deep effects make sure we heed that knowledge and stay alive. However, civilization has abused that adaptation to hold our food supply hostage, as it were, redefining food to a very narrow selection — a selection it can control. Such is the foundation of civilization, and such is the very thing that collapse threatens.

Such collapses have happened before, so we need not reach blindly for some idea of its implications. Many primitivists have expressed fears that, desperate and starving, a "land grab" may ensue; farmers may begin tearing into the forest for more land; people will flee the cities and the wilderness will collapse under the weight of so many human refugees fleeng their

218

collapsing civilization. Such fears seem logical — far more logical than the assertion that people will simply "choose" to die — but they are also unprecedented. Every prevous collapse has seen a *contraction* of farmland, not an expansion. For the most part, those lands not currently under cultivation are left wild for a reason — usually, that they are useless for cultivation. Even the most ignorant farmers know this; even dead farmland without the fossil fuel-based fertilizers need to eke crops out of it are better than the "useless," uncleared land beneath our forests. Our zombie movies provide a picture of popular psychology in the kind of catastrophe collapse entails. We do not "run for the hills"; we run to the cities for help.

Always, however, there is a small minority that chooses to separate itself from civilization and live another, more sustainable way. The Pueblo people retain almost no memory of the Hohokam, the Anasazi, and the other civilizations that preceded them, before they collapsed in the same horrific manner. Those who survived were those who left civilization behind to live a different way, a sustainable way. If they are "Noble Savages," it is only because of how savagely natural selection did its work — leaving only the most noble to survive. Yet in their myths, many of the Pueblo seem to echo this sentiment exactly. They tell a story that this is not the first world humans have lived in; several worlds have passed before, only to be destroyed by the decadence of humanity. Yet, each time, some minority remembered the ways of their ancestors, and they were permitted to pass into the next world. Natural selection eliminated the civilizations of the Hohokam and the Anasazi; it allowed the Pueblo to survive because they found a new, sustainable way to live.

Ultimately, there is a merciless elegance to the horror of collapse. Its destruction is not arbitrary or random. Every individual human being will be presented with a choice, as to whether or not we wish to die. We will have to choose, whehter we will remain civilized even unto death, or whether we will choose to find a new way to live. It *is* a choice. The Greenlanders, the Hohokam and the Anasazi all *chose* to die as civilized men, rather than imagine a different life. They were aware of alternatives that lurked on their periphery. They probably did not understand it as a choice, nor did they ever really concieve of the alternative. The choice was made on a much deeper level. For them, there was never any other choice — they were civilized. So they were born, and so they would die. Nothing else was even concievable. A choice made from such deep convictions that it never enters the conscious mind is a choice, nonetheless.

The collapse will be natural selection in its most amoral, merciless form. We cannot — must not — take away any individual's choice. That choice is the last sacred thing we have left. We cannot choose death for them through violence; yet it would be just as wrong to force them to choose life. Nearly all of our species will likely choose to die, just like every other time the choice has been posed. That cannot be changed. What we *can* change is ourselves, and our own choice. We can help as many people as we can to understand the situation we now face, and the choice that they must make. We cannot choose for them — but we can make sure they understand that they do have a choice. We will always be a fringe of a fringe, but every last individual we can reach is a whole world of possibilities we have saved — as the Talmud teaches, "whoever saves one soul, is regarded as if he had saved a whole world." (Mishna Sanhedrin 37a)

Thesis #29: It will be impossible to rebuild civilization.

Previous collapses often set the scene for another "rise" to civilization. The fall of Rome shapes the Western imagination's idea of collapse, with the descent into the barbarism of the Dark Ages, the long gestation of the Middle Ages, and the final rebirth of "civilization" in the Renaissance. However, as Greer points out in "How Civilizations Fall: A Theory of Catabolic Collapse," the Western Roman Empire suffered a maintenance crisis, not a catabolic collapse. So the question remains, is this *a* collapse, or *the* collapse? Are we merely facing a momentary downturn in a new sine wave of complexity, or does this collapse represent the end of civilization once and for all?

In *Of Men and Galaxies*, Sir Fred Hoyle obviously confuses civilization for intelligence, but that error notwithstanding, the following observation speaks to one of the essential problems that will face any civilization that will hope to succeed us:

« *It has often been said that, if the human species fails to make a go of it here on Earth, some other species will take over the running. In the sense of developing high intelligence this is not correct. We have, or soon will have, exhausted the necessary physical prerequisites so far as this planet is concerned. With coal gone, oil gone, high-grade metallic ores gone, no species however competent can make the long climb from primitive conditions to high-level technology. This is a one-shot affair. If we fail, this planetary system fails so far as intelligence is concerned. The same will be true of other planetary systems. On each of them there will be one chance, and one chance only.* »

It is important to remember that the various facets of complexity are inextricably linked, one to another. As Joseph Tainter remarked in "Complexity, Problem-Solving and Sustainable Societies": "Energy has always been the basis of cultural complexity and it always will be." He further oberseved in *Collapse of Complex Societies*:

« *A society increasing in complexity does so as a system. That is to say, as some of its interlinked parts are forced in a direction of growth, others must adjust accordingly. For example, if complexity increases to regulate regional subsistence production, investments will be made in hierarchy, in bureaucracy, and in agricultural facilities (such as irrigation networks). The expanding hierarchy requires still further agricultural output for its own needs, as well as increased investment in energy and minerals extraction. An expanded military is needed to protect the assets thus created, requiring in turn its own sphere of agricultural and other resources. As more and more resources are drained from the support population to maintain this system, an increased share must be allocated to legitimization or coercion. This increased complexity requires specialized administrators, who consume further shares of subsistence resources and wealth. To maintain the productive capacity of the base population, further investment is made in agriculture, and so on.* »

The illustration could be expanded, tracing still further the interdependencies within such a growing system, but the point has been made: a society grows in complexity as a system. To be sure, there are instances where one sector of a society grows at the expense of others, but to be maintained as a cohesive whole, a social system can tolerate only certain limits to such conditions.

Thus, it is possible to speak of sociocultural evolution by the encompassing term 'complexity,' meaning by this the interlinked growth of the several subsystems that comprise a society.

So, complexity is a function of energy throughput, and all the facets of complexity are interlinked. The question of whether or not a civilization will be capable of rising again is a question of how much energy will be available to it.

First, we must understand what kind of collapse it is that we face. A prolonged maintenance crisis like the fall of Rome would allow time for adaptation, but it is more likely that we face a sudden, catabolic collapse. The difference, as Greer explains in the paper cited above, is driven by the sort of diminishing returns on complexity that we have already discussed at length. Rome faced a maintenance crisis. It was beyond the point of diminishing returns, but the ecology and resources available in Europe were still sufficient to support a civilization. Rome collapsed under its own weight, moreso than from any kind of environmental stress or resource depletion. Thus, its collapse centered primarily on scaling back complexity and breaking down into smaller, more manageable kingdoms. In this scenario, energy throughput is reduced because complexity must fall to a more economic level. It is the price of complexity that is driving the process, so it levels out at a lower — but still civilized — level.

222

That is not the case with catabolic collapse. Catabolic collapse takes place when reductions in collapse are driven by a shortfall in energy throughput. That can be the result of desertification, sustained drought, loss of agricultural land, massive mortality from war, famine or disease, climate change, or a necessary fuel source's production peaking. While it is true that our complexity has passed the point of diminishing returns (*see* thesis #15), and we are dealing with the cost of that, we have not yet shown many signs of a maintenance crisis. Rather, the perils we face — such as global warming, mass extinction (*see* thesis #17), and peak oil (*see* thesis #18) — are causes of catabolic collapse. Our shortfalls in complexity will likely be triggered by shortfalls in energy throughput. As Greer describes the process:

« *A society that uses resources beyond replenishment rate (d(R)/r(R) > 1), when production of new capital falls short of maintenance needs, risks a depletion crisis in which key features of a maintenance crisis are amplified by the impact of depletion on production. As M(p) exceeds C(p) and capital can no longer be maintained, it is converted to waste and unavailable for use. Since depletion requires progressively greater investments of capital in production, the loss of capital affects production more seriously than in an equivalent maintenance crisis. Meanwhile further production, even at a diminished rate, requires further use of depleted resources, exacerbating the impact of depletion and the need for increased capital to maintain production. With demand for capital rising as the supply of capital falls, C(p) tends to decrease faster than M(p) and perpetuate the crisis. The result is a catabolic cycle, a self-reinforcing process in which C(p) stays below M(p) while both decline. Catabolic cycles may occur in maintenance crises if the gap between C(p) and M(p) is large enough, but tend to be self-limiting in such cases. In depletion crises, by contrast, catabolic cycles can proceed to catabolic collapse, in which C(p) approaches zero and most of a society's capital is converted to waste.* »

Of course, many of the survivors will want to rebuild civilization. The nature of catabolic collapse, however, will leave them with precious little to start with. As a self-reinforcing cycle, catabolic collapse is as unstoppable as the anabolic growth that currently drives us into ever-greater complexity. Both are self-reinforcing feedback loops, and both must run their course before any other direction can be taken. So we need not consider the case of an "interrupted" collapse, where civilization is rebuilt from the remains of the old. This will not be a return to the Dark Ages; it will be a return to the Stone Age.

How we be so sure of this? The current state of civilization is dependent on resources that are now so depleted, that they require an industrial infrastructure already in place to gather those resources. When coal was first used as a fuel, it could simply be picked off the ground. Those surface deposits were quickly used up. When those were gone, coal mining began. It was more costly, but as coal became a necessary fuel, the cost was justified. The shallowest mines were exploited first. As they ran out, miners turned to deeper and deeper mines. Today's mines are often hundreds of feet below ground, with access tunnels that must burrow through miles of earth. Mining so far below the earth is a dangerous job, made possible only by industrial machinery for ventilation, stabilization, and digging. We can fetch this fossil fuel only because we *have* fossil fuels to put to the task.

Again, the issue of peak oil leaves significant quantities of oil still in the ground. But it is deep in the earth, or under the sea, and often of a poorer quality, requiring more refinement. We can drill and refine this oil only because we have industrial equipment to build rigs and power refineries for the task. Any interruption in our civilization's supply of fossil fuel would require any effort to rebuild civilization to start from scratch. Catabolic collapse is precisely such an interruption.

Civilization, as we have seen, is only possible through agriculture, because only agriculture allows a society to increase its food supply — and thus its population — and thus its energy throughput — and thus its complexity — so arbitrarily. That level of complexity provides the agricultural society the ability to achieve other levels of complexity, such as crafting metal tools, state-level government, and advanced technology. Civilization only began when agriculture became possible, but does that mean that civilization can *only* appear based on agriculture? Yes, it does. Every culture must have some means of gathering food, and every means of gathering food can be placed into one of two categories: those where the people produce their own food, i.e., "cultivation," and those where they do not. The latter is referred to as "foraging." There is an enormous diversity under that heading — far more than deserves such a bland, umbrella term, but all such forms share a number of things in common. Because the amount of food they consume depends on the amount of food available in their ecosystem, there is a caloric limit of how much they can consume. They cannot raise their food supply, because their food supply is not under their control. Cultivators can be further subdivided between those who operate above, and below, the point of diminishing returns. Below the point of diminishing returns, cultivators are called horticulturalists. Horticulture also places a caloric limit — however many calories can be produced below the point of diminishing returns. To produce more than this would require working above the point of diminishing returns, at which point they cease to be horticulturalists, and instead become agriculturalists. Agriculturalists can increase the number of calories they produce simply by increasing their inputs — thus, only agriculturalists can arbitrarily increase their energy throughput, so only agriculturalists can start a civilization.

Given that, how plausible is agriculture after the collapse? Again, all but impossible. Plants, like any other organism, takes in nutrients, and excrete wastes. For plants, those are nutrients they take out of the soil, and waste they put into the soil. In nature, what one plant excretes as waste, another takes in as nutrients. They balance each other, and all of them thrive. But monoculture — planting whole fields of just one crop — sets fields of the same plant, all bleeding out the same nutrients, all dumping back in the same wastes. It is precsely the same effect as filling an empty room with people and sealing it completely off. Eventually, the entire room will be full of carbon dioxide, and there will be no more oxygen. Monoculture does to topsoil what locking yourself in a garage with your car engine running does to a human. Koetke's "Final Empire" highlighted the importance of topsoil to life on earth, and the devastating impact agriculture has had on that topsoil:

« In 1988, the annual soil loss due to erosion was twenty-five billion tons and rising rapidly. Erosion means that soil moves off the land. An equally serious injury is that the soil's fertility is exhausted in place. Soil exhaustion is happening in almost all places where civilization has spread. This is a literal killing of the planet by exhausting its fund of organic fertility that supports other biological life. Fact: since civilization invaded the Great Plains of North America one-half of the topsoil of that area has disappeared. »

As that happened, we also invented ever more powerful petrochemical fertilizers to offset the death of the soil, giving the illusion that all was well. The Dust Bowl arose because our innovation was outpaced by the devastation. We quickly got back on top of it, leading us to the current situation. The Great Plains are essentially a desert. We grow most of the world's corn on a thick layer of oil we have laid over its soil, long ago bled to death by the first wave of farmers in America. In "The Oil We Eat,"

Richard Manning dramatically illustrated how much our "breadbasket" now relies on oil when he wrote:

« *Corn, rice, and wheat are especially adapted to catastrophe. It is their niche. In the natural scheme of things, a catastrophe would create a blank slate, bare soil, that was good for them. Then, under normal circumstances, succession would quickly close that niche. The annuals would colonize. Their roots would stabilize the soil, accumulate organic matter, provide cover. Eventually the catastrophic niche would close. Farming is the process of ripping that niche open again and again. It is an annual artificial catastrophe, and it requires the equivalent of three or four tons of TNT per acre for a modern American farm. Iowa's fields require the energy of 4,000 Nagasaki bombs every year.* »

Iowa is almost all fields now. Little prairie remains, and if you can find what Iowans call a "postage stamp" remnant of some, it most likely will abut a cornfield. This allows an observation. Walk from the prairie to the field, and you probably will step down about six feet, as if the land had been stolen from beneath you. Settlers' accounts of the prairie conquest mention a sound, a series of pops, like pistol shots, the sound of stout grass roots breaking before a moldboard plow. A robbery was in progress.

The Fertile Crescent was not always a cruel joke. It was turned into a desert by agriculture in the very same way. At the moment, 40% of the earth's surface is covered in farmland; most of that is no longer arable after being farmed for so long. Of the 60% that remains, most of it was never arable to begin with — that is why it was not farmed. The domesticable crops are a small subset of all the plants that exist, and they are disproportionately cereal grains, making them both small in number, and lacking in diversity. They tend to be low in nutritional content, and extremely tempermental, requiring very specific climate and soil conditions. Beyond simply lacking the soil they require, they will not have the climate they require, either.

In thesis #6, we made reference to Ruddiman's "long Anthropocene" hypothesis, arguing that the Holocene interglacial was artificially extended by the deforestation caused by early agriculture. If Ruddiman is right, then an interruption in agricultural production would result in the resumption of hte Pleistocene ice age. However, that case is complicated by the more recent trend of global warming. Mounting evidence suggests that the massive increases in the scale of anthopogenic atmospheric change introduced by the Industrial Revolution may not simply have offset the earth's natural cooling trend, but may have begun to *reverse* it. Regardless of which scenario follows the collapse, ice age or global warming, the one thing that will not be possible is a continuation of the *status quo*. No matter what follows, we will see the end of the Holocene, and with it, the end of any climate capable of supporting agriculture on any significant scale.

We are therefore talking about a complete break with the end of our current civilization. Whole generations will pass before it becomes feasible again. What, then, of the distant future, when another interglacial occurs, or when global warming stabilizes? Will we be able to rebuild civilization then?

After the passage of millennia, the soil may well heal itself, and the necessary climate may return. In that scenario, agriculture may be possible in those same areas, and under the same conditions, that it first occured. Flood plains at a given climate are necessary. It needs to be an annual flood, and it needs to deposit new soil, to compensate for the depletion of the soil on a regular basis — but not so regular that the fields are flooded while the crops are still growing. And, they will need to exist in areas where domesticable plants live. All in all, a very precise set of circumstances already.

If agriculture does begin in such areas (and there can only be a dozen or less in the whole world), they will find themselves limited below a ceiling we did not suffer. In the course of our civilization, we used up all of the surface and near-surface deposits of all the economically viable metals on earth. The simple physical property of pounds per square inch will limit the technology of our little kingdoms to the Neolithic. No plow, however ingenious, can ever be made out of rock. In some directions, complexity will be allowed to flourish. In other directions — particularly lever-based machines, tools, and weapons — we will be very tightly circumscribed by the lack of any feasible materials. That limitation on technological complexity will necessarily limit all other forms of complexity, as well — as discussed above, while some levels can gain complexty at the expense of others, that can only happen within certain parameters. This is why the Neolithic never saw state-level governments; only with the beginning of the Bronze Age did we see that development. Likewise, the lack of metals will continue to limit technological development after the collapse — and by limiting technological development, it will limit all other forms of complexity.

The role of human ingenuity is marvelous, but not all-encompassing. Not every problem can be solved simply by the application of wits. Ambition and wits existed in plenty throughout the Paleolithic, yet we never developed the technology or complexity necessary to build a civilization, because complexity advances as a single thing, and always as a function of energy. The lever and the wedge are ultimately necessary — in the form of the plow and the sword — but these are not effective unless made of a material that can withstand sufficient pressure. The only such materials on earth are metals now buried so deep underground that only an industrial infrastructure can fetch them.

Our future Neolithic kingdoms will thus be constrained by problems of scale inherent to such low levels of complexity, lacking the technology to communicate quickly or easily, without effective weapons to suppress rebellion, without complex bureaucracies to administer large territories. They will effectively be limited to small city-states, incapable of expanding beyond that for the same problems of scale that inhibited so many of the civilizations of Mesoamerica, but moreso.

There is the minor question of civilization's waste, however. While mining the earth for metals may not be possible, mining our waste may be far more feasible. Of course, unattended metals rust quickly, and become unusable after a generation. However, our landfills preserve the garbage within remarkably. Might potential future civilizations mine landmills for new metals? There is, of course, an inherent limitation to such a proposition, in that the rate of that resource's replenishment is zero. Even fossil fuels have *some* replenishment rate. Any such resources will quickly be depleted — such a civilization might have a chance for a brief flash of glory, barely entering something akin to a Bronze Age level of complexity before burning itself out.

With the passage of gelogical ages, though, this will pass. Fossil fuels will be replenished, and metal ores will rise to the surface. After ages of the earth have passed, and another ice age comes, and then an interglacial, then, if there are still humans so far into the future — this is a matter of at least tens of millions of years, far longer than humans have so far survived — then there *might* be another opportunity to rebuild civilization then, but that will be the first chance we have after this collapse.

Thesis #30: The future will be what we make of it.

In his *Occasional Discourse on the Negro Question*, while arguing for the re-introduction of slavery, Thomas Carlyle played on Nietzsche's term, "the gay science," and gave us the derogatory title of economics: "the dismal science." Caryle used that same term when writing about Malthus' theories, calling them, "Dreary, stolid, dismal, without hope for this world or the next, is all that of the preventative check and the denial of the preventative check." In *The Collapse of Complex Societies*, Tainter worried that his idea of complexity subject to diminishing marginal returns would make archaeology economics' heir to the title. The idea that we are not in control of our own destiny is depressing to us. We rebel against determinism not because we can prove it is untrue, but because it frightens us to think of ourselves as mere cogs in a machine beyond our power. These theses may seem dismal in their predictions of inevitable collapse and a future created by deterministic, materialistic forces beyond our control. They should not be. This is, as another translation of Nietzsche's original phrase would read, a "life-enhancing knowledge." The greater moral of this story is not that our lives are bound by diminishing returns, but that the future will be what we make of it.

For millennia, civilizations have struggled to explain the misery their "superior" way of life creates, and across time and space that blame has been consistently heaped upon our flawed and sinful nature. In that view, our misery is not our fault; it is simply because we were made badly. This is a very dismal view. It is our nature to be miserable, and we cannot escape it. Yet, the many cultures that do live happily stand as a living testament against that excuse. They live well, and happily, and have so for millions of years. Their mere existence proves that humans are not flawed. We are not damned to destruction, or eternal unhappiness.

Collapse was not always inevitable. It is the consequence of agricultural life. When we decided to live in this way, only then did collapse become inevitable. The way we choose to live has consequences.

The first Inka's father prophesied that after five kings, the ancestors would stop listening to his people, and their way of life would end. The Inka founded the empire in order to keep a flow of sacrifices, begging the ancestors to stop time, to cheat their fate. The fifth king — Atahualpa — was pulled from his litter at Cajamarca by Spanish *conquistadors* in 1532. Qin Shi Huang, the first emperor of China, followed a brutal policy that began the Chinese tradition of alchemy, in pursuit of an elixir of life so that he could cheat his own death. The Egyptian pharoahs used pyramids and buried boats and mummification in hopes that they would live forever. Again and again, among the autochthonous civilizations, we see an explicit desire in their very foundations to cheat the natural cycle of life and death — to become the one thing in all of history that lived forever, that took without ever giving back. We see echoes of that same sentiment in our own civilization today. We look at the earth around us as a resource to be exploited; taking care of it is, at best, an act of charity. Even in death, as a final act of spite, we seal ourselves in boxes and poison our bodies with chemicals to hold off as long as possible the moment when we will be forced to give something back to the community of life that fed us, gave us water and air to breathe, and supported every endeavor we ever undertook.

Such attempts are not without their consequences. The cycles of life cannot be cheated forever. The longer we do manage to hold that moment off, the more dire those consequences would be. Collapse is a special case of overshoot — and the more we overshoot, the more drastic the consequences. But we are not bound to an eternal cycle of complexity and collapse. Ever-escalating complexity must always end in collapse — that is the consequence of such unsustainable madness. But we are not inherently mad — and no one forces us down the road of ever-escalating complexity.

In fact, as we saw in the previous thesis, that road will be all but cut off. Complexity may be subject to diminishing returns, but many other things are not. The forager spectrum spans from the Inuit, to the !Kung, to the Kwakiutl, to the Pygmies. How much more diverse might the foragers of the future be? Will there be Huns thundering across the plains of Kansas, or an Iroquois-like Confederacy practicing permaculture across upstate New York?

The future promises us lives as humans were meant to live them — free, respected as persons, respected as peers, subject to none. It promises us a true community — something most of us have never really experienced. It promises a mind-boggling diversity of belief, tradition, culture and lifestyle.

For ten thousand years, we have been caught in a positive feedback loop of ever-escalating complexity. Our lives have been created by the consequences of our ancestors' actions, and we have had little choice but to find our way within the ever-constricting confines of that destiny. That was the dismal reality of our parents, and their parents, and that is the dismal reality that has shaped us and brought us to this moment.

But now, collapse is upon us. It has already begun. The choice is ours, whether we will remain true to that culture that bore us and die with it, or whether we will choose to create a new future — a new culture. With collapse, the long curse visited upon us by our Neolithic ancestors finally ends, and we will become the first generation in ten millennia to truly claim its own destiny. Collapse will be the most horrific crisis any animal has ever faced, but with it also comes a great opportunity to claim our own future. The possibilities are limitless; the diversity of the future that awaits us is infinite.

There is a strikingly widespread astrology amongst many American tribes. The Milky Way is associated with the *axis mundi*, the world tree, the same mythological archetype as the Norse Yggdrasil, the Slavic Oak, or the Hindu *banyan*. The area about the North Star is considered "the Heart of the Sky," or the door to the underworld. When the sun rises in the Milky Way on the winter solstice, it is said to climb the World Tree, to open the door of heaven, and begin a new age of the world. It was this atrological interpretation that laid the framework of the Inka's prophecy, and the basis of the Mayan calendar. Interestingly, the Mayans predicted the end of this fourth world, and the beginning of the next, fifth world at precisely such an astrological event — in 2012.

By 2012, if peak oil, global warming or mass extinction will have any role in civilization's collapse, it will be well underway. By 2012, we will likely be embroiled in world-wide recession and constant warfare. By 2012, the collapse of our globalized civilization should be undeniable — and those of us who wish to find a new way to live should be able to find that the beginning of collapse has left enough space for us to do just that. By 2012, curiously enough, the door of heaven may well be open for anyone who wishes to pass through it and create the future.

What we do after that, is up to us…

Contact :

wildmanspath@protonmail.com

www.ingramcontent.com/pod-product-compliance
Lightning Source LLC
Chambersburg PA
CBHW060616290526
45793CB00001B/49